FootprintFrance

Brittany

Wendy Mewes

Introducing
the region

About
the region

Ille-et-Vilaine

Côtes d'Armor

Finistère

Practicalities

Morbihan

Contents

About the author

Writer and walker **Wendy Mewes** lives in the wilds of Finistère. A love of history and landscape drives the themes of her published work, which includes *Discovering the History of Brittany*, *Walking the Brittany Coast*, *Crossing Brittany* (a travelogue based on walking the Nantes–Brest canal) and *The Five of Cups*, a novel set in the Monts d'Arrée.

She runs the Brittany Walks organization (brittanywalks. com) and works extensively in promoting the understanding of Brittany's history for anglophones through talks, courses and guided events. She has been filmed for regional TV in France, and broadcasts a series on Breton history for local radio. Her blog Brittany Blues (wendymewes.blogspot.com) looks at the quirks and foibles of working in the context of Brittany's heritage.

Acknowledgements

Wendy would like to thank all those in tourist offices who offered help and advice, especially Gaël Turotte at Malestroit, Véronique Kahn at Vitré, Anca Boata at Rennes and Julie Gardy and Martine Dugué at Pontivy. Charly Bayou and Mireille Deschiens at the Musée de la Batellerie were also kindness itself. Special thanks go to friends who contributed in many supportive ways, especially Lesley Rice

for her hospitality and wide knowledge of nature and birdlife, fellow travel writer Vicki Trott, Karen and Graham Wetherick, Phil Roe and Rosie Neal for great eating, Jeanne le Bourgeois and Harold Mewes for helpful fact-finding. Jennifer and Martin Green, and Anne Marhic and Pascal Barret contributed much with their own images of Brittany, and staunch Breton support and debate came from Ronan Kergourlay, Youenn Quéffélec and Hervé Le Guen, while Maryvonne Strulliou's culinary expertise was invaluable. Finally Yves Marhic with his remarkable knowledge of Breton language, history and culture was as generous as ever with his time and goodwill.

About the book

The guide is divided into four sections: Introducing the region; About the region; Around the region and Practicalities.

Introducing the region comprises: **At a glance** (which explains how the region fits together); **Best of Brittany** (top 20 highlights); **Month by month** (a guide to pros and cons of visiting at certain times of year); and **Screen & page** (a list of suggested books and films).

About the region comprises: **History**; **Religion in Brittany**; **Art & architecture**; **Brittany today** (which presents different aspects of life in the region today); **Nature & environment**; **Festivals & events**; **Sleeping** (an overview of accommodation options); **Eating & drinking** (an overview of the region's cuisine, as well as advice on eating out); **Entertainment** (an overview of the region's cultural credentials, explaining what entertainment is on offer); **Shopping** (the region's specialities and recommendations for the best buys); and **Activities & tours.**

Around the region is then broken down into four areas, each with its own chapter. Here you'll find all the main sights and at the end of each chapter is a listings section with all the best sleeping, eating and drinking, entertainment, shopping and activities and tours options.

Map symbols

 l'Information
Information

 Gare
Train station

○ Endroit d'intérêt
Place of interest

Gare routière
Bus station

🏛 Musée/galerie
Museum/gallery

Ⓜ Station de métro
Metro station

Théâtre
Theatre

Ligne de tram
Tram route

✉ Poste
Post office

 Marché
Market

✝ Eglise/cathédrale
Church/cathedral

✚ Hôpital
Hospital

Mur de ville
City wall

⊞ Pharmacie
Pharmacy

🅿 Parking

🎓 Lycée
College

Picture credits

Front cover Lighthouse in a Britton landscape, Franck Boston/Shutterstock
Back cover 1 Medieval houses in Vannes, Elenathewise/istock
Back cover 2 Sardine tins at Penn sardine shop, Jean-Daniel Sudres/Hemis.fr
Inside back cover Provence vineyard, Paul Atkinson/Shutterstock

Wendy Mewes: pages 12, 13, 28, 42, 45, 56, 59, 61, 63, 67, 73, 75, 77, 79, 91, 93, 96, 97, 101, 102, 104, 105, 107, 108, 109, 110, 111, 112, 114, 115, 116, 123, 131, 136, 137, 142, 148, 150, 151, 152, 157, 160, 161, 162, 163, 165, 170, 174, 177, 184, 189, 190, 192, 206, 207, 209, 212, 239, 248, 255, 256

Robert Le Gall: page 258

Roger Moss: page 251

Hemis.Fr:
Bertrand Gardel: pages 22, 86, 146, 156, 200, 228; Bertrand Rieger: pages 14, 44, 159, 186, 195, 204, 215, 225, 238, 244, 252; Camille Moirenc: pages 46, 196, 232; Christophe Boisvieux: pages 53, 54, 80, 144, 240, 246; Emmanuel Berthier: page 95; Frances Wysocki: page 6; Franck Guiziou: pages 10, 31, 84, 178, 266; Hervé Hughes: pages 140, 180, 202, 222; Jean-Daniel Sudres: pages 48, 64, 78, 82, 126, 130, 132, 134, 172, 175, 218, 226, 236; Jean-Baptiste Rabouan: page 113; Jean-Marie Liot: page 1; Patrick Frilet: page 267; Pawel Wysocki: page 41; Philippe Roy: page 268; René Mattes: page 70, 265; Sandrine Rabouan: page 279

Istock:
alohaspirit: page 38; ballycroy: page 262; clodio: pages 18, 243; digital_eye: page 106; Elenathewise: page 234; jethic: pages 85, 100; Maica: page 21; vlevelly: page 51; Wlzz: page 188

Shutterstock:
Alonbou: pages 231, 245; Christian Musat: page 276; Claudio Giovanni Colombo: pages 25, 34, 135, 182; David Hughes: page 19; Elena Elisseeva: pages 26, 273; Fred Goldstein: page 277; Jakez: page 181; Jo Chambers: page 16; minik: page 199; Shutterschock: page 230; southmind: page 66; vgm: page 281

Tips Images:
Imagestate: page 154; Photononstop: page 11

Alamy:
Sébastien Baussais: page 119

Le Ménage
de la Vierge

Contents

Chaos of rocks, Huelgoat, Finistère.

Introducing the region

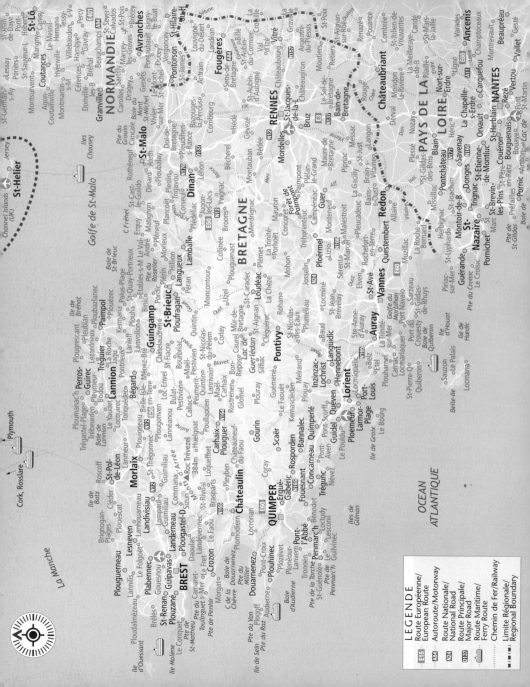

Introduction

Brittany is part of France and yet it retains a distinctive, individual character. Celtic roots and a vibrant heritage are revealed in song and dance, colourful festivals and local costumes with their famous lace headdresses. History lovers will find castles, medieval houses, chapels and standing stones at every turn, and the remarkable coastline, with its islands, forts and lighthouses, recalls long conflicts with England as well as the Atlantic Wall of the Second World War.

Brittany is a perfect arena for active holidays, whether you want any form of water sports or walking, cycling and riding. Many long-distance footpaths and former railway tracks criss-cross the immensely varied countryside, with its lakes, forests, wild heaths and the craggy peaks of the Monts d'Arrée. Beautiful rivers, such as the Oust and the Aulne, form part of the Nantes–Brest canal, which runs right across the region. The peace and tranquillity of the sparsely populated countryside can be enjoyed at any pace, with lively cities like Rennes, Quimper and Vannes providing a contrast with plenty to see and do by day and night.

So whether you want an energetic holiday or a cultural one, or simply to lie on a beach and sample as many crêpes and local ciders as possible, Brittany offers relaxation or stimulation to order.

At a glance

A whistle-stop tour of Brittany

Brittany's chequered relationship with France has dominated the history and economy of the region. Until the 20th century Nantes was the major city and present-day Loire-Atlantique was Breton territory. That all changed after the war, although many still regard the 'historic Brittany' (five departments) as the real thing. The Breton-speaking area of Basse Bretagne or Lower Brittany extended westwards from St-Brieuc to the whole of Finistère, which remains the most traditional Breton area. In Haute or Upper Brittany French was the dominant language with Gallo, a dialect deriving from Latin, surviving in places to the present day.

Brittany is in many ways quite distinct from the rest of France, with its Celtic culture, particular religious traditions and a peasant cuisine based on pancakes called crêpes or *galettes*. It's not a wine-producing area, but has excellent local ciders and beer.

Ille-et-Vilaine
The eastern area – modern, prosperous and vibrant Ille-et-Vilaine – was a kind of buffer zone between Brittany and France, controlled by the Franks around AD 800. The ninth century saw an expansion of Breton dominance to include Rennes and Nantes (the latter now being outside Brittany again in Loire-Atlantique). The fine fortresses of Fougères, Combourg and Vitré bear witness to the frontier nature of this area, and the beautiful beech

Town hall, Rennes.

Perros-Guirec, Côtes d'Armor.

Forêt de Fougères was a regular venue for clashes between salt-smugglers and customs officers.

The chain of castles once served to protect Rennes, now a large university city and the capital of Brittany. It's also the smallest city in the world to have an underground system. The Parliament building, completed in 1655, was badly damaged by fire during a fishermen's demonstration in 1994, but is now wonderfully restored. Despite disastrous fires in the 18th century, many medieval houses are preserved in the old town north of the cathedral.

St-Malo, the ferry port with its walled city on the north coast, upholds the maritime heritage of Brittany, which has been home of corsairs, merchants and explorers over the centuries. To the east is the Bay of Mont St-Michel, with its World Heritage Site (technically just over the border). The coast here is renowned for its shellfish, especially the oysters of Cancale.

On the western border with Morbihan, the Forêt de Paimpont is today also known as Brocéliande and has many Arthurian connections. The Château de Comper is now an evocative centre of Arthurian studies. Apart from the romance and magic of the setting, it's excellent walking and riding territory. The department's Neolithic treasure is a megalithic feast of menhirs and dolmens on the high plateau at St-Just, not far from Redon, the canal centre of Brittany.

Côtes d'Armor
This department was called Côtes du Nord until the 1990s when it was deemed necessary to shed a rather wintry image. Armor, the land of the sea, has

Tréguier.

a stunning northern coastline, with its craggy cliffs – wild around Cap Fréhel, the highest in Brittany near Plouha and the most exotic along the Pink Granite coast around Perros-Guirec, where the fantastically shaped rock formations draw visitors from all over the world. In summer this whole area is packed with people and, inevitably, cars. The Côte de Goëlo offers many sandy beaches and friendly traditional family resorts.

The only large town of Côtes d'Armor is St-Brieuc, buried deep in a double valley below the motorway flyover. It has a small medieval quarter, dominated by the somewhat prison-like Cathedral of St-Etienne. Livelier and more appealing towns are Lannion in the west and Dinan on the eastern border of the Rance. Tréguier, a centre of the Trégor region, is a gem of a place.

Inland, there are no big towns south of Guingamp and it is much less densely populated than the coastal area, with rocky, undulating countryside, granite villages, isolated chapels and many Neolithic standing stones or burial places. Right in the centre of Brittany, the vast Lac de Guerlédan provides a focus for active holidays with its forested surroundings, swimming beaches and sailing opportunities.

Finistère

The westernmost department of Brittany has the best coastal variety of all, with the endless beaches and towering cliffs of the Atlantic shore. The Crozon Peninsula and Cap Sizun provide the finest sea views, walking and water-based activities that anyone could wish for. Northwest of Brest is the westernmost point of France at Pointe de Corsen, and also the tallest standing menhir in France near St-Renan. Brest itself is essentially a modern university city, but there's plenty of interest with three port areas and the well-preserved château housing a maritime museum.

In the south of the department, Quimper could not be more different – compact and bright, with a really enjoyable medieval centre of ultra-modern shops and a breathtaking cathedral. The town of

Pink Granite Coast.

Pont l'Abbé just to the south is the heart of Pays Bigouden, a distinctive area with a long maritime history and still strong on Breton traditions today.

In the centre of Finistère, the Monts d'Arrée are the highest hills in Brittany. They're hardly mountains, but look impressive in the range of lonely schist peaks and empty moorland, set around the bowl of a reservoir and topped by the tiny chapel of St-Michel. There is plenty of scope for cultural or activity holidays in this extremely quiet area, which deserves to be better known, not only for its landscape but also as the home of some of the earliest established eco-museums in France. Just to the north is the old town of Morlaix, sacked by the English in 1522, but now more peaceably the first stop for those off the ferry at Roscoff. The ancient centre has some extraordinary old houses that you won't see elsewhere, and delightful twisting stepped passageways wiggling across the hillsides. Easily accessible from here are the *enclos paroissiaux* (parish closes), a phenomenon of religious architecture that draws visitors from afar. St-Thégonnec, Guimiliau and Lampaul-Guimiliau are close enough to visit in succession. Most of central Finistère is part of the regional Parc Naturel d'Armorique.

Introducing the region

Morbihan

The Gulf of Morbihan, said to have an island for every day of the year, is almost an inland sea that has emerged since Neolithic times with rising water levels. The New Stone Age remains on the islands of Gavrinis and Er-Lannic were on the mainland when originally erected. Boats go to the Ile-aux-Moines and Ile d'Arz from Arradon and Larmor Baden. Nearby Carnac is a world-famous heritage site known for its astonishing miles of megaliths. Erdeven and Locmariaquer are further exceptional Neolithic sites, on each side of the crooked finger of the Quiberon Peninsula. Here there is a marked contrast between the family beaches on the sheltered east side and the wilder west, a favourite surfing area. From Quiberon itself, at the end of the peninsula, boats run to the island of Belle-Ile. The coast outside the Gulf is not especially memorable, being relatively flat and quite built-up.

Vannes is a beautiful city, with extensive medieval remains, including large sections of the original town fortifications and gates. Sights include the Cathedral of St-Pierre, a fine archaeological museum in the 15th-century Château Gaillard and La Cohue Musée des Beaux-Arts. Inland Morbihan has much rural beauty in the form of river valleys, wooded hills and sleepy villages. Pontivy is the main town of

Covered gallery of engraved stones at the Gavrinis burial mound, dated 3500 BC, Morbihan.

the interior, with its imposing medieval château contrasting with the rather monotonous regularity of the Napoleonic quarter. The canalized Blavet river here goes north to Lac de Guerlédan and south to Hennebont. To the south and west of Pontivy, the areas around Castennec and Le Faouët are especially attractive.

Five special little towns lie almost in a line in the northeast of Morbihan. Each has its own distinct atmosphere and architectural delights – Josselin's Rohan château, Lizio's period houses, Ploërmel's strong ducal legacy, Malestroit's medieval centre and interesting church and, finally, Rochefort-en-Terre, perhaps the prettiest village in Brittany.

The lowdown

Money matters
Brittany is generally a relatively cheap place for visitors, especially outside the main towns and away from the coast. Even privately owned castles and museums are likely to charge little more than €5 for entry. For refreshments and visits, €45 per person should be enough for a day.

Opening hours
Monday is often closing day for shops, museums and other attractions, and lunchtime closing for most things is usual, except in July and August. Many chapels are closed for most of the year but an enquiry at the nearest house or Mairie will sometimes produce a key. Advertised opening times are usually, but not always, reliable in the main tourist season, but may be changed without notice in the winter months.

Tourist passes
Each department has a passport or similar scheme where linked sites have reduced entry after the first use and at least one free visit if you go to all the relevant places. Some large towns, such as Quimper, have a similar discount offer for main places of interest. Areas with good outdoor facilities may offer a discount scheme for following more than one activity or booking multiple sessions.

Tourist information
The regional committee for tourism has a useful website for all styles of holiday – bretagnetourisme.fr, and bretagne.com is also helpful. Each town has its own website/tourist office.

The *Central Brittany Journal*, an informative English-language monthly magazine available in most newsagents, has a good What's On feature.

Best of Brittany

Top 20 things to see & do

1. St-Malo's Grande Plage.

❶ St-Malo

This magnificent walled city, symbolic of St Malo's proud and independent spirit, is seen to best effect on approach by boat to the harbour. It was painstakingly reconstructed after being almost destroyed in Second World War bombing. From this port, boats went off to fish for cod in Newfoundland in the 16th century and corsairs like Robert Surcouf ranged the world's oceans. Page 96.

❷ Château de Fougères

A fabulous frontier fortress, immensely imposing in stature, despite being located below the High Town. This is truly a paradise of exploration for

castle lovers of all ages, and the exceptional-quality, modern presentation gives visitors a real experience of the life and turbulent times of the château. Page 106.

❸ Forêt de Paimpont

A magical setting for Arthurian connections, this beautiful forest is known more commonly these days as the Forêt de Brocéliande. Here, Merlin was bewitched by the fairy Viviane, who brought up Lancelot beneath the waters of the lake by the Château de Comper. Miles of paths invite exploration, but beware the Valley of No Return. Page 110.

➍ St-Just

A remarkable megalithic site, little visited in comparison with other better known places. Here, on a high granite plateau, a whole succession of alignments and burial chambers unfolds across the wild landscape, and you will often be alone when trying to sense the arcane connection between Neolithic man and his beliefs. Page 117.

➎ Nantes–Brest canal

Some of the most beautiful stretches of this remarkable waterway are in western Morbihan, around the Ile-aux-Pies and Malestroit. A monument of 19th-century economic and social history, the canal has reinvented itself for modern times as an exceptional leisure resource. The continuous towpath is perfect for walking, cycling or simply dawdling along looking at wildlife and nature. Page 118.

➏ Côte de Goëlo

With the highest cliffs in Brittany near Plouha, glorious beaches, secluded coves and a series of pretty ports, this stretch of coastline has everything to offer for a family holiday or for those interested in outdoor activities. Following the coastal path along the green heights provides panoramic views and seascapes in the Bay of St-Brieuc. Page 136.

➐ Tréguier cathedral

This glorious cathedral contains the tomb of St-Yves, patron saint of Brittany, a lawyer famous for his impartial treatment of both rich and poor. Lawyers from all over the world attend the Pardon of St-Yves in May each year, when the relic of his skull is taken in procession to Minihy where he was born in 1250. Page 145.

➑ Pink Granite Coast

Weird and wonderful best describes the remarkable rock formations along this section of the northern coast, and the glowing pink of the granite only adds to the spectacle. Names like The Tortoise and Napoleon's Hat give an idea of what to expect, but it's the sheer size and scale of this geological wonder that's dazzling. Page 146.

➒ Dinan

The famous duel of honour between Bertrand du Guesclin and Thomas of Canterbury during the 14th-century Wars of Succession was fought here in 1359. The heart of the old city retains a fantastic feast of colourful medieval buildings, surrounded by nearly two miles of towering ramparts that now provide a scenic walk with views down to the port far below. Page 148.

➓ Fort La Latte

A wild and romantic setting for this coastal castle, dating back to the 14th century and impregnable from the sea. In modern times it has proved an irresistible setting for film-makers: *The Vikings* (1957), starring Kirk Douglas and Tony Curtis, was shot here. There are breathtaking views across to the impressive Cap Fréhel from the keep and ramparts. Page 154.

⑪ Cathedral of St-Corentin, Quimper

According to legend, King Gradlon called on St-Corentin to be the first bishop of Quimper in the fifth century. Building of the current cathedral started in 1239 but was delayed by the turbulence of war and plague in the 14th century. On resumption, the nave was added at a crooked angle, an oddity which only enhances the radiance of the interior today. Page 183.

⑫ Menhir de Kerloas

This is the tallest upright standing stone in France, at almost 11 m. Legend said that hidden treasure beneath the menhir was revealed when the stone went off to drink from the ocean on the first stroke of midnight on Christmas Eve. However, since it returned on the second stroke, no one ever had time to get rich and stay alive. Page 194.

Introducing the region

⑬ Camaret

One of the most attractive ports in Brittany, Camaret has a long fishing tradition and a reputation as *the* place for lobsters. At the end of the natural curving cob is the glowing Tour Vauban, which fought off an English attack in 1694. Brightly painted houses, swimming beaches and superb coastal walks along the cliff paths add to the attraction. Page 197.

⑭ Morlaix

This fascinating town, long a trading contact and rival of England, is often overlooked by tourists getting off the ferry at Roscoff and whizzing past on their way south. The ancient centre is dominated by the towering granite viaduct which brought the Paris–Brest railway line in the 1860s.

9. Dinan.

Don't miss the unique architectural form of the *maisons à pondalez*. Page 206.

⑮ Monts d'Arrée

These 'mountains' are in fact the highest hills in Brittany. The bleak moors and craggy peaks often rise out of waves of thick mist over the basin of the reservoir at the heart of the American regional park. Beware the black dog roaming the marshes at night! The mystical atmosphere is heightened by the little chapel of St-Michel, a lone sentinel on its hilltop. Page 208.

⑯ Huelgoat

An enchanting forest surrounds the famous 'chaos' with its vast granite boulders, which have tumbled into incredible shapes. It's only too easy to believe the legends of giant hands being involved, and discarded lovers thrown into the chasm of the Gouffre. Less dramatically, you can follow the little canal through the woods to the remains of one of the oldest lead/silver mines in France. Page 209.

⑰ Vannes

The treaty making Brittany part of France was signed here in 1532, and many of the impressive fortifications with towers and monumental gates from that date survive, together with a large medieval quarter of half-timbered houses. Look out for the symbolic *Vannes et sa femme*. And when you tire of culture and history, enjoy a drink in the lively port area, gateway to the Gulf of Morbihan. Page 232.

⑱ Gulf of Morbihan

Whether you want to take a tour by boat, walk the coastal path, explore the Ile-aux-Moines or visit the world-famous Neolithic tomb on the island of Gavrinis, the Gulf offers you its calm waters and constantly changing seascapes. Page 235.

10. Fort La Latte.

⑲ Carnac

A heritage site with the most extensive Neolithic remains in Europe. Thousands of standing stones range across the countryside, interspersed with burial chambers and tumuli, giving the impression of a mecca of the New Stone Age, a focal point for the ceremonial celebrations of early man. Page 241.

⑳ Rochefort-en-Terre

The most beautiful village in Brittany, with stunning architecture and award-winning displays of flowers. Strolling the cobbled streets is like viewing an architect's sample book with superb period details from different centuries. It is also a centre of arts and crafts, so added appeal comes from the great variety of shops, galleries and restaurants. Page 257.

Month by month

A year in Brittany

It's difficult to generalize about the weather in Brittany – it varies enormously from region to region, from coast to inland and even from one side of a hill to the other. Generally, the south and east are warmer and less wet than the areas closer to the Atlantic coast.

January & February

This is the quietest time of year in Brittany, with many hotels, restaurants and attractions closed, except in school holidays. It can be very cold in mid-winter, usually with a few short periods of snow in the west and centre, and rain is to be expected. 1 January is a public holiday, and most places will be extremely quiet during the rest of the month.

February is still cold and can be very wet, but recent years have had long, clear spells. Many footpaths are affected by poor weather, but there are plenty of places, such as canal towpaths and old railway tracks, where walking and cycling at this time of year are perfectly possible. The hunting season finishes at the end of February.

Mardi Gras marks the beginning of Lent, celebrated publicly with feasts, music and masked balls, and privately with family parties. The burning of the stuffed figure of *Den Paolig* (the Devil) used to be the traditional climax of the fête, which is no longer an official public holiday.

March & April

In March the weather is unpredictable, torn between early spring and a late blast of winter, sometimes within a single day. Snow is still possible, and winds can be very strong, especially those blowing in from the Atlantic, so care is needed if walking the cliff paths. Around the spring equinox, high tides on the Atlantic coast are an impressive sight, especially in flatter areas like Penmarc'h. Many attractions and museums will be open at certain times during school holidays, if Easter is early.

In April, signs of real regeneration in the plant world bring a little lift and outdoor activities start. With Easter, the pace of life increases and the cycle of festivals begins. Prices are usually low season, so it's a good time for budget holidays or a city break, where uncertain weather is less likely to spoil things and cultural venues are open. More accommodation is generally available, and many campsites are open.

A cycling holiday in Brittany is glorious in May and June.

May & June

These months often bring the most pleasant weather of the year, and it's a good time for walking and activity holidays. In May nature is at her most bountiful with the apple blossom out and all the trees finally in full leaf. Most accommodation providers are open for business and many of the attractions are open morning and afternoon, with a long break at lunch. May has three public holidays, so be prepared for closures on those days. The great Pardon of St-Yves in Tréguier is on the third Sunday in May.

June is often hot, and more people come out to enjoy the countryside. Visiting the islands is to be recommended, as seas are usually quite calm and visitor numbers fairly low. People do swim in lakes and the sea at this time, but you may want to give the water another month to warm up. Cycling is very popular here and you will also find a lot of cyclists out on the roads from now onwards. The last Sunday in June sees the Pardon de Ste-Barbe at Le Faouët.

July & August

July is probably the hottest month of the year. This is traditional French holiday time and Brittany comes vibrantly to life – after the Bastille Day celebrations on 14 July the pace of festivals hots up – the third week sees the fantastically popular Vieilles Charrues music festival in Carhaix-Plouguer, and the Festival de Cornouaille in Quimper. One of the great religious celebrations, the Pardon of the Black Madonna in Guingamp, takes place in early July.

As it is the busiest part of the tourist season, expect higher prices for accommodation,

Religious pardon, Côtes d'Armor.

especially around the coast. Generally you will be able to find places to stay in central Brittany without too much difficulty.

In recent years August weather has been disappointing, but 15 August, Day of Assumption, sees many religious processions (pardons) regardless, followed by dancing and feasting. The major Interceltic Festival takes place in Lorient in the first half of the month. Beaches in the main resorts will be crowded but you don't have to travel too far from such centres to find a more secluded spot, as one thing Brittany is certainly not short of is coastline.

The main advantage of this high summer season is that everything is open, including many chapels closed for the rest of the year, but the top attractions – like Océanopolis – will be very crowded. Many French tourists arrive in August, often to second homes around the coast. As French visitors tend to favour afternoons to get out and about, try to plan morning visits if possible to avoid the crush. Advance booking is advisable for taking trips to the islands, but be prepared for crowds in small spaces.

September & October

This time of year is recommended for outdoor activities, as the weather is often good and certainly mild enough to enjoy life in the open air. Off-season accommodation has often been a problem in Brittany, but that is slowly improving. Some campsites, with very affordable cabins to let, are now open all year round.

September usually sees a drop in accommodation rates, at least in the second half of the month, and there should be little problem with availability. Some museums and attractions will close at the end of the month, so check carefully when planning. There are many important pardons in September, such as the Blessing of the Sea at Camaret on the first Sunday.

The hunting season begins usually on the last weekend in September. On public land each commune will then have allocated days, which usually include Sundays, when hunting is allowed – ask for precise details at the local Mairie if it could affect you.

October is well into autumn weather-wise, with nights drawing in quickly and the temperature dropping. All Saints is an important time in Breton society with the cleaning and decorating of family graves on 31 October. School holidays at the end of the month means many attractions are open for two weeks. Seasonal festivals revolve around the apple and chestnut, with a month-long 'Mois du Marron' at Redon. There are also cultural events such as the British Film Festival in Dinard and the Atlantique Jazz Festival in Finistère.

November & December

Early winter is generally wet rather than cold, but winds can be strong, especially near the coasts. In November mist often lies over the shoreline and low ground. The Monts d'Arrée are particularly atmospheric in this respect, and there you can also see millions of starlings doing their evening dancing swoops as dusk spreads over the hills. La Gacilly has wisely invented a Fête de la Soupe for warming a wintry month.

In December the Transmusicales festival in Rennes livens up the early part of the month. There are many Christmas craft markets, and the Château de Trévarez in Finistère always has a special exhibition and beautiful decorations.

Christmas has become considerably more commercialized in recent years, but it still retains an air of genuine good cheer and festivity. A Christmas Eve family get-together is traditional, and Christmas Day is mostly a time for staying at home, although some restaurants, especially in hotels, will be open for lunch. Boxing Day is not a public holiday here, so most shops will be open and many museums and galleries too – it rather depends on which day of the week it falls.

Screen & page

Brittany in film & literature

Films

The Vikings
Richard Fleischer, 1958
Fort La Latte was used for filming various battle scenes in *The Vikings*, which starred Kirk Douglas and Tony Curtis.

Lancelot du Lac
Robert Bresson, 1974
This heavy version of the Arthurian legends used Breton scenery.

Tess
Roman Polanski, 1979
This lush production of Thomas Hardy's classic *Tess of the d'Urbervilles* was partly filmed in Locronan, Finistère.

Western
Manuel Poirier, 1997
A road movie filmed in Brittany and starring the Catalan actor Sergi López.

Books

Fiction
Canterbury Tales
Geoffrey Chaucer, 14th century
Chaucer's Franklin's Tale tells the story of Dorigen, a lady of Penmarc'h, who employs a sorcerer to magic away the black rocks of this southwest tip of Brittany to bring her husband home safely.

Les Chouans
Honoré de Balzac, 1829
An atmospheric if romanticized account of Chouan activity, set mainly in Fougères, where Balzac wrote much of the text.

Le Blé en Herbe/Corn on the Blade
Collette, 1923
A steamy tale of adolescent passions set on Brittany's northeast coast. Later filmed for the cinema (1954) and TV (1990).

Non-fiction
The House of Tides
Kenneth White, 2000
A multi-layered look at local life, thought and language from the creator of 'geopoetics'.

The main square in Locronan, a location for the film *Tess*.

The Next Moon
Ewen Southby-Tailyour and André Hue, 2005

A thrilling true account of resistance activity at St-Marcel from André Hue, who was parachuted into this camp. He subsequently received the DSO and Croix de Guerre.

The Price of Water in Finistère
Bodil Malmsten, 2005

Swedish poet Bodil Malmsten takes a sharp, idiosyncratic and highly amusing view of her new life in Brittany.

Discovering the History of Brittany
Wendy Mewes, 2006

A guide to the events and characters that have shaped Brittany's complex history.

Crossing Brittany
Wendy Mewes, 2008

A travelogue describing the author's walk across Brittany along the Nantes–Brest canal.

Early visitors to Brittany

Arthur Young recorded his experiences of Brittany while on his tour of France studying farming methods, just before the French Revolution – his *Travels in France* was published in 1792.

Augustus Trollope, brother of the famous Anthony, made a trip to Brittany in 1841 and wrote a detailed description and assessment of the places and people he encountered: "It is impossible to conceive a more striking contrast than that which is observed on passing from busy, bustling, thriving Normandy, to this sombre land, where every thing seems to belong to and to speak of the past. It is like walking into a past century, and leaving the noisy, active living world behind one. The general features of the country, too, contribute their share to produce this effect. The scattered nature of the population, the utter and unmitigated desolation of the vast moors, above all, the stupendous monuments of a period lost to history, which are encountered at almost every step, give to the scene a death-like stillness, which weighs upon the spirits, and turns thoughts to the silent past."

Heather blooming among
megalithic monuments.

Contents

About the region

History

Ankou.

Celts & Romans

From around 750 BC peoples from the east of Europe and the Black Sea area gradually infiltrated northwest France. These are often referred to collectively as Celts, although their connections were probably cultural rather than racial. How many of them actually reached Brittany is debatable, but their cultural influences certainly permeated the peninsula, which embraced five tribes – the Osismes, Vénètes, Coriosolites, Riedones and Namnètes. Brittany was Armor, land of the sea. Finds of coin hoards and jewellery indicate the fine quality of their metalworking, and they had many trading links with Cornwall and the rest of Britain. Their polytheistic religion, reverence for nature and priestly class of Druids left a legacy that survived through the centuries. Their main structural survivals are the many Iron Age fortified peninsulas to be seen around the coast of Brittany.

Megaliths

Brittany has some of the most important Neolithic sites in Europe, including the alignments at Carnac and the tallest standing stone (nearly 11 m) in France in northwest Finistère (page 194). Burial sites from as early as 6000 BC are numerous enough to suggest a sizeable early population in the peninsula. And from an even earlier time, long before the channel separated Great Britain from the continent, there is evidence of habitation and the use of fire at Menez Dregan, with a date around 450,000 BC.

The main characteristics of the New Stone Age (c 5000-2000 BC) are that man began to settle on the land, clear forests, grow crops, tend animals, make pottery and weave fabric. Although these people have not left us any domestic buildings in Brittany, their monuments in stone show a remarkable mastery of construction and a high degree of social organization. We do not know exactly what their intentions were or what practical use the structures had, but group celebrations on a large scale were clearly the purpose of alignments such as those at Carnac and St-Just. Here, there are long rows of raised stones and burial places over a wide area, so the sites must have been a focal point for worship, community activities and the cult of the dead for many centuries. Elsewhere menhir ('long stones' in Breton) often appear to stand alone in the countryside, but so many have been lost that these may well have been part of related chains stretching for very long distances. They probably served as boundaries, directional markers or indicators of sacred burial sites. There are many forms of burial chambers to be seen in Brittany, most commonly dolmen (stone tables) or elongated allées couvertes (covered passages). These were often reused over hundreds of years, so objects excavated in them may date from different periods. The use of metals came with Bronze Age developments, when burial mounds tended to be more singular, suggesting a more hierarchical society, with important leaders receiving special round tombs.

Despite a propensity for tribal warfare, the Celts were ultimately no match for Roman military organization. Julius Caesar had a fleet built to challenge the most powerful tribe – the Vénètes – at sea in the Gulf of Morbihan (see page 235), and after his victory the Roman province of Armorica was established. It is doubtful if many Romans settled here, but the benefits of Roman civilization were certainly felt by the wealthier strata of the tribes who would have provided the local officials and built villas in the Roman style. A well-preserved bath complex at Hogolo on the northern coast reflects a new standard of living for some.

Remaining evidence of Roman occupation is not as widespread as one might expect, but there are some exceptional sites such as Corseul (see page 152), with its octagonal Temple of Mars, and a fish-processing factory at Douarnenez (see page 203).

The age of saints

The story of Brittany really begins in the fifth and sixth centuries with the influx of migrants from Great Britain in the aftermath of Roman imperialism and the solid spread of Anglo-Saxon culture across England. Contacts between the two countries had been established for thousands of years – the journey was only a day's sail in good conditions and similarities of language indicate close communication. In fact the fusion of indigenous dialects with the speech of the incomers is the origin of the Breton language. The name Brittany means Little Britain.

The territory at this time was divided into a series of small kingdoms. According to legend this was the Age of Saints, when Celtic monks and their followers primarily from Ireland and Wales crossed the channel to settle and build religious foundations. Stories of arrivals in stone boats probably reflect a scribal linguistic confusion of the Latin cumba (small boat) and old Breton koum (valley or hollowed-out stone trough). Generally the newcomers appear to have been well received, but the mixture of history and legend characteristic of this period is well illustrated by tales retaining hints of some localized opposition. Stories tell of saints such as Ronan and Ké being attacked and vilified on arrival.

There was a marked difference between the east and west of Brittany – the terms Haute and Basse Bretagne being used in the sense of nearer and further. Nearer, of course, meant nearer to seats of power elsewhere, whether Rome or Paris, as the empire of the Franks began to expand all over France. After the conversion of Clovis in AD 496, this meant the official Christianity of the Roman church. The east of Brittany developed under the influence of the Romans and then the Franks, with the resultant use of Latin and Gallo, a language derived from Latin. The Church of Rome held sway here with bishops of Breton sees appointed by the Pope under the authority of the Metropolitan bishop of Tours. In the west, matters were very different. The new religious leaders were simple holy men, sometimes hermits rather than worldly officials. They lived among their people and in nature, until drawn into political life by kings, such as Gradlon of Quimper, who persuaded St-Corentin to give up his rural life and become bishop of a new cathedral. If there were attempts to stamp out paganism (as tales of saints exorcizing the land of fierce dragons tend to suggest), then total success appears to have eluded the early Christians, given the mass of 'pagan' detail in decorative religious sculpture right up to the 17th century.

The emergence of Brittany

As the Franks began to expand their control throughout what is modern France, and powerful emperors such as Pepin the Short and Charlemagne sought domination, conflict with Brittany was inevitable. What is now eastern Brittany, roughly the department of Ille-et-Vilaine, became a sort of buffer zone, with Frankish lords installed to defend or attack as required. In the early ninth century, Louis the Pious made forays into Brittany against war-like leaders such as

Morvan, whose territory was around Langonnet but, while the army of the Franks could use sheer weight of numbers to overcome the Bretons in open fighting, they could not triumph against the sort of guerrilla tactics employed in the undulating hills and sinuous valleys of the interior. Each time authority seemed to have been imposed and Louis focused his attention elsewhere, there was trouble. Eventually he tried another tack and appointed a Breton, Nominoë, as Count of Vannes and *missus imperatoris*, the Emperor's representative. Peace was maintained in this way for Louis' lifetime, but when Charles the Bald took over, he was soon at loggerheads with Nominoë, who led Breton raids into the border lands. At the battle of Ballon (Bains-sur-Oust) the Bretons scored a stunning victory and Charles had no choice but to come to terms. Nominoë's son Erispoë kept up the same momentum and Charles had to grant him the title king and give up the lands of Rennes and Nantes. This period saw the naissance of a Breton state.

The Viking menace soon distracted both Bretons and Franks from their hostilities. Towns, villages, abbeys and islands were raided, with much destruction of resources, and more significantly, an exodus of nobles to France. Their later return brought French language and political influences to the detriment of Breton development.

A telling victory over the Vikings by Alain the Great at Questembert in AD 888 brought a temporary lull, but the horror was not over. After Landévennec Abbey was sacked in AD 913, the abbot called on another Alain, grandson of the first, who had been brought up at the court of Athelstan in England. Alain Barbetorte, as he became known, finally managed to put an end to the Viking threat in Brittany and made Nantes the new capital of his dukedom.

Menhir de Kerloas.

About the region

Normans & Plantagenets

Feuding rivals after his death brought more outside interference in Brittany, as William of Normandy battled around Dinan in support of a contender to the dukedom. Later, many Bretons were to cross the channel with him on the 1066 invasion of England, and subsequently held lands there in reward for their prowess.

The Plantagenets were next to try for control in Brittany, with Henry II using Conan IV, a weak duke, to rule indirectly before coming in person to besiege nobles opposed to his puppet. He finally arranged for his son Geoffrey to marry Conan's daughter and become duke in 1175. After Henry's death, French King Philippe Auguste, supported Arthur, Geoffrey's son, against the English King John. John had Arthur murdered, but Pierre de Dreux, cousin of the French king, married Alix, Arthur's half-sister, and became duke.

So in 1213, Brittany was already inextricably linked to France. The supremacy of the duke did not go unchallenged, and the lords of Léon and Penthièvre constantly strived to retain autonomy and fortify their territories. The successors of Pierre de Dreux brought a degree of stability and prosperity to Brittany, but when Jean III died in 1341 without naming an heir, all hell broke loose.

Wars of Succession

There were two claimants to the duchy, both related to Jean III. Jean de Monfort was his half-brother, and Jeanne de Penthièvre his niece. She was married to Charles de Blois, nephew of the king of France, so French support was assured for their side. Most of the high nobility also supported them, while Jean de Montfort, on the other hand, could call on English troops thanks to his connections with Edward III, and on much of Basse Bretagne.

The armed conflict, part of the Hundred Years War, caused appalling damage and loss of life on Breton soil for more than 20 years. Jean de Montfort was tricked into custody in Paris, then freed by the efforts of his wife after the Treaty of

Malestroit in 1341. He died soon after his release, but the war continued and Charles de Blois was captured in 1347, then kept prisoner in England for years. The famous Battle of the Thirty (see page 253) took place in 1351 near Josselin, with Beaumanoir's Breton side victorious and 18 English captives later ransomed. Jean de Montfort's son took up his father's cause and a decisive battle was fought near Auray in 1364. Charles de Blois was killed and the king of France finally had to acknowledge Jean IV as duke of Brittany.

The struggle with France

A period of stability under the Montfort dynasty enabled trade to flourish, especially during the long rule of Jean V (1399-1442), despite a final Penthièvre flurry of revenge when they captured the duke and held him prisoner for four months. When he was freed, their estates were confiscated, but the continuing antagonism of certain noble families did much to undermine Brittany's independence and security.

Tensions with the French court came to a head in the time of Duke François II. Louis XI laid claim to Brittany, and François called on the Breton council *Les Etats de Bretagne* to ensure the rights of his two daughters, Anne and Isabeau. He hoped to marry Anne to the Austrian emperor Maximilian, to keep the French out, but many of the Breton nobility, looking to their own advancement, sided openly with France. Armed conflict ensued and the French were victorious in a decisive battle at St-Aubin-du-Cormier (see page 105) in 1488.

François died soon after and Anne, aged 11, became a political pawn. Her supporters engineered a marriage by proxy to Maximilian but Charles VIII, newly crowned king of France, marched into Brittany and forced an annulment before marrying Anne himself. To keep Brittany firmly in French control, a clause in their wedding contract said that in the event of his death, Anne must marry his successor. When Charles did die suddenly, Anne became the wife of the new king, Louis XII.

As Duchess of Brittany, Anne was a popular figure, later taken as a symbol of her region's independence from France, although the political reality was rather different. Patron of the arts and religiously devout, Anne toured her duchy to rapturous welcomes and lavish gifts. Her image today remains a powerful evocation of medieval Brittany at its height. But of her eight children, only two girls survived infancy and she feared for the future of Brittany. Rightly so – Anne died in 1514 and Louis a year later, but he insisted before his death on the marriage of their daughter Claude to François d'Angoulême, heir to the French throne. Claude could not be expected to resist the pressures of French dominance, and in 1532 an act of Union was signed at Vannes (see page 233), making Brittany part of France. Important special privileges retained were exemption from military service outside Brittany, trials for Bretons before Breton courts, and no imposition of new taxes without the consent of the *Etats*. It was the end of an era, but the culmination of a long trend of Frenchification among the Breton upper classes.

Prosperity & war

A new period of peace and stability fostered Brittany's Golden Age of prosperity and artistic development. Towns and villages were permanent building sites as cathedrals, chapels and houses sprang up. The linen trade with England continued to flourish with Morlaix, Guingamp and Quintin much occupied in its execution. Fishing was also a major prop of the economy with boats from St-Malo and the Côte de Goëlo making the long journey to Newfoundland for cod as early as the 1520s.

Brittany got a new Parliament body in 1552, as the main court of justice for the region. Rennes, now the capital, was the location, with a suitably fine building later erected to house it (see page 90).

The Wars of Religion, which affected much of France, once again brought soldiers and destruction to Brittany. The Duke de Mercoeur,

governor and fanatical Catholic, set up his power base around Nantes in defiance of the French king, Henri IV, and the proclamation of tolerance for Protestants. He was determined to stamp out Protestantism in the region. Although most of Brittany was Catholic in faith, some powerful noble families, like Lavals and Rohans, were Protestant and this had some effect through their wide land-holdings. Towns like Brest and Rennes remained loyal to the king, as did the Breton Parliament.

Between 1589 and 1598, war raged across the region. Foreign soldiers poured in, the English in favour of the Protestant cause and the Spanish to support the Catholics. The Pointe des Espagnols in the Crozon Peninsula is an echo of a fortress from this period. St-Malo declared its independence as a Republic, which lasted four years before they surrendered to the king. In 1593 Henri IV converted to Catholicism to put an end to the war. He came to Brittany and accepted the surrender of the Duke of Mercoeur. The Edict of Nantes (1598) granted freedom of worship to Protestants.

Revival

The post-war relief was deep, and new expressions of counter-reformation religious faith burst out in further construction of convents and chapels. In western Brittany the extraordinary parish closes (see page 210), exquisitely decorated church precincts, came to life. There was also a revival of the missionary spirit, largely fuelled by Michel le Nobletz, born in Finistère in 1577. He travelled in western Brittany teaching and encouraging the poor to adhere to the Catholic faith. He used painted maps to represent biblical stories and parables (these *taolennou* were painted on wood or animal skins) in the same way that the stories of Jesus' passion on the calvaries were used to teach often illiterate parishioners. Père Julien Maunoir was le Nobletz's energetic successor, bringing thousands back into the fold but, coming from eastern Brittany, he did not speak Breton. A quick learner, he was soon able to continue the work, but the official story went that an angel had touched

About the region

Parliament building, Rennes.

him on the lips and given him the gift of speaking Breton at once.

The early part of the 17th century saw a development of the ports and naval facilities of Brittany under the auspices of the new governor, Cardinal Richelieu. In 1631 Brest was designated as the main military port, to take advantage of its vast protected roadstead or Rade. Lorient was created in 1666 as a place of naval construction and a home for the trading organization *Compagnie des Indes*, and Nantes was an already an important international trading centre.

The beginning of the end

As early as 1632 there were signs of tension in the terms of the Union, as the *Etats* made formal complaints to Louis XIII about the amounts of money being demanded by the crown as 'gifts' in breach of the original agreement, whereby their assent was required. It was glossed over on this occasion but this was to become the recurrent theme of relations between France and Brittany.

The determination of Colbert, finance minister of Louis XIV, to wrest money through taxation drove the first nails into the coffin of Brittany's traditional economy. Taxes on tobacco and stamped paper for legal transactions were announced without the agreement of the *Etats*, which led to rioting in the streets of Rennes and Nantes. The unrest spread to rural areas, particularly in western Brittany with the revolt of the Bonnets Rouges in 1675. After negotiations with the English and Dutch, this uprising found itself leaderless when Sebastien Le Balp was murdered by an aristocratic prisoner.

The peasants of Pays Bigouden were determined to pursue their claims to justice and protection from the abuses of the nobility. Rallying to the summons of church bells, they seized the towns of Pont l'Abbé and Concarneau before the Duc de Chaulnes arrived to ruthlessly quash the rebellion. In Combrit where the local lord had been murdered, 14 peasants were hanged from the same tree in reprisal. The bell towers of churches at the heart of the rebellion were taken down as a symbolic punishment – the church of Lambour in Pont l'Abbé (see page 187) remains an evocative reminder today. Rennes was also penalized, with the Breton Parliament exiled to Vannes until 1690.

Signs of unrest

The 18th century saw increasing social and political tensions in Brittany. The growth of towns and mercantile trade brought divisions between urban and rural areas and priorities. The gulf between rich and poor was felt by the peasants struggling with burdens of cultivation, taxation and obligation. The development of a commercial class who had money but little power was also an issue simmering below the surface. Louis XIV died in 1715 but his successors continued to make demands as European conflicts increased military spending. English blockades of Breton ports and raids on the land were a constant actual and psychological battle.

During the Seven Years War (1756-1763) St-Malo was a target for English attacks. Failing there, they landed further west and were surrounded when attempting to re-embark at St-Cast, with more than 2000 casualties (see page 153).

Nantes was now the second port in France and made much of its wealth from the slave-trade, with boats taking goods to Africa to exchange for slaves then moving on to the West Indies to exchange slaves for luxury goods like sugar to bring back to Nantes. Shipbuilding was also important there, and at Brest where the arsenal employed nearly 5000 people. Meanwhile Breton corsairs confronted France's commercial rivals, the English and Dutch, in the Channel and on the high seas worldwide.

An event of 1764 brought political tensions to crisis point. In the so-called Affaire de Bretagne, there was a clash between La Chalotais, president of the Breton parliament and the Duc d'Aiguillon, Commander-in-Chief of the region. Louis XV intervened to poor effect: when the Bretons refused to obey him, he resorted to the extreme of dissolving Parliament. La Chalotais was arrested and imprisoned, accused of political incitement, but his support held firm and eventually the new king, Louis XVI, freed him in 1774 and restored the rights of Parliament.

French Revolution

Initially the French Revolution was generally favoured in Brittany for obvious reasons. Many were tired of what they saw as the oppression and injustice of the nobility and no one was keen on the constant demands for money to fund French quarrels. The earliest clashes of the Revolution took place on the streets of Rennes, and Bretons were at the forefront of the revolt in Paris, through the influential Club Breton. Guy Le Guen de Kerangall from Landivisiau made an influential speech against the nobility in the French Assembly.

Early moves by the Revolutionary authorities in Paris to recognize regional differences by producing decrees in various languages, including Breton, were reassuring. The Breton representatives agreed to cede the special privileges Brittany had enjoyed since union in 1532 – what need was there in the new age of equality and republicanism? The Breton Parliament and the *Etats* were formally abolished in 1789. Brittany was divided into five departments – Côtes-du-Nord (now Côtes d'Armor), Finistère, Morbihan, Ille-et-Vilaine and Loire-Inférieure. As there was only to be one bishopric per department, four were lost at Dol-de-Bretagne, St-Pol, St-Malo and Tréguier.

It was largely the issue of religion that changed a swathe of public opinion in Brittany. In 1791 all clergy were pressured to swear an oath of allegiance to the Republic. Some 75% in Brittany refused and were ousted from their parishes. Many went into hiding and still gave secret mass for their loyal followers. When anti-clerical measures began to come into force, and peasants realized they were no better off than under their noble masters, many pockets of resistance to revolutionary ideas grew

up. As early as 1791 the Marquis de la Rouërie had founded a Catholic, anti-revolutionary, pro-monarchy movement around Fougères. This soon fizzled out with his death, but the Chouan uprisings further south in the Vendée found an echo in certain parts of Brittany. Morbihan was a stronghold for Chouan bands, who mostly worked independently. One leader, Cadoudal, was part of a plan to land English forces at Quiberon to support the Chouans. This was a tragic failure as the attackers were hemmed in on the peninsula and then forced to surrender or were killed by General Hoche (see page 239).

When Prussia and Austria began hostilities against France, Bretons were called up into the French army, as their old exemption was lost. Many young Bretons preferred to go into hiding or join Chouan bands rather than leave their homeland. In 1800, the bishop of Quimper, who had voted for the decapitation of Louis XVI, was murdered on the road by Chouan activists. When Napoleon came to power he sent troops to put an end to Chouannerie once and for all. Pontivy, the military centre in Morbihan where the counter-revolutionaries were most active, was renamed Napoleonville. Cadoudal was eventually arrested and executed in 1804. The Emperor took some steps to calm the situation. His Concordat with the Pope in 1801 allowed priests to return, and he gave a short exemption from service outside Brittany to those of military age.

Another consequence of European opposition to the Revolution was the construction of the Nantes–Brest canal. It was given the go-ahead by Napoleon as a strategic defensive measure for cross-Brittany transport at a time when the English were blockading Breton ports. It was to link the arsenals at Nantes, Brest and Hennebont (in conjunction with the Blavet canal) and provide a secure internal supply route. In fact the canal's main use on completion 30 years later was commercial rather than military.

The first half of the 19th century was a challenging one in Brittany. No longer with special privileges, Bretons found their culture and language under threat in an era of conformism and uniformity. The Church, mainstay of Breton's strong social cohesion, faced hard challenges within a secular state. A decree of 1793 said that teaching should be in French only and, as much education in Brittany was delivered by Breton-speaking priests, it seemed to be an anti-clerical measure.

Political parties gradually emerged, with the Blues, who were republican, progressive and hostile to traditionalists and the Church, and the conservative Whites, aristocrats and clergy who had the support of many dependent peasants. An exception was in the Monts d'Arrée, where some of the poorest people in Brittany took the side of progress. Area support for these groups pretty much mirrored current 21st-century voting, with Léon, Morbihan and eastern Ille-et-Vilaine essentially with the conservative Whites, and the rest of Finistère and the Trégor with the Blues.

Economic progress was mixed. Traditional industries such as the cloth trade and foundries were in decline and agriculture suffered from a lack of manpower as foreign wars continued to rage. Even in the 1840s people were dying of famine and pestilence, and rural life was grim. Inland ports such as Morlaix and Redon declined as ships got larger, while Lorient flourished.

Communications improved as the Nantes–Brest canal was finally finished in 1842 and the railway pushed its way into Brittany; by 1865 Quimper, Rennes and Brest were linked to the main French network, and numerous branch lines in the latter part of the century saw commercial and touristic development for places like Douarnenez, Roscoff and Dinard.

Agriculture began to expand with better fertilization available, and more land came under cultivation. But overall there was a decline in the numbers of the rural population as larger towns, like Rennes, grew. In the latter part of the century as many as 300,000 Bretons left Brittany for Paris, other large towns or abroad.

The end of the century saw a great revival of antiquarian interest in the 'Celtic' aspect of Breton development. The URB (Union Régionaliste Bretonne) formed in 1898, to study Breton language, folklore and oral traditions.

Industrially, as factories grew so did disputes between bosses and workers. Unions began in the 1890s and strikes became common, often leading to violence. Politics saw the formation of the earliest Breton Nationalist Party (PNB) in 1911. Numerous Bretons lost their lives on the battlefields of the First World War, which also saw the arrival of many foreigners – workers, refugees, the wounded, American soldiers – in Brittany. The most elaborate Great War memorial in Brittany is at St-Anne d'Auray in Morbihan.

Moving towards modernity

Between the wars, Brittany had France's first communist mayor at Douarnenez in 1921, but political power swung between conservatives and socialists. The Breton nationalists, although few in number, were conspicuously active, blowing up a statue in Rennes representing the union of Brittany and France.

The white and black flag (*Gwenn ha du*) regarded today as the Breton standard was created in 1926 by Morvan Marchal, a nationalist, with its symbolic reference back to the medieval days of Breton 'independence'. The hermines are from the duchy's coat of arms and the black bands represent the five bishoprics of Haute Bretagne and the white those of Basse Bretagne.

In the Second World War Brittany was taken over by the Germans in June 1940. About 150,000 soldiers of three army corps came in as the last British troops left, sabotaging the ports as they went. Submarines were soon operating from Brest, Lorient and St-Nazaire, which all became the targets of allied air-raids. Remains of the defensive structures of the Mur de l'Atlantique are still visible

Gwenn ha du, the flag of Brittany.

around the coast. Many groups of resistance fighters were active in Brittany, often working in conjunction with allied parachutists. A small number of extreme nationalists, like Olier Mordrel, collaborated openly with the enemy. The Museum of the Resistance at St-Marcel in Morbihan (see page 256) presents a vivid picture of these hard times of occupation. Liberation began in July 1944 as the allied forces moved steadily west. Some places, such as Quimper, drove the Germans out themselves.

The terrible destruction of Brest, St-Malo and Lorient led to many years of reconstruction. Nantes had been taken from Brittany by the Vichy government during the war and this was cemented with the creation of the new department of Loire-Atlantique, head of Pays de la Loire in 1957. In 1950, CELIB (Comité d'étude et de liaison des intérêts bretons) was set up to attract investment into Brittany, with car manufacturers and telecommunications companies later established at Rennes, Vannes and Lannion. Today, the food industry is the largest industrial sector, with shipbuilding and other branches of nautical science also important, along with marine and health technology. The region is renowned for its high standards of education, training and research centres.

Brittany remains the main French fishing area, but numbers involved in the industry have gradually dwindled in the last 50 years. Farming, on the other hand, has modernized and expanded to a powerful agricultural lobby in the most prolific vegetable-growing area in France, which also produces a large proportion of the nation's milk, pork and chicken.

Modern Brittany is far from just a quaint setting for all those standing stones and Celtic tales. Yes, it's a rich land of the imagination and a fertile source of oral tradition, but also a complex, diverse and ever-evolving reality, where history gives legend a run for its money and contemporary culture thrives.

Religion in Brittany

Appreciation of Brittany's distinctive heritage starts with religion. The region has the largest concentration of religious monuments in Europe, and the faith of the people has fuelled much of their history right from the start.

The seven Founding Saints of Brittany and the cathedrals associated with them have a particular place in the Breton pantheon. St-Pol (St-Pol-de-Léon), St-Malo, St-Brieuc, St-Samson (Dol-de-Bretagne) and St-Tugdual (Tréguier) were Welsh incomers, while St-Patern (Vannes) and St-Corentin (Quimper) were natives of the peninsula. In medieval times the Tro Breiz was an important pilgrimage around Brittany, which visited each cathedral, a custom that has been revived recently as a religious or walking exercise covering more than 600 km. Tales of miracle-working by the saints, such as driving out dragons, are probably symbolic stories of attempts to put an end to local paganism.

These saints are 'unofficial', never sanctified by the Roman Catholic hierarchy. The legacy of the simple, intimate faith they embody remains today in the extraordinary number of wayside crosses (marking pilgrims' routes), chapels and sacred springs (*fontaines*) with a saint's statue, where the waters had healing powers. The tradition of pardons, religious processions on saints' days, is still flourishing mainly in the west, when traditional banners are carried and the faithful – or horses, or even inanimate objects – are blessed. The rural nature of these religious practices is clear in traditions such as the butter pardon of St-Herbot, at which cows' tail hairs are still offered.

The different developments of eastern and western Brittany throws up important contrasts – the official church of Rome held sway in the east via the Romans and the Franks, while Basse-Bretagne to the west was converted by hermit-

The language of faith

Statues were easily recognizable to the often illiterate faithful by the simple addition of symbols related to their subject's life. So St-Laurent is always shown holding a grill, reflecting his martyrdom, St-Roch points to a boil on his leg from endurance of the plague, and Ste-Marguérite stands over the dragon that swallowed her and then thought better of it when she tickled his inside with her cross. Ste-Anne is always portrayed as a tall woman, with veiled head. Children enjoy looking out for these identifying signs!

priests of Ireland, Wales and southwest England with their Celtic practices. Place names starting in Plou (parish), Lan and Loc (holy places) reflect the development of this western area. Here, people retained a close and very human relationship with their saints, calling on them for favours and even resorting to 'punishments' like turning statues to face the wall if their demands remained unmet.

The early saints had a greater hold over the hearts and imaginations of the Bretons than any rivals the official Catholic church could produce, although the cult of Mary or Notre Dame is ubiquitous. Her mother, Saint Anne, also has a high profile here – there's a local legend that she visited the Bay of Douarnenez. Her status as the female patron of Brittany has led to an association with medieval ruler Anne de Bretagne, who has strangely acquired a saint-like image in notions of Breton identity.

Stone stories

The widespread presence of Neolithic monuments in Brittany sparked a multitude of stories in the days before history and archaeology could explain their original context. In the 19th century, the megaliths became anachronistically associated with the Druids, regarded as sites of ritual sacrifices and debauched pagan revelry in popular imagination. Many alignments today still have local names like Druids Cemetery and Druids Row. The stones are also often associated with the *korrigans*, ugly, mischievous and downright dangerous gnomish imps of Breton legend, who were said to live in or around them.

Similarly, legends evolved to explain the very existence of the stones, thought to have been humans originally. So a drunken wedding party was literally petrified by an angry priest, dancing girls were punished for their levity, or Roman soldiers were turned to stone by a saint they were chasing.

Such was the power of superstition over the common people, that Christianized menhir are

Death

Christianity never managed to oust the fascination with death common in Celtic cultures, and Death looms graphically in Breton legend and belief. The usual manifestation is Ankou, Death's skeletal assistant, who drives his cart in search of victims. His skull image, sometimes with killing arrow, is portrayed on many ossuaries in Breton church enclosures. The legendary entrance to the Celtic underworld was said to be the Yeun Ellez in the marshes of the Monts d'Arrée, where the lonely landscape has given rise to many tales of danger for the unwary traveller (see page 209).

common, with a cross or religious engravings added to standing stones – such as the Menhir de St-Uzec (see page 144) – to reclaim the stones for the Church and turn the tide of pagan practices.

Pardons are religious processions held on saints' days.

Art & architecture

Quimper Cathedral.

Brittany has never been a place of ostentatious domestic architecture, but the channelling of money and faith into community projects was common. The greatest glory of Breton art and architecture finds its expression in religious structures, from the grandest cathedral to the simplest wayside calvary. Wherever you turn in the region, there will be a church spire, a little chapel, or a finely carved sculptural group on a *calvaire*. Dark, abiding Kersanton stone was most sought after for the statuary of this work.

Architecture

From Neolithic to Roman

In the 19th century the megaliths were believed to be associated with the Druids – hence stories of sacrificial stones. Only with more sophisticated dating techniques was their much earlier origin revealed. The oldest remains are burial places (6000-3000 BC), usually given the name dolmen (stone tables), a reference to the simplest structure of uprights and roof stones. In fact, many styles developed over time with passageways leading to the funerary chamber or multiple chambers. Some of the earliest relics are cairns, most famously at Barnenez, a collection of chambers covered by a huge mound of small stones, and the tumulus, a mound covered by earth, such as the Tumulus de Kercado at Carnac. The Musée de Préhistoire at Carnac (see page 242) demonstrates how burial practice developed. Carved decoration on the interior stone faces is the earliest artwork in Brittany, with fine examples on the island of Gavrinis (see page 235) and the Table des Marchands at Locmariaquer (see page 243). Here, geometric patterns and representational shapes such as axe heads can be seen. Elsewhere, pairs of bumps imaginatively claimed to represent goddess breasts, with oar and shield-shaped objects common motifs.

Some standing stones (menhir – long stones) were also once decorated, but exposure has generally destroyed the details. An exception is at St-Samson-sur-Rance. The purpose of their erection is generally uncertain, but use as territorial, positional or directional markers seems likely, or ceremonial where large groups – alignments – are found. The wonders of Carnac are world famous, but there are also spectacular creations of stones at Erdeven, Monteneuf and St-Just.

While the Iron Age Celtic tribes notoriously have not left permanent structures, apart from hill-forts, even the Roman occupation of Brittany has comparatively few remains. The site of Corseul, once Fanum Martis (shrine of Mars), is interesting, with the foundations of a street with shops and private houses remaining. A short distance away is the remarkable octagonal Temple of Mars – hence the town's former name. Carhaix-Plouguer is also producing more and more evidence of its Roman town, which had an aqueduct built in the third century AD, bringing water from 27 km away. There are well-restored baths at Hogolo on the coast of Côtes d'Armor, and an elaborate series of stone tanks for producing *garum*, the fish sauce so beloved by the Romans, at Douarnenez (see page 203).

Brittany rocks

Brittany's architecture is dominated by granite, a durable material, but only worked with effort. It has a wide colour range, depending on the mineral make-up, from the most common grey, to pink and a warm yellow in the Trégor region. Schist, a softer stone, has always been used in all types of building and appears from grey-brown to blue-green, and even a distinctive purplish variety in the area west of Rennes. It also provides the characteristic thick roof tiles.

Religious architecture

Almost nothing survives from the Age of Saints or formatory period of Brittany, as many of the earliest churches were destroyed during the Viking incursions. From the 11th century, the first stone-built edifices appeared in Romanesque style with high rounded arches and carved capitals, small upper windows and a sobriety of decoration, the idea being that worship did not need distraction. A few fine examples remain, in part if not whole, at the abbey of Redon and St-Gildas-de-Rhuys.

The advent of Gothic design in the 13th century brought light sweeping into the churches, with high arched windows in the characteristic pointed shape. The cathedral at Quimper and the chapter house at the Abbaye de Beauport illustrate the beauty of the fine stone tracery and vaulting of this style.

The development of Flamboyant Gothic in the late 15th and early 16th centuries gave free rein to the imagination of architects and sculptors. In religious buildings, much is remarkably lacking the constraints of the Catholic Church. Secret medieval jokes are not so secret in these days of binoculars and zoom-lenses, so look up at lofty gargoyles and the decorative details of interior beams for some amusing surprises and a riot of lively detail.

The sublime and original Breton contribution came from the 16th-century fervour of the Counter-Reformation and the development of the parish close (see page 210). A precinct wall

About the region

Carved sculptures, Côtes d'Armor.

Within Breton churches, the greatest show is in ornate and brightly-coloured altarpieces, which developed in detail and display in the 16th to 17th centuries. Typical subject matter is the life of the patron saint of the church, the Rosary or the Assumption of the Virgin Mary. The best are in the parish closes, but the most extraordinary of all must be Mary and her baby lying in an actual double bed above the altar at Le Yaudet (page 143). Statuary and relics of saints have always been of prime importance in Breton churches, but many were lost or destroyed at the time of the Revolution.

Some churches still retain remarkable rood screens, with the greatest of these (unusually) in wood, such as that at Loc-Envel (see page 158). Painted wall-frescoes and ceiling panels have also been discovered in some churches, hidden under later whitewash or panelling. Kernascléden (page 249) is famous for the Dance of Death above the nave, with skeletons gripping humans of all walks of life by the hand.

Externally, churches developed steadily over the centuries. When parish councils could no longer meet on the stone benches in the porches and secure storage for treasures was needed, sacristies were a common addition behind one side of the altar. Spires were often a major feature of the church – in northwestern Brittany the most familiar is the Beaumanoir style with square towers, hexagonal spires and a round stair tower alongside. Some beautiful spires in open stonework, like that of Bulat-Pestivien, and a Renaissance dome effect can also be seen, although Brittany clung to its traditions, and this style of architecture is mostly manifested in additions rather than grand conceptions.

The Revolution and its anti-religious measures saw many churches fall into disrepair or private hands, or plundered for building stone. At the end of the 19th century when congregations were again on the increase, new churches were often built and old ones destroyed or remodelled. If you want to see what modern architects made of a religious challenge, visit the amazing post-war church of St-Louis in Brest (see page 191).

encloses the church, cemetery, calvary and ossuary. Access was through a triumphal arch, symbolic of triumph over death for the righteous, but architecturally an echo of those of victorious Roman generals. The figure of Ankou, the skull-like sidesman of Death, sometimes appears in decorative detail on the ossuary. At Lanrivain, this still contains neatly sorted bones and skulls, and at St-Fiacre, the little skull-boxes sit in a row on a stone shelf.

The art of the calvary also developed at this time. Once brightly painted, these elaborate structures figure scenes used for teaching an illiterate congregation about the life and Passion of Christ, and also, at the top, the ultimate lesson of the resurrection, the triumph of faith over death. The finest can be seen in the parish closes of northern Finistère, see pages 210-213.

Châteaux and defensive structures

The earliest castles were little more than wooden towers on raised mottes, as shown on the Bayeux tapestry, when William of Normandy came to Brittany to oust Duke Conan II. Stone began to be used from the 12th century – a tower base at the impressive castle of Fougères (see page 105) may be the one dismantled by Henry II in 1166. In this border area between Brittany and France, château-fortresses were of great importance and this is the best place to study the history of castle development, which can be read at Fougères and Vitré in the various defensive enclosures and the changing shape of the towers, from rounded to horseshoe, to deal with the new demands of artillery offensives in the 15th and 16th centuries. Perhaps the finest example of early coastal defences is to be seen at Fort La Latte (see page 154), which proved invulnerable from the sea.

From the 13th century towns too were encircled by stout defensive walls, essential in the torrid times of medieval conflicts. The ramparts of Dinan (see page 149) cover almost 3 km today, and other good examples can be seen at Vannes and the small *ville close* of Concarneau.

The Wars of Succession and Wars of Religion both caused great damage to châteaux owned by the nobility. Being on the wrong side in a conflict often led to the building's punitive or symbolic dismantlement; this happened to several towers at Josselin, but this château retains a superlative Flamboyant-Gothic interior façade (see page 253). Others, such as Hunaudaye, suffered damage at the time of the Revolution when Chouan resistance led to reprisals. The finest of ruined castles with elements from the 13th to 16th centuries can be seen at Tonquédec (see page 144). The ducal château of Suscinio (page 237), in an odd position on the marshes in the Gulf of Morbihan, suffered more from neglect than attack, but has now been well restored. The Renaissance château is rare in Brittany but there are fine examples at Châteaubriand and Kerjean in Léon, which employed the talents of the parish close craftsmen.

Château at Josselin.

Coastal protection & defence

The chain of fortifications built by Vauban, Louis XIV's royal engineer, to protect the coast against European rivals during the 17th and 18th centuries are impressive proof of architectural development. Many of these structures were utilized by the occupying Germans in the Second World War. Remains of their defensive chain, the Mur de l'Atlantique, is all-pervasive, with bunkers and gun-batteries littering the coasts. The museum of the Battle of the Atlantic is actually in a bunker near Camaret, and Fort du Dellec near Brest, where the Germans took over a Vauban installation, is now part of a public park.

An early fire tower survives at the Abbaye St-Mathieu (see page 195) and the lighthouses that came to succeed this warning system began at the end of the 17th century with Le Stiff (1699) on the island of Ouessant. The great age of lighthouses came later with Eckmühl (1897) and the tallest in Europe at Ile Vierge (1902), which can both be visited. These remain an enduring symbol of Brittany and its staunch maritime identity.

Vernacular architecture

Granite and schist in all variations of colour dominate the architecture of houses in Brittany. Slate roofs are the norm, although thatch was favoured in areas of marshland in the east. The minor Breton nobility was never very rich and rural *manoirs* are usually small, even if they show a refinement of decorative detail.

Remains of some of the earliest stone houses, with 12th-century Romanesque façades, can be seen at Dol-de-Bretagne (see page 101).

In towns where space was at a premium, the narrow upwards elongated house was the answer. Early 16th- to 17th-century half-timbered

Pont-Aven.

merchants' houses still brighten the old centres of places like Rennes, Quimper, Vannes, Morlaix and Malestroit. These *pan de bois* constructions have timber frames with plastered lathe infill. Some were pillared and recessed at ground level to create a covered walkway, but few of these *maisons à porche* survive intact. One twist on the essential design is found only in Morlaix where two examples of the *maison à pondalez* style (see page 208) can be visited. Many of these houses were later faced with slate, which was more fireproof and less demanding to construct.

Building in stone increased in the 17th century, with finely proportioned granite houses of the period, best seen (outside the cities of Quimper and Rennes) in the small towns of Locronan (Finistère) and Lizio (Morbihan). St-Malo has a wealth of restored 18th-century wealthy traders' houses. In the Monts d'Arrée there is a style of peasant-farmer dwelling often called, for reasons obscure, a *maison anglaise*. This may be because of the wealth that came from the linen trade with England, or a linguistic confusion. The Maison Cornec (1702) in St-Rivoal (see page 209) is typical with its covered outside stair and *apoteis*.

Art

Brittany is more famous for inspiring art than producing native artists, and is known for its *art populaire*, which is rooted in landscape and custom, rather than grandiose themes. The Romantic movement of the late 19th century saw revived interest in its Celtic past – the megaliths, Druid rituals and pagan folklore. Paintings of pardons, washerwomen and village weddings give much detail of costume, architecture and rural society, often romanticized. The Pont-Aven school and later Nabis, such as Maurice Denis, gave a new attention to many aspects of the landscape.

Some native 20th-century artists stand out. Mathurin Méheut (1882-1958) was born in Lamballe

Pont-Aven School

This little river town developed into an artists' colony in the 19th century, attracting first Americans, then a group including Gauguin, Emile Bernard, Maurice Denis and Paul Sérusier in the 1880s. They developed a new style – sometimes called Synthetism – in rather flat, boldly blocked and coloured renderings of local landscape and life. Examples are to be found in every major art gallery in Brittany.

If you want to visit Pont-Aven with its town art museum and many private galleries, it is a 30-km drive from Quimper, a very pretty place, and famous for its biscuits as well as painters. A tourist honey-pot destination, it is always packed in high season.

where there is now a museum dedicated to him in the Maison du Bourreau. His themes are inspired by Breton dependence on the sea, and his striking paintings of fishermen and boats show outlines in a few swift dark lines in angular shapes, then overlaid and rounded with bright strokes of colour.

Surrealist Yves Tanguy (1900-1955) was of Breton parentage and spent much of his childhood in Brittany. Later, he produced many works around the Bay of Douarnenez where his ashes were eventually scattered.

The Musée des Beaux Arts at Quimper has a section devoted to Max Jacob (1876-1944), a native of the city. He was an artist, writer and visionary who was also a leading figure of bohemian Paris and a close friend of Picasso, Matisse and Modigliani.

Where to look

The art galleries in Vannes, Rennes, Quimper and Brest have good collections of Breton painting and paintings on Breton subjects. Other places where art has an emphasis are Le Faouët and Pont-Aven. For modern working artists in many media, it's worth visiting the centres of Pont Scorff, La Gacilly and Rochefort-en-Terre.

Brittany today

Port Haliguen, Quiberon.

Dynamic culture

Music, dance, storytelling and performance art thrive throughout Brittany's packed festival calendar, which provides endless possibilities for burgeoning local talent and high-profile performers. Brittany is remarkably open and receptive to outside influences as well as proud of its own incredibly diverse cultural scope. This first became a focus for preservation and development in the late 19th century when all things Celtic became popular. More recently a major revival in the 1970s stimulated a new vibrancy and creativity, drawing on old traditions to create new forms and contexts. The magazine review *Ar-Men* is at the forefront of exploring all aspects of Breton history and culture.

The real Brittany

The issue of what constitutes the 'real' Brittany is still alive and kicking. Historically Nantes was the capital city from the time of Alain Barbetorte in the

10th century until the 20th century, when it was severed by the Vichy government, an arrangement confirmed in 1957 with the creation of the Loire-Atlantique region with Nantes at the head. Unionists want this dismantled to reunite the two parts of Brittany. The Nantes–Brest canal has become something of a symbol of this unity as it crosses the whole territory of 'historic Brittany', linking the lost limb with its body. Many still routinely regard Loire-Atlantique as part of Brittany.

The ubiquitous black and white Breton flag (*Gwenn ha du*) was originally created in the 1920s by Morvan Marchal, at a time when nationalism was a theme in European politics. Still regarded as a symbol of Breton independence by nationalists and separatists, the flag has come to be a vivid emblem of the region's distinctive individualism, see page 37.

British inhabitants

Brittany today is home to thousands of British people, particularly in the central part of the region where house prices are much cheaper than the desirable coastal zones. Although the positive tide of incomers has subsided somewhat in recent years, Brittany continues to be an affordable foreign location, conveniently close to friends and family back across the channel. Some villages have high percentages of British inhabitants, and there's even an English monthly magazine, *The Central Brittany Journal* (including a What's On section), which has done great work towards helping incomers to integrate. The same is true of the AIKB, Association Intégration Kreizh Breizh (aikb.fr), based in Gouarec, which has an excellent programme of cultural events as well as an advisory service and language lessons.

Anyone who wishes to find out about Brittany and participate in local events can expect a warm welcome from the Bretons.

The Breton language

There are many classes available for those who wish to learn Breton today. This language, a Brythonic tongue related to Welsh and, more closely, Cornish, is spoken now by about 250,000 people, mainly in Finistère. The western part of Brittany, Basse Bretagne, was settled in the fifth and sixth centuries by incomers from southwest England and Wales. Their speech, blended with that of the indigenous population, formed Breton. Earliest examples of writing date from the ninth century, but it was mainly an oral culture, passed down the generations. In eastern Brittany, French, Latin and Gallo were spoken. Once Brittany became part of France, the hold of French increased among the aristocracy, and after the French Revolution, which initially supported regional languages, Breton suffered serious persecution. Its preservation lay largely in the hands of peasants and the clergy, who continued their defiance by teaching it in schools and holding mass in their own language. But conformity was imposed by the state, and from the 19th century right up until the 1950s, children were punished in school for uttering a word of their own tongue, and made to wear humiliating symbols like wooden sabots round their neck. A law of 1951 finally allowed teaching in Breton, and soon there were Breton-language radio and TV. The association Dastum now works to preserve oral traditions by recording songs and stories handed down over generations.

There are essentially four dialects of Breton from the districts of Cornouaille, Léon, Trégor and Vannes, with distinctively different accents. This also accounts for varied spellings of Breton words you may still see. During the 1940s, however, a unified version was developed and imposed, with the intention of strengthening the language's future. Many of the older generation cling proudly to their birth dialect, but the Breton you will find today, that taught in bilingual Diwan schools or used in public service, is the official Brezhoneg.

See page 280 for a Breton glossary and more language information.

Nature & environment

The Armorican peninsula on the edge of France occupies a transitional position between the colder north and warmer south, leading to a special range of fauna and creating an important refuge for many overwintering birds. Known as a land of granite and schist, the soil is acidic and traditionally poor until the extensive use of seaweed-based fertilizer began a crucial revitalization that has turned Brittany into one of the most productive agricultural regions. There's much of geological interest here, from the formation of the Gulf of Morbihan, to the extraordinary shapes of the Pink Granite Coast, the pillow-lavas of the Crozon Peninsula and the marine grottoes of Morgat.

Coast

The traditional picture of Brittany is that of its fabulous coast – more than 2000 km of heavily indented shore, punctuated by ports, beaches, dunes, islands and lighthouses. And being on the northwest tip of France means that the sea is on three sides. So Armor, the land of the sea, has been the predominant image of this region for hundreds of years. It is a birdwatcher's paradise, with numerous reserves for the 17 species of nesting seabirds and many other visiting migrants. As well as numerous varieties of gulls, cormorants, terns and guillemots, you might see choughs, puffins, razorbills and overwintering spoonbills. In the Atlantic waters off Finistère, seals are common, and dolphins often entertain visitors taking boats to the islands of Molène and Ouessant.

There are more than 600 varieties of seaweed on Breton coasts, many harvested for fertilizer, or for cosmetic or culinary purposes. Old stone ovens sunk into the ground that were used to burn the seaweed can be seen in many places along the coastal path in the west. There are centres of interpretation for this unusual industry in Lannilis and Plouguerneau in northern Finistère, where there is still activity on a significant scale. The prolific species *ulva lactuca* (sea lettuce) is a recurrent problem in certain areas with shallow bays and weak currents, since it creates a line of smelly green scum around beaches as it rots. You will often see daily clean-up operations in tourist areas.

The state of the tides certainly affects the appearance of coastal areas, and also activities, so it's important to check the daily times by buying a timetable from a newsagent or consulting the tourist office when planning days out. Some bays, such as those of St-Brieuc and St-Michel, have very long tide recessions, leaving miles of sand and no sign of water at low tide. Estuaries can also be little more than mud-banks when the water is low.

The cliffs and dunes are ecologically sensitive areas, and it is important to respect the advised paths in these areas to avoid further erosion. On the Atlantic coast, especially in the vast, exposed Baie d'Audierne, the salt-resistant marram grass

Brittany's coastline.

and long-rooted sea-kale and samphire are planted to help stabilize the dunes. Natural, defensive pebble-banks here were badly undermined when they were taken away and used to make concrete during the German occupation.

In general the south coast is fairly flat in contrast with the north and west, where long stretches of high cliffs are to be found around Cap Fréhel, on the Côte de Goëlo around Plouha, the Crozon Peninsula and Cap Sizun. The striking shapes and colours of the famous Pink Granite Coast in the north contrast with a softer shoreline around the Gulf of Morbihan. Most dramatic of all is the Atlantic exposure of western Finistère, where waves drive in from the vast ocean.

Interior

The interior, the Argoat or land of the woods, is also rich in its variety of landscape from high granite plateaux or *landes*, covered in heathland, to the beautiful river valleys so common here. Brittany has always been known for its granite base, but this is by no means ubiquitous and many areas are based on varieties of schist and quartzite. The extraordinary natural phenomenon of the granite 'chaos' can be seen at Huelgoat or the Gorges of Corong and Toul-Goulic, formed from magma pushed to the surface and then weathered over millions of years into huge boulders that have finally tumbled into strange formations like a giant's fantasy lego.

The forested area of oak, beech and chestnut that once spread across Brittany, providing material for ship-building and clog-making, is now largely denuded with rich remnants here and there across the peninsula such as the Forêt de Fougères, the Forêt de Paimpont, the area around Huelgoat and the Forêt de Cranou. Many conifer plantations have been added in recent times. In areas of intensive agriculture the glorious hedgerows and *chemins creux*, sunken lanes, have sadly been lost.

In the west, the Monts d'Arrée, the highest hills in Brittany, are a stark series of schist and quartz crests, the slopes covered with wild moors of gorse and heathers, and below, in a delicate ecological balance, the *tourbières* or peat-bogs that harbour such plants as the flesh-eating drosera and spaghnia moss.

As far as mammals go, wood and scrubland hide plenty of roe deer, wild boar (*sangliers*) and foxes in the rural areas, and pine-martens can also be seen. Aquatic mammals such as otters survive in areas of pure water, and the canals attract many coypu. Special breeds of domesticated animals to look out for include black or dark brown Ouessant sheep, and *pie noir* (piebald) cows, which are a fairly small, horned Breton variety. There are many native breeds of horses, cows and goats at the nature reserve of Menez Meur (see page 209).

Minerals were once widely exploited in the interior of Brittany, with the largest lead/silver mines in France in the 18th century near Poullaouen in Finistère. The canals, waterwheel and mine-shafts can still be seen in the forest of Huelgoat. Iron working was a major source of employment with forges largely sited near the resources of forested areas – the Forge des Salles (see page 164) near Bon Repos in Côtes d'Armor preserves such a production village of the 18th and 19th centuries.

In general, the landscape of eastern Brittany and northern Finistère is much more highly cultivated and undistinguished than the green, wilder heart of the centre and the wide open spaces of mid-Finistère.

Waterways

Water is never far away in Brittany, with many glorious rivers, and some large estuaries. In the west these are known as Abers, like the Aber Wrac'h and the Aber Ildut. In the ambitious 19th-century programme of canalization, large rivers such as the Oust, Blavet and Aulne were utilized, with artificial stretches constructed to connect the relevant valleys. The Nantes–Brest canal runs right across Brittany, with the Ille-et-Vilaine canal running north-south in the east and the Blavet linking Pontivy and the south coast in the centre.

Brittany has had more than its share of ecological disasters, with the wreck of the *Amoco Cadiz* in 1978 spilling oil along hundreds of kilometres of shoreline. The anchor of that ill-fated ship now stands on the quay at Portsall, a constant reminder of the destructive 'black tides' on the northern coast. In 1999 the *Erika* repeated this nightmare, breaking up off the southwest of Penmarc'h after an abortive attempt to reach the Loire estuary.

The most pressing current environmental issue is the high level of nitrate in certain rivers, resulting from intensive use of pesticides. Initiatives are in place to tackle this where required, but elsewhere the pure quality of the water is indicated by the presence of otters and beavers, especially in Finistère. Breizh Bocage is a programme to protect water from pollution by re-planting and encouraging hedging and scrubland around intensively farmed terrain. There are also increasing numbers of migratory salmon and eels in rivers like the Aulne and the Elorn. You will see fish ladders on many locks in the Nantes–Brest canal, although many fishermen would like to see the rivers revert to their natural state.

Energy

Development of new sources of energy is another big issue, with Brittany lying at the edge of French networks. The first nuclear power station in France was built in the 1960s in the underpopulated Monts d'Arrée in Finistère, but this was decommissioned 25 years ago. Popular protest and mass demonstrations prevented the siting of a second nuclear plant near the Pointe du Raz in 1980.

Today, wind farms are increasingly common in line with a major development plan, but with the great potential of marine energy, as shown by the barrage of the Rance, there is also current investigation of underwater *hydroliennes*, with promising initial results at Benodet.

Sept Iles, Côtes d'Armor.

Regional parks & nature reserves

The Parc Naturel Régional d'Armorique was created in 1968 and runs across Finistère, taking in the islands of Ouessant and Molène, the Crozon Peninsula and Rade de Brest and the Monts d'Arrée. In addition to an exceptional variety of terrain, there are many centres of interpretation, such as the nature reserve at Menez Meur and the Maison des Mineraux near Crozon, which explains the geology of the area.

The Parc naturel marin d'Iroise is a new intitiative, and France's first marine park. This is to cover 3550 sq km of sea and shore on the west coast from Ouessant to the Ile de Sein (excluding the Rade de Brest). The purpose is to concentrate on maintaining a balance between protection and development, with tourism and the fishing industry represented alongside environmentalists. It will also facilitate nature and ecological studies.

Bird reserves

Birdwatchers will want to make a trip to the reserves of the Sept-Iles, near Perros-Guirec, or the Réserve de Goulien on Cap Sizun. For further information, consult bretagne-environment.org, bretagne.lpo.fr and bretagnevivante.asso.free.fr.

Festivals & events

Celebrating a pardon.

January

Dance Ska La (second half of January)
Rennes, myspace.com/bananajuicerecords.
Three days of ska-reggae-rock organized by
Banana Juice.

February

Les Hivernautes (third week)
Quimper, hivernautes.com.
With rock, hip-hop and electro-jazz musicians.

Route du Rock (third week)
St- Malo, laroutedurock.com.
Smaller version of the summer rock festival,
see page 56.

April

Spi Ouest-France (early April)
La Trinité-sur-Mer, spi-ouestfrance.com.
Major sailing event with many classes of entry.

May

Fête de la Morue (third week)
Binic, ville-binic.fr.
Lively celebration of the town's maritime traditions.

Pardon of St-Yves (third Sunday)
Tréguier.
This important pardon for Brittany's patron saint has a huge procession, with lawyers from around the world attending their special patron's festival.

La Semaine du Golf (second half of May)
Gulf of Morbihan, semainedugolfe.asso.fr.
A two-year cycle (next 2011) for this vintage boat festival with vessels of all kinds, from bi-planes to pleasure craft, plus concerts, walks and exhibitions.

June

Le Pardon de Ste-Barbe (last Sunday)
Le Faouët.
The Pardon of Ste-Barbe, with the idyllic country setting of her famous chapel.

July

Pardon de Notre-Dame de Bon-Secours (first Sunday)
Guingamp.
A nocturnal candle-lit procession honours Notre-Dame de Bon-Secours, otherwise known as the Black Madonna, with the unusual statue on parade.

Les Tombées de la Nuit (early July)
Rennes, lestombeesdelanuit.com.
At the beginning of the month, this event gets summer in the city off to a flying start with acrobats, clowns, mime artists, comedians and music.

Grand/Petit Tromenie (second Sunday)
Locronan.
This pardon has a procession up to the chapel above the town each year. Every six years it takes a much longer form, celebrating an early Christian religious tour said to be based on a sacred Celtic space, with a popular walking event.

Les Vieilles Charrues (third week)
Carhaix-Plouguer.
Brittany's answer to Glastonbury. This famous music festival attracts international artists such as Bruce Springsteen and Breton stars, as well as new bands and local talent.

Grand Pardon Ste-Anne d'Auray (26th)
Ste-Anne d'Auray.
The Feast of St-Anne is marked by the biggest of the religious pardons in honour of Brittany's female patron saint.

Festival de Cornouaille (second half of July)
Quimper, festival-cornouaille.com.
Quimper devotes itself to a lavish celebration of Breton culture, with pipe bands, concerts, dancing and parades.

Jazz à Vannes (second half of July)
Vannes, T02 97 01 62 40.
Long-established jazz festival kicks off at the end of the month.

Fête de la Crêpe (late July)
Gourin, fetedelacrepe.free.fr.
Celebrates the humble crêpe.

Art in the Chapels
artchapelles.com.
In July and August this superb venture arranged in circuits in northern Morbihan sees contemporary art featured against a background of ancient, religious buildings.

About the region

Festival du Chant de Marin (first weekend)
Paimpol, paimpol.net.
Held every two years (next 2011) this celebrates the maritime tradition of the area with artists from all over the world, on the loose theme of sea shanties.

Arts dans la Rue (early August)
Morlaix, artsdanslarue.com.
Street theatre and performance art in Morlaix and the surrounding district.

Festival du Bout du Monde (early August)
Crozon Peninsula, festivalduboutdumonde.com.
Summer music-fest of international appeal, where big stars mix with local talent.

Festival Interceltique (first half of August)
Lorient, festival-interceltique.com.
The biggest and boldest of the Celtic events, celebrating the diversity and similarity of all the Celtic cultures, featuring Brittany, Scotland, Ireland, Wales, Cornwall, the Isle of Man and Galicia. Each year focuses on one region.

Festival Arvor (mid-August)
Vannes.
Celebration of Breton music and dance.

La Route du Rock (mid-August)
St-Malo, laroutedurock.com or routedurock.free.fr.
One of the top pop-rock events in Brittany.

Son et Lumière (mid-August)
Bon Repos, pays-conomor.com.
A dramatic and colourful look at the area's legends and history, held after dark in the grounds of a ruined abbey near Lac de Guerlédan.

Fête des Lavoirs (15th)
Portrieux.
Celebration of the town's 50-odd *lavoirs* along the river, with washerwomen in costume, songs, dance and fireworks.

Pardon de Notre-Dame de la Joie (15th)
Penmarc'h.
At the southwest tip of Brittany, this well-attended pardon emanates from the chapel by the sea, a focus of maritime ex-voto offerings.

Festival de la Danse Bretonne et de la St-Loup (second half of August)
Guingamp, dansebretonne.com.

Festival Fisel (second half of August)
Rostrenen, fisel.org.
Dance festival.

Fête de l'Oignon Rosé (second half of August)
Roscoff, roscoff-tourisme.com.
Around the old port, this popular event pays tribute to the local speciality that sent the Johnnies across the Channel, selling onions to the British from their bicycles.

Grand Prix de Plouay (second half of August)
Plouay, comitedesfetes-plouay.com.

Traditional costumes at a pardon.

Three days of competitive cycling, culminating in the Grand Prix Ouest-France.

Les Filets Bleus (second half of August)
Concarneau, filetsbleus.free.fr.
This event recalls attempts made in 1905 to raise support for fishermen, impoverished by the failure of sardine shoals. Now a lively, colourful festival with pageants and music.

Astropolis (date varies)
Brest, astropolis.org.
A four-day feast of electro-music.

September

Blessing of the sea (first Sunday)
Camaret, camaret-sur-mer.com.
Pardon and benediction, honouring those lost at sea, with gathering of boats and the local lifeboat.

Pardon de Notre-Dame du Roncier (7th-8th)
Josselin.
Torch-lit evening procession and mass, repeated in the day.

Foire Biologique (mid-September)
Mur-de-Bretagne.
Fair with a huge range of organic products.

Pardon de Notre-Dame de Tronoën (third Sunday)
Tronoën, Pays Bigouden.

Feast of Archangel St-Michel (Sunday nearest 29th)
Mont St-Michel.

October

Pardon de Notre-Dame des Marais (first weekend)
Fougères.

British Film Festival (early October)
Dinard, festivaldufilm-dinard.com.
A traditional event for Dinard, with dozens of British films old and new shown in various venues.

Quai des Bulles (early October)
St-Malo, quaidesbulles.com.
An unusual event, drawing large crowds into the world of the comic strip.

Atlantique Jazz Festival (second half of October)
Finistère, atlantiquejazzfestival.com.
A wide range of music within the genre.

La Route du Rhum (late October)
St-Malo, routedurhum-labanquepostale.com.
The transatlantic race starts from St-Malo with pomp and celebration.

Mois du Marron & Bogue d'Or (all month)
Redon, tourisme-pays-redon.com.
A month-long celebration based on the chestnut, with a varied programme of gastronomy, walks, concerts, competitions and events for children.

November

Fête de la Soupe (second half of November)
La Gacilly, T02 99 08 21 75, paysdelagacilly.com.
Go around the town trying all the soups on offer before voting for your favourite.

December

Transmusicales (early December)
Rennes, lestrans.com.
International artists and music for all tastes.

Noël à Trévarez
Château de Trévarez, near Châteauneuf-du-Faou, cdp29.fr.
This château always puts on a good Christmas-themed exhibition and celebration.

Sleeping

Brittany has a good range of accommodation – hotels, B&Bs/ *chambres d'hôtes, chambres chez l'habitant*, gîtes and campsites can all be found in most areas. There is a much greater choice in the summer season, however, and many establishments in all those categories are closed for up to six months of the year. It's not difficult to find a historic building to stay in as more and more *manoirs* offer *chambres d'hôtes* or gîtes in converted outbuildings. If you'd like something a bit different, some campsites now offer yurts or restored gipsy caravans – at the Domaine du Roc in Morbihan, you can even stay in a cabin in the tree-tops. If you're planning a walking or other activity holiday outside June to September, it is best to get organized and book in advance as the limited accommodation available can get filled up quickly. Similarly, if you're looking for something on the coast in high season you'll need to book early for the best places.

Booking

It is always advisable to book in advance, but between June and September you should have little difficulty finding something on the spot as long as you are prepared to travel a little inland from the coast. Many hotels offer online booking, but it is always worth phoning for special deals and offers, especially for families.

Tourist offices will have lists of rooms available according to your criteria, and some actually book places for you. If travelling in the summer months, booking in advance is sensible, especially if you want a good coastal spot. Single-night bookings may be refused in July and August in B&Bs and some hotels.

Costs

Accommodation is more expensive on the coast and in large towns, but overall prices are generally cheap. You can expect to pay between €50 and €90 for a double room, and even the most luxurious hotel is unlikely to take you over the €200 mark. A sea view or balcony/terrace will add a few euros to the tariff. Prices are highest in July and August, with mid-season from May to June and September. Low season is in autumn/winter and often excludes Christmas to New Year.

In hotels breakfast is not included in the price of the room and this can be a significant extra cost, from €5 up to €15 per person. It may be worth refusing the option and going to a nearby bar for coffee, picking up fresh croissants from a bakery on the way. On the other hand, a lavish hotel buffet breakfast can keep you going all day. The B&B/ *chambres d'hôtes* room tariff nearly always includes breakfast, which consists at the most basic of bread

Maison d'hôtes Tara, Tréguier.

and jam, with possible additions of cereal and croissants. Expect to pay €45-75 for an en suite room. Rooms *chez l'habitant,* where you may have to share a bathroom or toilet, are likely to be cheaper.

A local *taxe de séjour* (usually €0.2-1.50), which goes to the municipality towards infrastructures relevant to tourism, may be added to the bill in hotels, furnished rooms and on campsites. It is applied per adult per night in season (and not extended to children).

Hotels

A huge variety of hotels is available, from château-style or spa luxury with all the facilities

and gourmet dining, down to the simple country *auberge* with a few rooms above the bar. The star grading system is from one to five – anything with two stars should be more than adequate, with TV and a small desk/table area in the room and often toiletries and hairdryers in the bathrooms, which are often shower only. Wi-Fi is found in many hotels.

Individuals should look out for the offer of a *soirée étape* (sometimes only for business customers) – you pay a single price for room, dinner and breakfast and it's usually a real bargain. Hotels without a restaurant often offer this in conjunction with a local place to eat. A hotel with a restaurant offering *demi-pension* usually has a good-value evening menu for residents only, rather than dining *à la carte.*

Useful websites

- accueil-paysan-bretagne.com
- bretagnealaferme.com
- chateaux-story.com
- clevacances.com
- etaphotel.com
- gites-de-france.com
- hotelformule1.com
- tourismebretagne.fr

Hotel chains include the ubiquitous Logis de France (independent hotels conforming to a quality standard that is usually reliable), but there is quite a variation in terms of ambience and individuality. For budget holidays there are more options these days with the likes of B&B, Etap and Formule 1. These are essentially motels, with, for example, limited reception hours (automated opening facilities otherwise), drinks machines and basic meal dispensers. Rooms are usually adequate if on the small side, and better for the odd night when travelling than for a week's relaxing break. If it's comfort you're after, the top end of the price range includes Oceania, Best Western and Kyriad chains.

Tipping is not expected in hotels.

d'hôtes, you eat the evening meal with the family, but this is only usually a service if there are no restaurants in the vicinity (a rare case) or if the proprietor is a passionate cook. Breakfast may include local or home-made products. Many B&Bs offer a corner kitchen where guests can prepare simple meals in the evening (and the use of the garden for eating outside). Hosts generally do not expect full-scale cooking to take place here.

As far as quality marks go, *Clévacances* is a recognized label for B&Bs (up to five letting rooms), with a system of keys from one to four, reflecting the comfort and amenities of each room.

More and more B&Bs do not take single-night bookings in the summer months.

Bienvenue à la ferme is an organization assuring standards for accommodation on working farms, where the whole rural experience is part of the package. (As well as *chambres d'hôtes*, this may include camping and gîtes). Often walking routes are offered or riding organized, and farm produce will be available, as well as visits to see the animals.

Accueil Paysan Bretagne is a similar network with accommodation in authentic rural working households, where food and/or drink are often produced on the premises.

B&B/Chambres d'hôtes

The quality of *chambres d'hôtes* is naturally variable, but you can usually expect a private or en suite bath or shower room and toilet. There may also be a guest lounge. Furniture and furnishings vary greatly, with comfortable chairs, writing tables and televisions not necessarily as standard. Tea/coffee-making facilities are not common, except in British-run places. Wi-Fi is sometimes, but not often, available in B&Bs. If the size of a room or a particular facility is important to you, do ask specifically when booking. Note that it may be necessary to share facilities such as a bathroom in a room *chez l'habitant*. If establishments offer *tables*

Self-catering

Self-catering options include gîtes (which are often run by British owners these days) and caravan/chalet rentals on the numerous campsites. The latter is a useful aid for walkers on long-distance paths outside of the summer months (when single-night bookings may be refused). A gîte may be next to the owner's home, on a farm, in a complex of converted outbuildings or a single cottage on its own. The *gîte rural,* as the name suggests, is out in the countryside.

Gîtes usually have well-equipped kitchens, sitting areas, TVs and local tourist information for you to make the most of your stay. Outdoor space will have garden furniture and often a BBQ.

Washing machines/dishwashers are common, but ask beforehand if they are essentials for you.

Expect to pay from €500-1000 for a week in high season.

Gîtes de France has thousands of graded properties throughout Brittany. There is also the *Clévacances* quality mark, using keys (one to four for studios and apartments, one to five for gîtes). The Clef Verte (green key) scheme is a rare award for ecological quality.

A *gîte d'étape* is a hostel with basic accommodation for walkers, cyclists and riders who are journeying around and looking for a cheap night's stay. Facilities vary, but there'll be a kitchen, dormitory (sometimes single/double rooms too) and shared bathrooms. Usually breakfast and packed lunches will be available, and maybe an evening meal if booked in advance. The *Rando Accueil* (rando-accueil.com) mark should guarantee knowledgeable hosts and good standards of accommodation.

Youth hostels (*Auberges de Jeunesse*) are another good bet for cheap accommodation (see auberge-de-jeunesse.com), and are not only open to young people. There's a Pass Bretagne that offers a sixth night free after getting five stamps from different establishments in the scheme (see breizh-trotters.com).

Another increasingly popular choice is to rent an apartment or studio in a *Résidence* building, frequently situated in a town or by the coast. This is a compromise between hotels and self-catering, with different levels of extra services, from babysitting to provision of meals. Room size varies considerably, so check in advance to avoid disappointment on arrival. Many residences have organized outings and entertainment in the summer months, and some include restaurant or bar services then too. Kitchens will be fully equipped if you prefer to cook for yourself. Many offer baby equipment, down to the last dummy and even a pushchair, to save bringing everything with you.

Camping

There are numerous campsites in Brittany, mostly on the coast but also often by rivers. Many small towns and villages have municipal sites, open only from June to September and good value for basic amenities. Larger commercial sites have caravans, chalets and mobile homes (or even yurts occasionally) to rent by the week, but out of high season you can also find these useful for an overnight stop. Cabins in the trees are the latest thing, and more sites will soon be offering them.

Arranged activities for children are another advantage for this type of well-organized accommodation. Larger sites will also have some sort of shop and a swimming pool. Few sites are open all year round, but March to October is getting more common.

The typical cost is €15-20 a night for pitch, car and two people, plus a few euros extra for children, pets, electricity and so on.

Yurt, Fougères forest.

Eating & drinking

Brittany is a cheap place to eat and you will never be far from a restaurant or crêperie where you can get a meal for less than €20. Lunch begins at midday, when a great flock of white vans descend on the little restaurants offering the best *ouvrières* deals, a meal with drinks for about €10. In towns many office workers regularly eat lunch out, so restaurants can be crowded. It is not so common to dine out in the evening, except in large towns, but popular places will be busy from 2000 onwards. The good news is that it's rare to find a service charge here, and tipping is not expected in a regular way, although rounding up the bill is a nice gesture if you are satisfied.

Crêpes & galettes

Brittany has a tradition of peasant cooking – cheap, filling dishes, easily prepared over cottage fires. Crêpes and *galettes* (pancakes) are ubiquitous now, with many different recipes and textures according to different regions or even villages. The Breton-speaking western part of the region uses the term crêpes (being most like the Breton *krampouz*), while *galettes* for the savoury version is more common in eastern Brittany. The use of *blé noir* (buckwheat) flour is traditional for savoury fillings. This is the basic Breton flour, historically important because it grew well and quickly in poor soil. *Froment* or white flour is mostly used for dessert crêpes.

Many people eat several crêpes at a sitting. If you visit a Breton home, be prepared to start with a plain buttered dark pancake, move on to a few with meat and eggs and then get set in for the jam and fruit delights. Don't count, just eat! In the markets you can buy freshly made crêpes and marvel at the dextrous skill of the cook. The traditional fillings are basic farm staples – ham, bacon, sausage, eggs – and then there are all manner of fishy options such as scallops, smoked salmon or even sardines. Desserts mostly centre around apples and pears, chocolate and caramel, honey and jam, with flambéed versions too. If you don't like the commercial whipped cream that sometimes swamps these, ask for your crêpe *'sans chantilly'*. In most crêperies you can choose your own combination of ingredients from a list. Like everything else, the crêpe has developed, and modern attempts at originality may produce extraordinary options like fig and foie gras. Occasionally crêpes come with a green salad or you can ask for one, but otherwise there is no garnish, and no bread is served with the meal. Main course salads are usually on offer in crêperies too, and sometimes omelettes.

If you want to try creating a crêpe meal in your self-catering accommodation, you can buy fresh

La Kabane, Forte la Latte.

crêpes from many bakeries or in packets (hand or machine made) from supermarkets.

Fish & shellfish

Fish is the other staple of the Breton diet in this major fishing area of France. Shellfish (*fruits de mer*) is the thing to try, with vast arrays piled on huge plates, especially in restaurants around the coast. Dining rooms are often filled with the sound of cracking, clattering and slurping – at one Brest restaurant you just get a board with a crab and a mallet. *Coquilles St-Jacques* (scallops) are the speciality of the region (and the symbol of the Santiago de Compostela pilgrimage trail), and the best are to be found in the Bays of St-Brieuc and Morlaix in the north, and Concarneau in the south. You will find them served with and without the orange-coloured part of the coral, and the simplest cooking – generally pan-fried in a little butter – is the best way to appreciate the flavour. Another common offering is mussels, and you'll find *moules frites* (mussels with crisp chips) everywhere, or *moules à la marinière*, with a thin white wine liquor.

Other popular sauces for mussels include cream and curry. Mussels are often grown on stakes (*bouchots*) or lines of ropes, which you can see in coastal areas. *Moules* of the Baie de St-Michel were the first to be given an AOC (*appellation d'origine contrôlée*), a guarantee of quality and origin.

Contrary to the popular saying, it is possible to eat oysters (*huîtres*) in months without an 'r' in them, the traditional reproductive time. Oysters are produced in various ways, but the most sought-after is the flat Belon oyster from Finistère, at their best from September. The combination of fresh and salted water produces a fine flavour, usually likened to that of hazelnut. Cancale in the Bay of St-Michel is famous for its briny-flavoured oysters, which you can buy fresh from stalls. Deep-sea oysters are to be found around Paimpol.

Lobster (*homard*) is also popular, including the special deep-water *homard Breton,* which is blue in colour. Restaurants oftesn offer *homard l'armoricain*, lobster with a sauce of shallots, garlic, white wine, tomatoes and a hint of chilli.

Langoustines can be found in most coastal towns, as well as shrimps (*crevettes*) and prawns, spider crabs and rock crabs caught in pots like

Fresh lobster is a popular dish.

lobsters. At low tide you will see people out collecting *huîtres sauvages*, rock crabs, clams, cockles and all manner of other small shellfish from the rocks. There are restrictions on the sizes that can be taken and, if you decide to try yourself, you must replace any stone or rock so as not to disturb the natural ecological balance (and be sure you know the tide times).

Cotriade is a substantial fish soup with vegetables and potatoes, the name coming from the *Kaoter* cooking pot, but a general *soupe du poisson* made with whatever is available is commonly offered in coastal places. It usually comes with croutons, cheese and spicy *rouille* paste. Sardines are a staple catch and almost a historical symbol of Pays Bigouden; do try them freshly grilled at a port restaurant there. Brittany has always been at the forefront of the food conserving industry, and especially preserved fish, which is particularly successful for oily species such as sardine, mackerel and tuna. *Rillettes* are a sort of pâté of mashed flesh with oil and seasonings, which makes a perfect sauce for pasta with a little

thinning down, or a starter with bread. Smoked fish – mainly sardine, mackerel or trout – is also worth looking out for, whether from traditional smokehouses or simply hung up in a chimney. Tinned fish products, often preserved in a muscadet-based liquid, are perfect for picnics – you need nothing more than a rough country bread to dip.

The commonest white fish served in restaurants are *lieu jaune* (pollack), *cabillaud* (cod), *merlu* (hake) and *anglefin* (haddock), but if you get the chance, try the prized and delicate *bar* (sea bass) and *daurade* (bream). Red mullet (*rouget*) is also a treat, often served *en cocotte*, in a small casserole. Fresh-water fish include trout (*truite*) and salmon (*saumon*).

If you're self-catering, try to buy from a market or specialist *poissonnerie*, although good-quality fish is also available from supermarkets. At ports you can be sure of an extra-fresh catch just off the boats in the morning or evening. The *criée* is the name for the auction held when the boats return, and at certain ports the public can attend the sale

– it is part of some visits at Haliotika, the centre of discovery for the fishing industry at Le Guilvinec (see page 188).

Brittany has more than 600 varieties of seaweed (generally called *algues*) and, although they are not all edible, their use in cooking is increasingly popular. The flavour can be strong and *algues* should be used sparingly, but well-cooked as an accompaniment to fish or in omelettes and crêpes, it's delicious. The salty sea vegetable samphire also appears on menus, sometimes a bit on the vinegary side, but tasty when pan-fried with a hint of garlic.

Meat & vegetables

Pork, chicken and turkey are all commonly available on menus, as well as steak, either *entrecôte* or *faux-filet* (sirloin). Lamb is a traditional Breton meat, with those from Belle-Ile particularly well known for their flavour. Ask for meat *sanglant* (rare), *à point* (medium) or *bien cuit* (well done). *Plats du terroir* on a menu indicate tasty locally sourced ingredients.

There are many excellent cold meats (*charcuterie*) for sandwiches and to accompany salads. The local *traiteur*, who offers ready-prepared delicatessen dishes, will have a whole range of suitable picnic foods. The famous *andouille* sausage, a Breton speciality, with the best coming from Guéméné-sur-Scorff in Morbihan, is made from cows' intestines and has an intense, rich flavour. Thin slices are often used as a filling for crêpes. There is even a festival in its honour!

Another favourite with locals in western Brittany is Kig ar Farz (meat and stuffing), essentially a collection of boiled meats (pork, bacon, sausage) with cabbage or other vegetables, and buckwheat flour stuffing that has been cooked in a bag, in with the rest of the ingredients. You need a large appetite to work your way through this often stodgy speciality.

Brittany is also one of the most prolific vegetable-growing areas in France, especially Léon, northern Finistère. Brittany Ferries began life as a means of transporting vegetables to Cornish markets, and artichokes have long been flown to Paris and New York to supply top restaurants. Eating the artichoke is a time-consuming and fiddly occupation of peeling, sucking and dipping the fleshy based leaves.

Cauliflowers and the *oignon rosé* (pink onion) of Roscoff are the other bumper crops. Onion-sellers or Johnnies used to travel across the channel with their bikes and strings of onions to sell to UK housewives door to door: there is a museum of their history in Roscoff. The Coco de Paimpol, a small white bean from northern Côtes d'Armor (brought from South America early in the 20th century), is often found in restaurants, usually in conjunction with white-fleshed fish.

Fruit & nuts

Fruits tend to do best in the milder, drier southeast, but the strawberries of Plougastel in Finistère are famous worldwide, so try them fresh or in delicious jam. More exotically, Le Petit Gris de Rennes is a small flavoursome melon grown around the capital. Apples for cider-making and traditional cakes are the major fruit crop, especially in the valley of the Rance around Dinan, and Pays Bigouden in southern Finistère.

Chestnuts have always been prized for their nutritional value in a poor diet, and bread or savoury cake made from chestnut flour is delicious. The Redon area is the best place to sample *marrons* in cooking, such as in the Frigousse stew. Each October there is a festival in the town celebrating the chestnut and all its traditions – they even produce an aperitif from it. You'll see many hamlets called Quistinic, which means a place of chestnuts in Breton.

About the region

Dairy

While cheese is not a regional product for Brittany, there are many first-rate producers of organic goat's cheese to be found around the area, especially at regular markets. The monks at Timadeuc Abbey in Morbihan also produce a good cheese called Trappe.

Dairy products are generally excellent – salted butter has always been a vital part of the Breton diet, so important that it figures in religious rituals, such as the Pardon du Beurre at Notre-Dame de Crann at Spezet, with its butter sculptures. In the eastern part of historic Brittany, the salt-marshes, especially around Guérande, provided the perfect addition. Buttermilk (*lait ribot*) is also widely available and used in cooking.

Desserts & cakes

The traditional Breton dessert is the *far*, available on many menus and in almost every bakery (*boulangerie*). It is a solid custard flan of variable texture, sometimes plain, sometimes with prunes or other fruit for novelty value. The no-nonsense named *flan* is a cheap, often tasteless version.

The cake to try before all others is *kouign amann*, a round, dense product made from multiply folded bread dough, sugar and salted butter; very rich and satisfying. The real thing needs no addition, but you do sometimes see apple versions. The commonly found *gâteau Breton* has a hard exterior, a round form and very dense texture, and often a thin layer of jam-like filling, perhaps raspberry or prune.

Brittany is famous for its butter biscuits, a cheap and delicious souvenir to take home. The best are *palets*, thick circles that crumble in the mouth, and *galettes*, a thin, crunchier form. *Crêpes dentelles* are

Below: Special Brittany cake, *kouign amann*. Opposite page: A typical menu.

Breton far recipe

125g flour
125g sugar
1 sachet vanilla sugar
1 tsp baking powder
Pinch of salt
4 eggs
650ml milk
1 tbsp rum (optional)
250g dried prunes or apricots (optional)

Sieve the flour. Add the sugars, baking powder and salt. Beat in the eggs with wooden spoon. Heat the milk with the rum and fruit (if using), then remove the fruit. Beat the liquid into a batter and add the fruit before pouring into a greased baking tin. Bake for 30-40 minutes at 200°C (gas mark 6). Allow to cool before removing from the tin.

crispy biscuits in the form of a rolled crêpe, a speciality of Quimper, and also around Dinan, often served with ice cream.

Drinks

Cider is the staple drink to accompany crêpes and you will find little pottery cups (bolées) on the tables of most crêperies. You can buy a small jug (pichet) if you think a whole bottle may be too much. Cider is eligible for an AOC (Appellation d'Origine Contrôlée) and the best brands come from Pays Bigouden in Finistère and the Valley of the Rance near Dinan. Try to look for reputable makes such as Kerne (Pays Bigouden) or Cidre Val du Rance, or the AOC/Fermier label to avoid the industrial products on many supermarket shelves. And when out and

about, try a Breton kir, made with cider (instead of white wine) and the usual cassis.

Different areas use different varieties of apple, and the best cider is made from a single type, such as the guillevic apple grown mainly in Morbihan, which produces Royal Guillevic (look for the Label Rouge quality mark). In Morbihan a pear cider called poiré is also produced.

For stronger stuff, couchenn is a honey-based spirit, like mead or hydromel, while lambig is a fiery apple brandy, good to knock back in one gulp. The aperitif pommeau is made from the juice of cider apples and brandy, and sometime used in desserts.

Beer is also produced in Brittany, with growing popularity. You can visit the premises of Coreff, the best known, in Carhaix, for a tour and to buy the product, and also the Brasserie Lancelot near Lizio in Morbihan, which produces five regular brews. They also make a good Breton cola.

When Loire-Atlantique was part of Brittany, it could lay claim also to the robust wine Muscadet, from the Nantes area, which is the traditional accompaniment to shellfish. The white wine Gros Plant is also from the same region.

Menu reader

General

à la carte individually priced menu items
Appellation d'Origine Contrôlée (AOC) label of regulated origin, signifying quality; usually associated with wine, though can also apply to cider and regional foods such as cheeses
biologique/bio organic
carte des vins wine list
déjeuner lunch
dîner dinner or supper
entrée starter
hors d'oeuvre appetizers
menu/formule set menu
petit déjeuner breakfast
plat du jour dish of the day
plat principal main course
une carafe d'eau a carafe of tap water

Drinks (*boissons*)

bière beer (usually bottled)
bouteille bottle
un café/un petit noir coffee (black espresso)
calva (lambig in western Brittany) calvados (apple brandy)
chocolat chaud hot chocolate
cidre cider
un coca Coca-Cola
un (grand) crème a (large) white coffee
dégustation tasting
un demi a measure of beer (33cl)
demi-sec medium-dry – or slightly sweet when referring to Champagne
diabolo menthe mint syrup mixed with lemonade
doux the sweetest Champagne or cider
eau gazeuse/pétillante sparkling/slightly sparkling mineral water
eau plate/minérale still/mineral water
glaçons ice cubes
jus de fruit fruit juice
ker Breton cider and cassis
kir popular apéritif made with white wine and a fruit liqueur
lait milk
une noisette espresso with a dash of milk
orange pressée freshly squeezed orange juice
panaché beer/lemonade shandy
pastis anise-flavoured apéritif
pichet jug, used to serve water, wine or cider
poiré perry (cider made with pears rather than apples)
une pression a glass of draught beer
sec dry
sirop fruit syrup or cordial mixed with still/sparkling water or soda
un thé tea, usually served *nature* with a slice of lemon (*au citron*) – if you want milk ask for *un peu de lait froid*, a little cold milk.
une tisane/infusion herbal tea
un verre de... a glass of
un (verre de) vin rouge/blanc/rosé a (glass of) red/white/rosé wine

Fruit (*fruits*) & vegetables (*légumes*)

ail garlic
algues seaweed
ananas pineapple
artichaut artichoke
asperge asparagus
blettes Swiss chard
cassis blackcurrants
céleri-rave celeriac, usually served grated in mayonnaise

cèpes porcini mushrooms
champignons de Paris button mushrooms
châtaignes/marrons chestnuts
choux cabbage
citron lemon
citrouille/potiron pumpkin
courge marrow or squash
épinards spinach
fenouil fennel
fèves broad beans
figues figs
fraises strawberries
framboises raspberries
gratin dauphinois a popular side-dish of potato slices layered with cream, garlic and butter and baked in the oven
haricots cocos small, white beans
haricots verts green beans
lentilles vertes green lentils
mesclun a mixture of young salad leaves
mirabelles small golden plums
myrtilles blueberries/bilberries
noix walnuts
oseille sorrel, often served in a sauce with salmon
pêches peaches
petits pois peas
poireaux leeks
poires pears
pomme de terre potato, *primeurs* are new potatoes (or any early fruit or vegetable), and *frites* are chips (*chips* are crisps)
pommes apples
prunes plums
salicorne saltwort
soupe au pistou a spring vegetable soup with pistou
truffe truffle

Fish (*poissons*) & seafood (*fruits de mer*)

aiglefin haddock
anchoïade anchovy-based spread
anchois anchovies
anguille eel
araignée spider crab
assiette de fruits de mer plate of shellfish/seafood
bar sea bass (*bar de ligne* is wild sea bass)
bigorneau winkle
bulots sea snails/whelks
bourride white fish stew, thickened with aïoli
brochet pike
cabillaud cod
calamar/encornet squid
colin hake
coquillage shellfish
coquilles St-Jacques scallops
crevettes prawns/shrimps
dorade sea bream
homard lobster
huîtres oysters
lieu jaune pollack
lotte monkfish
maquereau mackerel
morue salt-cod
moules mussels
oursins sea urchins
palourdes clams
poissons de rivière river fish

poulpe octopus
poutines very tiny, young sardines
rascasse scorpion fish
rouget red mullet
Saint-Pierre John Dory
saumon salmon
soupe de poisson a smooth rockfish-based soup, served with croutons, rouille and grated gruyère cheese
soupions small squid
thon tuna
truite trout

Meat (*viande*) & poultry (*volaille*)

à point medium cooked meat (or tuna steak), usually still pink inside
agneau lamb
andouille/andouillette soft sausage made from pig's small intestines, usually grilled
bien-cuit well-cooked
blanquette de veau veal stew in white sauce with cream, vegetables and mushrooms
bleu barely cooked meat, almost raw
boeuf beef
boucherie butcher's shop or display
canard duck
charcuterie encompasses sausages, hams and cured or salted meats
chevreuil venison, roe deer
confit process to preserve meat, usually duck, goose or pork
cuisse de grenouille frog's leg
daube marinated beef, or sometimes lamb, braised slowly in red wine with vegetables
dinde turkey
escargot snail
faux-filet beef sirloin
foie-gras fattened goose or duck liver
fumé(e) smoked
gigot d'agneau leg of lamb
jambon ham; look for *jambon d'Amboise*, an especially fine ham
lapin rabbit
lièvre hare
médaillon small, round cut of meat or fish
mouton mutton
pavé thickly cut steak
pintade guinea-fowl
porc pork
pot-au-feu slow-cooked beef and vegetable stew
poulet chicken
rillettes a pâté-like preparation of pork belly cooked slowly in pork fat, then shredded; also made with duck, goose, chicken or tuna.
rillons big chunks of pork cooked in pork fat
ris de veau sweetbreads
sanglier wild boar
saucisse small sausage, dried (*sèche*) or fresh
saucisson large salami-type sausage, for slicing
veau veal

Desserts (*desserts*)

café gourmand selection of desserts with a cup of coffee included
chantilly whipped, sweetened cream
clafoutis dessert of fruit (traditionally cherries) baked in sweet batter, served hot or cold
compôte stewed fruit, often as a purée
crème anglaise thin custard; normally served cold
fromage blanc unsweetened fresh cheese, similar to quark, served on its own or with a fruit coulis – most people add a little sugar

glace ice cream (*boules de glace* is scoops of ice cream)
coupe glacée cold dessert with ice cream, fruit or nuts, chocolate or chantilly
le parfum flavour, when referring to ice cream or yoghurt
île flottante soft meringue floating on custard, with caramel sauce
liègeois chilled chocolate or coffee ice cream-based dessert topped with chantilly
pâtisserie pastries, cakes and tarts – also the place where they are sold
sabayon creamy dessert made with egg yolks, sugar and wine or liqueur
tarte au citron lemon tart
tarte au pomme apple tart

Other

aïoli garlic mayonnaise
assiette plate (eg *assiette de charcuterie*)
beurre butter
beurre blanc buttery white wine sauce often served with fish
bordelaise red wine sauce served with steak.
boulangerie bakery selling bread and viennoiserie
casse-croûte literally 'to break a crust' – a snack
crêpe large pancake served with various fillings; see also *galette*
croque-monsieur grilled ham and cheese sandwich
croque-madame as above but topped with a fried egg
en croûte literally 'in crust'; food cooked in a pastry parcel
escargots snails
fleur de sel speciality hand-harvested sea salt
forestière generally sautéed with mushrooms
fromage de brebis ewe's milk cheese
fromage de chèvre goat's milk cheese
galette large pancake served with various fillings; see also *crêpe*
garniture garnish, side-dish
gaufre waffle, usually served with chocolate sauce
pan bagnat sandwich version of *salade niçoise*, dressed with lashings of olive oil and vinegar
pâte pastry or dough, not to be confused with *pâtes*, which is pasta or *pâté*, the meat terrine
petits farcis usually small onions, tomatoes, peppers and courgettes stuffed with a mixture of veal, Parmesan and vegetables
pistou a basil and garlic sauce, similar to Italian pesto but without pine nuts or Parmesan/pecorino
riz rice
rouille saffron, garlic and paprika mayonnaise, served with *soupe de poisson* and bouillabaisse
salade verte simple green salad with vinaigrette dressing
soupe/potage soup
viennoiserie baked items such as croissants and brioches

Entertainment

Breton musicians.

There is always a great burst of energy when summer comes and the big festivals draw crowds from far and wide. However, the traditional year-round entertainment in Brittany is the *fest noz* or *fest deiz* (night or day fête), which brings together a local community to eat, dance and sing. Springing from the rhythms of rural life, this practice joins people of all ages in a carefree celebration. The *fest deiz* takes place in an afternoon, often following a religious pardon, while the *fest noz* generally begins late in the evening and continues until well after midnight. Food and dancing might be indoors or outside depending on the time of year. Breton dancing is fascinating to watch, but you will also be welcome to join the circle. There may be a musical accompaniment or simply two singers in a resonant form called *kan ha diskan*, call and counter-call.

Wherever you're based, there is sure to be one of these natural, easy-going events on in the vicinity as it's the main form of entertainment in rural areas. Another highly popular one, especially in western Brittany, is storytelling (*contes*). Large audiences gather in public halls or cafés/bars to hear *conteurs* recount contemporary fables, legends, humorous stories or morality tales. This is creative performance art – a good storyteller will captivate regardless of language barriers.

In the towns there will always be somewhere to have a drink in the evenings, and larger towns will have opportunities for music and dancing. Rennes and Brest have the best club scenes, and gay venues are mainly limited to these big cities. Where there's a student population or port area there'll be plenty of lively bars or *bars de nuit* that stay open much of the night. Irish bars often have Celtic music and impromptu jamming sessions.

The main cities have concert halls, theatres, cinemas and many cultural events. The large performance venues, where you can expect international performers and bands, are the Quartz in Brest, home of the internationally acclaimed Matheus ensemble and UBU at the Théâtre National de Bretagne in Rennes, with plays, ballet and dance also offered in both complexes.

Brittany is renowned for its prolific festivals, with music at the heart of most entertainment. Breton music thrives and develops, with its traditional forms based around the *biniou* (like bagpipes) and *bombarde* (wind instrument resembling an oboe). Other pipes, the accordion and violin are also used. The *bagad* is a band containing a variety of instruments. Don't miss an opportunity to hear the Bagad de Lann Bihoué, a forces pipeband from the naval air base near Lorient.

The most famous large festivals – such as the Interceltique at Lorient, the Festival de Cornouaille in Quimper and the Vieilles Charrues at Carhaix-Plouguer – have a great range of artists, both Breton and international. The Frères Morvan (freresmorvan.com) are a revered trio of singers who have been performing traditional songs around Brittany for more than 50 years. Tri Yann from Nantes are good exponents of more modern interpretations of the traditional repertoire, as well as producing original material. Popular singers who bring new elements to old traditions include Denez Prigent, Eric Marchand and Annie Ebrel.

Most towns have music in the streets in high season. The commercial port at Brest has free concerts on the quays every Thursday in summer with local musicians and international artists appearing. In St-Brieuc, Les Nocturnes on Thursday and Friday evenings offers rock, blues, soul and jazz-punk and more, as well as street theatre. Les Tombées de la Nuit in Rennes in July provides music, mime and comedy.

Some celebrations, such as the Mois du Marron (month of the chestnut) at Redon in October, manage to combine music, gastronomy and children's events. Gourin has a Fête de la Crêpe in July, when due honour is paid to the staple food of Brittany with competitions. The crêpe finds its way into most festivals in one way or another!

On a smaller scale, keep an eye out for a bar/café with the label Café du Pays. These establishments promote local products in the food they serve and the drinks on offer, like cider and beer. They usually also arrange a programme of events and music throughout the year.

Coastal resorts have their own particular brand of entertainment, with casinos being particularly popular in places such as Perros Guirec and St-Quay Portrieux, but you won't find much in the way of permanent fairground/amusement arcade-type offerings. Organized amusements for children of various ages are usually good in seaside areas, and opportunities for getting some physical exercise are never lacking.

Theme parks, while not especially sophisticated, are well done here, often with a strong educational element built in. Océanopolis in Brest (see page 194) is the front-runner, but children will enjoy places like the adventure park at Le-Roc-Saint-André, and there are also more unusual ideas such as the wolf museum in the Monts d'Arrée (see page 209) or the Labyrinthe in Crozon (see page 227), or a straightforward aquatic fun venue like Armoripark (see page 177).

To find out what's on, consult the local tourist office. Each district produces a detailed programme of events in the summer months with venues and content. Don't expect things to begin exactly at the stated hour – everything happens in its own time here, but patience is rewarded.

Shopping

Brittany is not historically a place where there has been a lot of wealth to be flaunted and even today shopping sophisticates may have to limit their activities to designer boutiques in cities like Rennes and Brest. By contrast, the artisanal tradition is strong, so arts and crafts of quality are widely on offer. The Ferme des Artisans near Mont St-Michel de Brasparts in Finistère is a large outlet for such products in the middle of unpopulated countryside.

Clothes

Clothes and shoes of traditional type, such as the fishermen's hardy smocks and stripy T-shirts, are on sale everywhere, but the quality is variable and it's worth holding out for the densest cotton in terms of durability and wind-proofing. Armor-Lux, which only uses fair-trade cotton, and Le Glazier are both reputable labels. Modern versions of peasant clogs (*sabots*) in wood or with leather uppers are often extremely comfortable. For something unusual, a hamlet called St-Antoine produces hemp in central Brittany (see page 176) and has a small range of quality clothes in this material and bales of cloth for making your own. Traditional lace, often in the form of tablecloths, can still be found in places such as Pays Bigouden, west of Quimper.

Food & drink

Every town and even some large villages have weekly or bi-monthly markets. Tourist offices will have maps or lists with details of the relevant days. Some are morning only, as far as food products are concerned, so get there early for your picnic ingredients. Cured meats, smoked fish and goat's cheese are good buys.

The *traiteur* will have a range of prepared foods like quiches, salads and filled pastries. There is also a dedicated organic movement here, with quality goat's cheese, vegetables and dense country bread available. Honey from native black bees is special, especially in areas of *landes* such as the Monts d'Arrée, where many types of heather flourish.

For food shopping, Brittany's markets are unbeatable, with fresh fish and shellfish playing a major part in any settlement within striking distance of the coast. Try oysters at Cancale or lobsters in Camaret. For taking home, the canned-fish product range is also vast, with some amusing twists, as shown by the Penn Sardin shop in Douarnenez. Shops selling regional products are increasingly common in tourist areas, and while some have chosen to add on a lot of tat, the core offerings of genuine Breton food products – such as biscuits, cake, preserved fish, cider and beer – are excellent.

Brittany is not a wine-producing area, so cider is the prize as far as drinks go. Avoid the many commercial brands and look for a *fermier* or AOC label to ensure quality and taste whether you prefer sweet (*doux*) or dry (*brut*). *Couchenn* (or hydromel), a mead-like drink made from honey, is another local speciality, as is *lambig*, a strong spirit made from apples. Breton beers are well worth buying: the best-known makes are Coreff and Lancelot, with a range of light and fuller brews.

Shopping hours

Shopping hours are getting increasingly complex. Some large supermarkets now remain open through the lunch hour, while others retain the traditional 1200 or 1230 closure until 1400. Most shops stay open until 1900, but do not expect to find anything open after that except in large towns. Bakeries may be open all day or take a break from about 1300-1600. Some supermarkets in towns or on commercial trading estates are now open on Sunday mornings, but until the Sunday trading laws change, most places are closed on Sunday afternoon. Many smaller shops, including bakeries, close all day on Monday, especially in rural areas.

Beer for sale at a brewery.

About the region

Souvenirs

There are many *biscuitières* offering visits and selling attractively packaged butter biscuits (*palets/galettes*). These and Breton cakes such as *kouign amann* are popular presents to take home, and often found in decorative boxes or tins with traditional designs of Breton life or the ubiquitous black and white Breton flag. Also look out for the Breton *caramel salé* or salted caramel, either in the form of toffee-like sweets or delicious sauce in a jar, for crêpes or ice cream.

For something completely different, there's a good variety of seaweed products, from edible to beautifying. Brittany has more than 600 varieties of seaweed and some excellent spa-type products can be found in coastal gift shops, like Océane Alimentaire (see page 225).

Some speciality products are useful for souvenirs, such as the range of Quimper pottery with its colourful peasant figures. Pottery with maritime and rural motifs is widely available and widely variable in quality. A set of attractive cider *bolées* and matching jug is a popular choice for drinking toasts to your Breton holiday back home. At the bottom end of the market, you will be sure to come across a plethora of 'Celtic' and 'Korrigan' themed goods, the main tourist marketing ploy, ranging from decent jewellery and interesting books to tacky knick-knacks. Anything black and white or with the symbolic Celtic (but non-Breton) triskel is likely to have a higher price.

Market stall, St-Quay Portrieux.

Activities & tours

Brittany's variety of landscape offers much in the way of physical activities, with limitless resources for water sports and a well-developed network of cross-country trails and waterways.

Breton cuisine

There's a surprising lack of development in gastronomic courses for anglophone visitors in Brittany, but various organized trails linking food-producers and cider-makers do exist in leaflet form, such as the **Route de Saveurs** (tregorgoelo. com/Route-des-saveurs-en-Tregor-Goelo) in Côtes d'Armor. There's a well-known cookery school, **Le Cercle Culinaire** (cercleculinaire.com), in Rennes, offering courses in French, and **La Cuisine Corsaire** (cuisine-corsaire.fr), in Cancale, offers food discovery courses for small groups.

Cultural tours

Details of guided tours of all the major towns and cities are available through the relevant tourist offices. In the summer season there will usually be an English-language option, especially in designated Towns of Art and History such as Rennes, Fougères, Dinan and Quimper. The emphasis of these events is often heavily architectural rather than anecdotal, but they certainly provide interesting insights into religious and public buildings. Another option is to hire an audio guide, for exploration at your own pace.

Cycling

Cycling is as popular in Brittany as the rest of France, with Breton Bernard Hinault an inspirational five-times Tour de France winner. The cycling capital is Plouay in Morbihan, which hosts a major Grand Prix each August (comitedesfetes-plouay.com).

Most tourist offices offer details of circuits in their area, often in a handy folder.

The **Randobreizh** (randobreizh.com) website helps in planning a cycling holiday, and includes information on ongoing development of Green Ways, which provide many new possibilities for avoiding roads with traffic, and the dozen VTT (*vélo tout terrain*), mountain bike stations spread across

Brittany, specialized centres that provide details of routes, hire of bicycles and facilities for cyclists. This website also has a useful list of bike-hire shops. **Breton Bikes** (T02 96 24 86 72, bretonbikes.com) in Gouarec offers well-organized cycling holidays in Brittany for beginners or more experienced riders.

Horse riding

The organization **Equibreizh** (equibreizh.com) has pioneered the development of riding trails right across Brittany. These are signed by the symbol of a black horseshoe on an orange background. A map of areas covered is available from tourist offices or you can consult their website. Various types of accommodation and pasturage/shelter for horses are available about every 30 km along the routes and within 1 km of the actual track. Many weekend or four- to five-day packages are offered by local equestrian centres in superb territory, such as the Forêt de Brocéliande, the Bay of Mont St-Michel and central Finistère.

If you'd rather admire horses than ride them, there are two National Haras (studs) in Brittany, at Lamballe (see page 175) and Hennebont, near Lorient. Here you can go on a tour of the stables, see how the horses are trained and cared for, and often watch displays.

The website cheval-bretagne.com may also be of interest if you want to find out more about magnificent Breton horses.

Walking

Brittany is a walker's paradise, with many long-distance paths – notably the GR34, around more than 2000 km of spectacular coastline – and thousands of local circuits covering heritage sites and diverse countryside. There are also hundreds of kilometres of Green Ways which can be used to link different parts of the region.

Green Ways

The *Voies Vertes* or Green Ways have been developed in recent years mostly from disused railway tracks and canal towpaths. They provide a network of long-distance routes for walking, cycling and riding. New sections are gradually being added – the website randobreizh.com has updated maps with details of each route, distances and accommodation along the way. A general map of the routes with English text has also been published.

About the region

Randobreizh (randobreizh.com) is the best French website for research, or try **Brittany Walks** (brittanywalks.com), which provides information for guided walks. Most large communes have a branch of the **FFRP** (Fédération Française de la Randonnée Pédestre, ffrp.asso.fr), which organizes regular walks and maintains the GRs.

See also page 80.

Water sports

With Brittany's coastline, you'll be spoilt for choice if water sports are your delight, and many lakes or municipal *plans d'eau* also have centres for sailing, canoe/kayak or even waterskiing. In every coastal centre there's a *centre nautique* to provide you with information, instruction, equipment and guided activities. Brittany is also the top sailing destination in France with many competitive events and courses. The website of **Bretagne Nautisme** (nautismebretagne.fr) has details of all the many possibilities, including windsurfing, kitesurfing, speedsailing, kite buggying and sand-yachting, which is especially popular on the endless beaches of the Atlantic coast in Finistère. The strong tides here also make for great surfing, with a focus at Pointe de la Torche. For more information, see surfingbretagne.com. Bretagne Nautisme also has a list of diving clubs, and you can get a glimpse of the underwater possibilities on the specialized website bretagne-plongée.com.

Below: Sea kayaing, Cap Fréhel. Opposite page: Walking in the Monts d'Arrée.

Wellbeing

Brittany, with its strong maritime traditions and prolific seaweed resources, has also developed a reputation for thalassotherapy, where the healing properties of seawater mineral salts are used to treat muscular and joint problems. Spas have burgeoned, especially in the coastal resorts, and they are increasingly popular as places of pure relaxation as well as treatment centres for specific ailments. Seaweed baths and mud baths, warm seawater pools, saunas and massages are among the many options that are on offer at these centres. Roscoff, Carnac, St-Malo, Dinard, Perros-Guirec, Douarnenez and the Presqu'île de Rhuys all have well-equipped spa centres. For more information, see thalasso-bretagne.fr.

Walking in Brittany

Brittany provides an amazing variety of landscape for all kinds of walking, from challenging to easy strolls. The coastline is exceptional, but the interior also offers a good choice, from verdant river valleys to open moors and wooded countryside.

The GRs are national footpaths organized by the **FFRP** (Fédération Française de la Randonnée Pédestre) that have red and white waymarks, while the **GPR** (red and yellow waymarks) are routes covering places of interest in a particular area. Each *commune* has local, organized circuits, marked in yellow, blue or green and usually shown on a leaflet from the Mairie or tourist office. **IGN** (ign.fr) maps are widely available in supermarkets and bookshops. Their Randonnée editions have major footpaths marked, but these are not always up to date, as things can change quickly on the ground. Long-distance paths or Green Ways, see page 79, are now in development to provide hundreds of kilometres of fairly level tracks using old railway lines and canal towpaths. An up-to-date summary can be found via **Randobreizh** (randobreizh.com).

Rural footpaths here are usually along communal tracks, the old inter-village routes, not across fields, so there's little problem about rights of way. It's important to take note of diversions marked during the hunting season (September-February), when some paths, especially through privately owned woods, will be closed.

The most spectacular route of all is the coastal path (GR34), former path of the customs officers, running for 2000 km around the Armorican peninsula from Mont St-Michel to just beyond the Gulf of Morbihan. Most of this is close to the shore, hugging the undulating cliffs and coves and providing stunning views of sea, islands and lighthouses. Recommended for a demanding hike are the Crozon Peninsula from Camaret to Morgat, the Cap Sizun peninsula from Douarnenez to Audierne, including the Pointe du Raz, the Cap Fréhel area, and the cliffs of Plouha on the Côte de Goëlo. If you want the stunning scenery without the constant ups and downs, the Pink Granite coast starting from Perros Guirec is a world-famous marvel and easy walking, or try the Gulf of Morbihan or the Finistère coast west of Roscoff.

Forest walking is often a good bet for family fun and there are many circuits, both easy and strenuous, in the Forêt de Paimpont with its Arthurian legends. The Valley of No Return may have an ominous name, but the scenery is superb.

Other options are the large beech forest at Fougères, and the area around Huelgoat, with its added bonus of an amazing granite 'chaos' with huge boulders in strange formations.

The Nantes–Brest canal running right across Brittany provides an unproblematic, pretty much level route for strollers or a long-distance option for hardy walkers ready to cover the 365-km length. A two-week holiday will nearly do it! Don't be deceived by the word canal – less than 20% is artificial, the rest is made up of glorious wide-flowing rivers including the Blavet and Aulne, and the route passes through attractive towns and past chapels and châteaux, as well as some of the loveliest natural scenery imaginable. One of the most beautiful sections is north from the Barrage de la Potinais not far from Redon, following the Oust through sheer granite cliffs and past the serene Île aux Pies.

For something completely different, the Monts d'Arrée in Finistère is an area of open moors and schist peaks, the highest in Brittany. Circuits there offer stony tracks, wooden walkways across peat bogs and the hilltops of Mont St-Michel de Brasparts with its little chapel or the rounded ridge of Tuchenn Gador. If you like heights, a long walk in central Brittany from Gouarec to Bon Repos via the Landes de Liscuis has high, sometimes steep, paths with stunning open views, past three Neolithic alley-graves. Nearby is Lac de Guerlédan with some easy paths on the northern shore, including sections suitable for the disabled, and a very undulating hike along the southern shore through the Forêt de Quénécan, with a welcome refreshment stop at the Anse de Sourdan.

If you're considering a walking holiday, recommended times would be May, June or September. The paths are never especially busy, but these months usually have the most pleasant weather and temperature for being outside all day. Plan ahead if you're looking for overnight accommodation on a long linear route, as some sections of the coastal path are well off the beaten track and available places can get booked up. It's also important to plan food and water provisions for the same reasons.

This is an incredibly diverse landscape. It's worth remembering that many of Brittany's special delights – lonely menhir, isolated chapels, dazzling promontories, little islands across narrow causeways that vanish at high tide – are only accessible on foot.

Contents

Ille-et-Vilaine

St-Malo, the library sign in the *ville close*.

Introduction

The best-known part of Ille-et-Vilaine is the maritime fringe of splendid St-Malo and the Bay of Mont St-Michel, but for once the coast is not the star, being only one corner of the large, populous area dominated by the regional capital of Rennes. This relatively small city has a strong personality shaped by its university and heritage of political muscle, with the former Parliament building and modernist Musée de Bretagne top cultural destinations. The same sense of confident wellbeing is shared by Fougères and Vitré, with their magnificent castles in the Marches of Brittany, historical border territory with France. This proximity may account for a more affluent and progressive feeling than in western Brittany.

In contrast to all that reality, there is the magical Forêt de Paimpont, where Merlin fell for the wiles of Viviane, and Lancelot grew up beneath the lake at the Château de Comper, now an Arthurian centre. Least well known, but set to become more popular with the growing interest in inland waterways, is the area around Redon, where the Nantes–Brest canal crosses the Vilaine. No part of Brittany is without its megaliths, and here is the unforgettable Neolithic site of St-Just, little visited on its lonely heath.

Cathédrale St-Pierre, Rennes.

What to see in…

…**one day**
You could spend a day in **Rennes**, visiting the innovative Musée de Bretagne, window-shopping or touring the famous Parliament building. Get active with a walk in the magical **Forêt de Paimpont**, or around the walls of **St-Malo** before hopping on the little ferry to **Dinard**. Or maybe take a boat on the river at **Redon**. Art lovers should head for the craft shops and studios of pretty, riverside **La Gacilly**.

…**a weekend or more**
Brocéliande is close enough to **Rennes** for an ideal city/country combination, so visit a gallery and the cathedral before heading off in search of megaliths in the woods and that elusive Holy Grail. A spell on the coast at the **Bay of Mont St-Michel** with oysters for lunch and a guided low-tide walk could be followed by a tour of the amazing castles in the **Marches of Brittany**.

Rennes

Rennes is the capital of Brittany, traditional seat of parliament for the region and a busy university centre. It's a modern business and communications centre and a cultural venue of note, with full programmes of contemporary art performances and quality museums. Music fills the streets in summer, and also in winter with the famous Transmusicales festival in December – the place is alive and kicking year round. Don't miss the stunning medieval quarter, which has the best food market imaginable on Saturday mornings.

You need at least a couple of days to sample all that Rennes has to offer, whether you're interested in art and architecture, history, shopping, bar-hopping or nightlife. And in July, with the festival Les Tombées de la Nuit, Rennes proves itself to be a city that really knows how to party.

The old district on Place Ste-Anne, Rennes.

To walk around Rennes is to enjoy a rare feast of architectural splendour. A huge fire devastated nearly 1000 buildings in 1720, leaving medieval streets intact to the west and a great space for redevelopment in new styles. The area around the Parliament building and the Hôtel de Ville has many fine examples of the neoclassical grandeur befitting a prosperous capital city.

A good place to start is the Chapelle St-Yves, adjoining the tourist office. This high, narrow building with a wonderful wooden ceiling houses a free exhibition introducing Rennes, taking the themes of water, wood, stone and metal to present architectural development, illustrated by the most interesting buildings.

The most atmospheric area is medieval Rennes, situated between the **Rue St-Yves** where the tourist office is, and **Place Ste-Anne** (map: Rennes, C1, p88) to the north. Highlights include the **Rue du Chapitre**, where you can dine in several medieval interiors and, for contrast, No 6, where you can enter the courtyard of the **Hôtel de Blossac** (c 1730) to see the sort of classical structures that were constructed for wealthy individuals after the great fire.

The **Rue de la Psalette** has possibly the oldest house in Rennes at No 12 and, just beyond, in **Rue Guillaume**, at No 3 is Ty Coz, the 'old house', with its sculpted figures on guard at the doors. It is now rather bizarrely a 'bar de nuit', lit in pink neon after dark. Opposite the cathedral, the **Rue des Portes Mordelaises** leads to the only remaining gate of the former city defences.

The **Place des Lices**, where the superb Saturday market takes place, has a line of some of the most remarkable houses of all, with their brown, latticed façades, echoed by the 19th-century diamond-patterned brick market halls.

Continue up to **Place St-Michel**, heart of the student area, and along rue St-Michel with its wacky houses leaning at different angles, to Place Ste-Anne, where there is a metro station. Under the creepered wall of Eglise St-Aubin this square has a

Essentials

❶ Getting around Rennes has a fairly compact centre north of the river, but as it's the smallest city in the world to have its own metro system (VAL), the three central stations can cut down on walking. A City Pass is available from the tourist office to give reduced entry to the main sights and metro/bus. You can pick up and drop off bikes around the city through the Vélo Star scheme (levelostar.fr); advance registration is required.

If you have a car you can park free on the outskirts and take the metro into the centre.

❷ Bus station Place de la Gare. There's a good local bus network (T02 99 30 87 80, star.fr). For regional bus travel, see page 274.

❸ Train station Place de la Gare. Paris is just two hours away by train (T3635 or sncf.fr for information). For regional train travel, see page 274.

❹ ATMs Banque Populaire, 4 rue de la Monnaie, CIC, 17 Quai Lamartine.

❺ Hospital CHU, 3 rue Henri le Guilloux, T02 99 28 43 21, chu-renes.fr.

❻ Pharmacy 13 rue de la Monnaie, Rue de Brilhac.

❼ Post office Place de la République, Place Ste-Anne.

❽ Tourist information Rennes: 11 rue St-Yves, T02 99 67 11 11, tourisme-rennes.com, ticket office T02 99 67 11 66, Monday 1300-1800, Tuesday-Saturday 1000-1800, Sunday 1100-1300, 1400-1800, July and August 0900-1900. Telephone-style audio-guides in English are available. St-Malo: T08 25 13 52 00, saint-malo-tourisme.com. Ille-et-Vilaine region: bretagne35.com.

Five of the best

Things to do in Rennes

❶ Tour the **Parlement de Bretagne**.

❷ Enjoy an aperitif in **Place St-Michel**.

❸ Picnic in the **Jardin du Thabor**.

❹ Visit the **Musée de Bretagne**.

❺ Go to the Saturday morning market at **Place des Lices**.

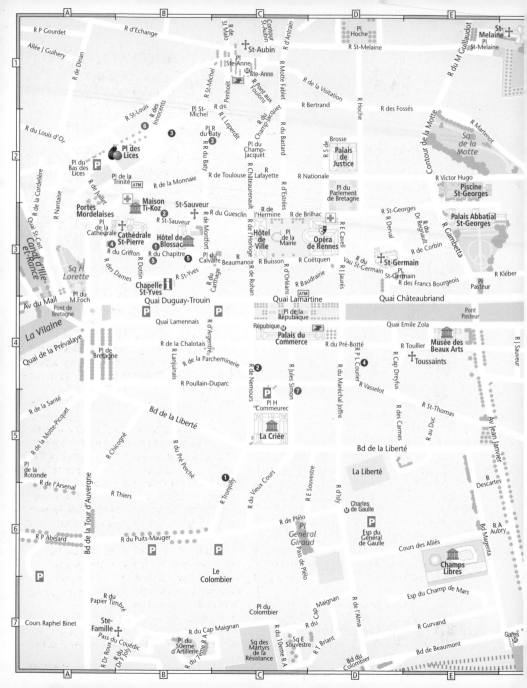

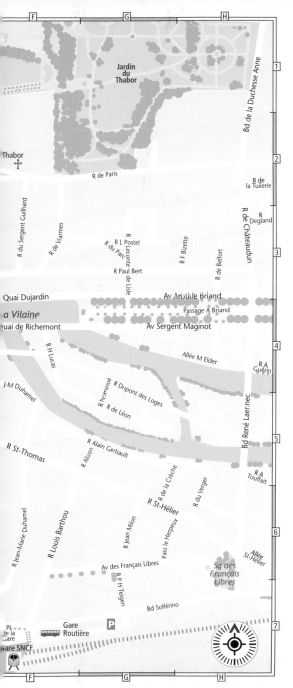

Rennes listings

ⓘ Sleeping

1 Hôtel Anne de Bretagne *12 rue Tronjolly* **C5**
2 Hôtel de Nemours *5 rue de Nemours* **C4**
3 Hôtel des Lices *7 place des Lices* **B2**
4 Mercure Centre Parlement *1 rue Paul Louis Courier* **D4**
5 Symphonie des Sens *3 rue du Chapitre* **B3**

ⓘ Eating & drinking

1 Auberge du Chat Pitre *18 rue du Chapitre* **B3**
2 Auberge Saint Sauveur *6 rue St-Sauveur* **B3**
3 Au Goût des Hôtes *8 rue Rallier du Baty* **B2**
4 Café Babylone *12 rue des Dames* **A3**
5 Crêperie Saint George *11 rue du Chapitre* **B3**
6 Le Cours des Lices *18 Place des Lices* **B2**
7 Le Daniel *19 rue Jules Simon* **C5**

rather seedy atmosphere by day, transformed into a vivid scene at night.

In contrast to medieval Rennes, neoclassical and modern Rennes can be seen in the heart of the administrative centre, which revolves around the **Place du Parlement de Bretagne** and the **Place de la Mairie**. Admire the uniformity of construction of the first, granite in the bottom half and lighter touffeau above. The little heads on each building were the trademark of architect Jacques Gabriel.

At the town hall you can go inside and see the Pantheon (immediately on the right), a war memorial room. On the first floor, ask to see the chapel, a 19th-century marbled affair under the central dome with a fine wall tapestry, although the altar has now gone. Beyond is the marriage room and the intimate petit salon with portraits of two famous mayors of Rennes – Leperdit (1793-1795) and Rallier du Baty (1696-1733).

Opposite is the 19th-century opera house, and, bringing unity to the ensemble, just across the river, the imposing **Palais du Commerce** is a reminder of Rennes' economic prosperity. This building was originally decorated by Isidore Odorico (1893-1945), whose mosaic style can be widely seen today around the city. If you're interested in modern architecture, the Cité Judiciaire (1984) is a stunning design conjuring up boats and castles simultaneously.

Le Parlement de Bretagne (Palais de Justice)

Place du Parlement de Bretagne, T02 23 20 43 28, parlement-bretagne.com.
Enquire at the tourist office for visits.
Map: Rennes, D2, p88.

To visit the Palais de Justice, the former Parliament building, you must book a guided tour at the tourist office. This begins in the Chapelle St-Yves with a film of footage of the fire of 1994, when a flare set off during a fishermen's demonstration led to disaster. It lodged in the roof, starting a smouldering, unseen fire in the attics where archives were kept. Much of the building was seriously damaged, works of art suffering equally from the torrents of water used by firemen. Restoration and renovation cost nearly €55 million.

   The building was constructed in the first half of the 17th century, originally accessed up a monumental external staircase, which was later destroyed. The internal decorative work continued for decades after, and when Parliament was exiled to Vannes in 1676 (see page 35), the state craftsmen left Brittany with some of the work unfinished. The courtroom ceiling panels have only clouds and no figures.

   The political context for viewing the splendour of the interior is that such luxury sent a clear message about the king's influence and power to the Bretons, and it directly showed the artistic sophistication of the French court in Brittany for the first time. The golden 'eye' ('spy') of Louis XIV – in the same room as a portrait of La Chalotais, the Breton noble who stood up against the royalist authority of the Duc de Aiguillon in 1764 – is a pleasing irony.

   The tour covers the Pas Perdus, a large reception hall, and then a series of incredibly ornate rooms, most strikingly the Grand'Chambre with its curtained boxes. In the actual court rooms, the incongruity between the modern 'office' furniture, including bullet-proof glass, and the sumptuous decor of the original building is the most amusing note of the visit.

Cathédrale St-Pierre, Rennes.

Around the region

Cathédrale St-Pierre

Carrefour de la Cathédrale.
Daily 0900-1200, 1500-1900.
Map: Rennes, B3, p88.

Behind a neoclassical façade with two towers and an enormous blazon of Louis XIV's coat of arms, the church has an odd entrance hall, created by the placing of the grand organ in the late 19th century. This version of the cathedral, after the Gothic nave was pulled down, was built mostly between 1816 and 1844, creating an Italian-style basilica.

The overall impression of the interior is heavy and dim. Painted panels of the ceiling and ambulatory dominate the decoration, the latter showing the founding Breton saints connected to eight Breton cathedrals. In the nave the thick pillars interspersed by chandeliers are stone, covered with stucco to look like marble. Everywhere are reminders that this is the metropolitan see, with former bishops' tombs (including one in the north transept pointing upwards) and coats of arms of Brittany, giving the sense of institutionalized and official faith rather than a place of private prayer.

The famous early 16th-century Flemish altarpiece is behind glass in the last side-chapel before the south transept. You need to put the light on to appreciate fully these gilded scenes from the life of the Virgin, including a graphic one of Jesus' circumcision, and angelic musicians playing to world-weary oxen. The figures are impressive in the detailing of fabric folds, headgear and pointed chins.

Eglise Notre-Dame en St-Melaine

Place St-Melaine.
Map: Rennes, E1, p88.

This huge former abbey church is a bit of a hotchpotch of styles. Much was destroyed in the fire of 1720, but Romanesque transept crossing arches and a clumpy Gothic-style nave remain. There are recently discovered frescoes and a wall-painting showing St-Melaine and praying Breton women. The lofty tower with its statue gazing out over the city dominates the landscape and the Thabor gardens.

Eglise St-Sauveur (Basilique Notre-Dame des Miracles)

Rue St-Sauveur.
Map: Rennes, B3, p88.

A focus for popular prayer in the old town, the cult of Notre-Dame des Miracles traditionally dates back to the saving of the city from the English siege in 1357. The statue of Mary sits in a cave-like niche, with ex-voto paintings showing old Rennes. The main altar has an overwhelming gilt baldachin (heavy canopy), like a fat sun bursting through heavy storm clouds.

Eglise St-Germain

Place St-Germain.
Map: Rennes, D3, p88.

This church, financed by medieval merchants, has some fine carved beams, but you will need very good eyesight to appreciate them. Otherwise there are the magnificent, Flamboyant-Gothic stained-glass windows, which were dismantled and recreated, out of order, from 1860.

Jardin du Thabor

Place St-Melanie.
Map: Rennes, G1, p89.

This 10-ha park, also known as Parc du Thabor, in the centre of the city, is much used by locals, students and visitors. It was laid out in the 19th century by Denis Bulher in the grounds of the former abbey. Here you will find plenty of places to stroll or picnic in the formal French-style gardens among fountains, statues and the shade of mature trees.

Musée des Beaux Arts

20 quai Emile Zola, T02 23 62 17 45, mbar.org.
Tue 1000-1800, Wed-Sun 1000-1200, 1400-1800.
€4.50.
Map: Rennes, E4, p88.

This palatial 19th-century edifice houses a core collection that was once the possession of the president of the Breton Parliament, Christophe de Robbien, until the upheaval of the French Revolution deprived him of it, to the ultimate benefit of the state. Italian and Dutch masters from the 14th to 17th centuries are well represented, and the 19th-century gallery includes examples of the Pont-Aven school (see page 47). There is also a small group of works by Breton artists with Breton subjects from the 19th and 20th centuries, typified by works such as Louis Garin's *Le Jour de Pardon* (1922).

Highlights include the *Tiger Hunt* by Rubens and an intriguing painting from 1575 of unknown authorship, *La Femme entre Deux Ages*. Don't miss the star of the show, the luminously beautiful *Newborn*, attributed to Georges de la Tour.

La Criée

Place Honoré Commeurec, T02 23 62 25 10, criee.org.
Tue-Fri 1200-1900, Sat and Sun 1400-1900, closed Mon and public holidays. Free.
Map: Rennes, C5, p88.

Rennes' contemporary art showcase is situated in part of the permanent market halls south of the river. It houses changing exhibitions – for example, disorder in response to social/political security and strictures by architect François Seigneur – and works by local artists.

Les Champs Libres (Musée de Bretagne, Espace des Sciences, Library)

10 Cours des Alliés.
Tue 1200-2100, Wed-Fri 1200-1900, Sat and Sun 1400-1900 (Jul and Aug opens at 1300).
Museums €4/€3, many free events (Pass €7/€5).
Map: Rennes, E6, p88.

This vast new building has brought together three important cultural elements, the Musée de Bretagne, Espace des Sciences and the public library, the latter in a central glass wedge that rises above the galleries. Inside is a sometimes confusing world of circuitous paths, empty spaces and hi-tech exhibits. There is also a regular

What the locals say

Rennes is a small town, so you keep meeting up with the same people. The street life is lively and there's always something going on. On Thursday night students gather around Rue St-Michel and the Place des Lices. *Le jeudi soir* is the time when everyone is out enjoying themselves. Lots go home at the weekend so it's quieter then.

We live in a little *commune* just outside Rennes and we're lucky to have good local transport. What's great are the bars – we really like Le 1929 (a bar with music) and the Sunset for its ambience and good coffee… and it's cheap!

Laure, Chloe and Marine, three young people about town.

Inside the Hôtel de Ville, Rennes.

programme of concerts, exhibitions and talks in the centre, and a café.

Musée de Bretagne The display of items on show is exceptional in terms of choice and quality, with English summaries in the labelling. Starting with archaeological finds from Paleolithic to Neolithic, the evolution of megalithic tomb-building is well presented, and there's an audio-visual station with legends of the stones described in Breton, French and Gallo. Two famous objects from the Gallo-Roman period to look out for are the goddess (Brigitte, or maybe Minerva) with swan headdress, and the sculpted lyre-player found at Paule.

The section on Brittany's formation and early Christianization includes a useful map with the distribution of place names beginning in *plou* or ending in *ac*, showing the distinct entities of western and eastern Brittany, one developing from incomers from Britain, the other under Roman and then Frankish interest. There are some superb pieces from later periods including religious statuary (a funny one of Ste-Marguérite emerging from the dragon) and carved coffer panels from the rich merchants of Léon.

The Dreyfuss affair has its own section. His second trial was conducted before a military tribunal in Rennes in 1899, and his lawyer was shot in the street here.

Overall this is an exceptional display and it is well worth taking a couple of hours here to find out about the origin and development of modern Brittany.

Espace des Sciences There are temporary displays on the ground floor and an interesting permanent section upstairs on the geology of Brittany, with rock samples and magnifying glasses provided. A booklet in various languages is provided for the Laboratoire de Merlin, a separate section where children (and adults) can carry out simple experiments. In term times there are likely to be parties of school children in the science areas, which have a strong pedagogic slant. On the top level is the Planetarium, with various showings about stars and the solar system.

Jardin du Thabor, Rennes.

St-Malo & around

This area is a very popular holiday destination for the coastal marvels of St-Malo and the Bay of Mont St-Michel, but there are many other sights worthy of attention. Cancale, the oyster capital of Brittany, is a must for sampling that quintessential taste of the sea, and a trip out onto the sands at low tide reveals an incredibly complex and diverse marine world. The speed of the incoming tide is legendary, and quite a spectacle in itself. Away from the coast, Dol-de-Bretagne has a glorious cathedral and the oldest houses in Brittany, plus a special Scottish connection, while across the Rance estuary, the traditional resort of Dinard is unique, with its British social and architectural heritage.

St-Malo.

St-Malo

Perhaps the most remarkable thing about St-Malo is that the magnificent walled city you see today is a reconstruction, painstakingly restored after the devastating bombing of the Second World War. But the town has always been known for a strong, independent spirit, admirably summed up by the famous motto '*ni français, ni Breton, Malouin suis*' (I'm neither French nor Breton, I'm Malouin). It has indeed been a place apart in many tides of Breton history, and was declared an independent republic during the Wars of Religion.

St-Malo's own flag still flies proudly from the château, and the town has a vibrant modern identity, home to an international festival of travel writing and one of France's best rock music events, rather suitable for an inner city (the Intra-Muros) known locally as *le rocher* (the rock). Today the port retains its importance in the French fishing industry, and also houses one base of Brittany Ferries. It's a confident sort of place, and they don't feel the need for many black and white Breton flags here.

Prosperity and audacity have been the key to St-Malo's sturdy individualism, based on maritime trade and the exploits of native corsairs all over the world, mainly against the English. From here René Douqay-Trouin set off before seizing Rio de Janeiro in 1711, and from here Jacques Cartier left on a voyage that resulted in the discovery of Canada in 1534. The town benefited from the natural protection of small islands and rocks, easily

Tour Solidor, St-Malo.

navigable for local experts, but a barrier for the enemy. The English regarded St-Malo as a 'wasp's nest' for its corsair strikes, and in 1693 devised the 'Infernal Machine', a ship charged with gunpowder and metal, intended to come right up against the walls before exploding, but it finally blew up on the rocks below.

St-Malo was in fact something of a late development. The initial settlement in the area was at **Alet**, a little promontory just to the west. This was a major base for the Coriosolites tribe and was then fortified by the Romans. It was here that Maclow, a Welsh monk and one of Brittany's founding saints, established his chapel, later destroyed by the Vikings and replaced by a Romanesque church.

Today a walk at Alet offers fantastic views of Dinard and St-Malo. Start from the ruined church and then take the Rue St-Pierre out to a viewpoint by the surviving bits of Roman walls. On top of the point is the Fort de la Cité, the prime spot for defences through the ages. An 18th-century fort was later adapted by the Germans, and a **museum**

Tip...

Arrive early to find good parking for St-Malo. Inside the walled city it is possible (€1.50 an hour), but it's easier to use an external car park, especially the Cale de Dinan, or near the tourist office in Esplanade St-Vincent. In July and August free buses run between the Parking Paul Féval and the Intra-Muros. The ferry port is within easy walking distance of the Intra-Muros and the train station is about 850 m away.

Around the region

(Apr-Oct, guided visits only, check hours, T02 99 82 41 74) of the war-time events of the area is now contained in a huge bunker on the site.

Continue right round to the Tour Solidor, an impressive 14th-century double-tower built after the Wars of Succession, where you can visit the excellent **Cap-Hornier Museum** (1000-1200, 1400-1800, Nov-Mar closed Mon and public holidays, €5.40).

The move east to the semi-island rock where the *ville close* now stands came in the 12th century, under the impetus of bishop Jean de Chatillon (or de la Grille) who is regarded as the second founder of St-Malo. The ramparts were built from the 14th century and the château soon after. Anne de Bretagne had the inscription "Whatever anyone says to the contrary (*quic-en-groigne*), I say this tower shall be built" set on the tower that still bears that name, though the words are long gone. Clearly even then Malouins were independent in their opinions.

The rampart walk today is less than 2 km. Start clockwise from the **Porte St-Vincent** with the port basins below, crossing the oldest gate (Grand'Porte), and then swing right past the statue of corsair Dougay-Trouin, admiring the typical 18th-century façades, and the resort of Dinard across the water (a regular ferry connects the two). Turning east at the little tower of St-Philippe, the statue of Jacques Cartier is ahead, and the sea-water swimming pool outside. When the tide is high the top of the diving board rises out of the sea like a strange monster.

This is the place to admire the offshore islands, especially Grand Bé, with the grave of writer Chateaubriand, which can be reached on foot at low tide. Petit Bé with its fort is behind. Robert Surcouf's statue commands his own terrace, reached by a wooden footbridge, before the Bidouan Tower, which you can climb for the views. After turning to the eastern side, the Fort National, also visitable depending on the tides, is before you. The walk finishes by the château.

Inside the walls, reconstructed 17th- and 18th-century houses line the straight streets, often a funnel for sea winds. There are many smaller details to appreciate in the backstreets. Don't miss the **Cour de la Houssaye**, where No 2, with its half-timbering and stair-turret, is known as the House of Duchess Anne. The **Rue des Vieux Remparts** preserves the memory of a Franciscan convent, with remains of a cloister visible through the gates of No 9 and a beautiful single room arch across the narrow street. The **Rue Mahé de la Bourdonnais** is named after another Malouin adventurer, once governor of Mauritius, thought to have been born at No 2, which has a finely carved Renaissance doorway of 1652. One half-timbered survival from the 17th century is the **Maison des Poètes et Ecrivains** at No 5 rue du Pélicot.

For something more modern, a courtyard in the **Rue Thévenard** has two enamelled creations from the 1950s of St-Malo and fish/seabirds, plus tiny statues of St-Malo and the whale, and Virgin and child on the arches.

The **Rue d'Orléans** and **Rue St-Philippe** have the finest façades of houses belonging to 18th-century *armateurs* (wealthy shipowners). Marvel again that all this was pieced back together in the 30 years following the war.

Cathédrale St-Vincent

Daily, closed 1200-1400.

Like much else in the town, the cathedral was badly damaged in the liberation of 1944. Entering today, one is immediately taken by the luminescence of the great window, the work of Jean le Moal in the late 1960s. The unusual lower level of the choir adds to its prominence. Here are the tombs of Dougay-Trouin, Jacques Cartier and

Tip...

Do the rampart walk in the evening and watch the sun setting over the water.

Jean de la Grille (behind a grill), as well as a golden reliquary containing bones of the latter in the south transept. The capitals of the columns in the nave are very finely carved with real and grotesque figures and animals.

Windows on the south side of the nave show the arrival of St-Malo and the blessing of Jacques Cartier on departure. The modern ironwork altar is worth noting, with each corner a stylized portrayal of the evangelists' symbols: man, lion, bull and eagle.

Musée d'Histoire

Château de St-Malo, T02 99 40 71 57.
1000-1200, 1400-1800, Nov-Mar closed Mon and public holidays. €5.20.

The entrance room contains a fine marble statue of Malouin hero, Douguy-Trouin. Upstairs there is a huge ship's figurehead of a corsair in amazingly lifelike detail, amidst nautical paintings and models. The little chapel has religious relics, and documents relating the sad story of Chateaubriand's search for his own island resting place, against town council opposition. "Everything has been difficult in my life, even my burial", he wrote.

There are three levels of exhibits in the *tour générale*, including the realities of fishing in the New World, and an interesting display about Malouinières. Look up at the wonderful ceiling of the top room, which contains paintings of St-Malo from the 19th and 20th centuries. Mathurin Méheut's 1944 offering shows the bomb damage the town suffered. A visit concludes in the *donjon* itself, with evidence of famous people in the town's history, such as a copy of Dougay-Trouin's memoirs, with a fold-out map of Rio.

Around St-Malo

The country area around the town – **Le Clos-Poulet** – contains many fine corsairs' houses called *Malouinières*. The tourist office has a leaflet with a driving or cycling tour of some of the best. The **Manoir de Limoëlou** (musee-jacques-cartier.com,

Jul and Aug daily 1000-1130, 1430-1800, Sep-Jun Mon-Sat, €4), house of Jacques Cartier who discovered Canada, is now a museum about his achievements.

Rochers sculptés, Rothéneuf

6 km northeast of St-Malo.
Daily 0900-1900, closed 1200-1400 in winter. €3.

The sculpted rocks are a true curiosity, both in their execution and inspiration. Carved over 25 years by a reclusive priest, Abbé Fouré, they represent the Rothéneuf clan of pirates and adventurers, who mostly came to a sticky end at the time of the Revolution. Dozens of individuals are shown in strange postures of life or death, such as the man lying with an arm round his dog, the sea monster, the cow and the Punch-and-Judy-type scene of a cruel husband. The location alone is worth a visit.

Pointe du Grouin & Cancale

Taking the coast road (D201) northeast towards Cancale via Pointe du Grouin provides great sea views across to the Channel Islands. The promontory is the best vantage point, and binoculars will be useful for watching birds on the reserve of Ile des Landes, where you may see shags and oystercatchers. The magical mound of Mont St-Michel lies to the east, and the hump of Mont-Dol inland.

Continue to Cancale, the oyster capital of Brittany, a narrow strip of a place nestling against a steep hill. Make for the Port de la Houle for the oyster stalls. But if you don't want to get caught up in seasonal traffic mayhem in such a confined space, carry on along the main coast road to find more oyster places, including a restaurant, a little further ahead. You can also visit an oyster farm, **La Ferme Marine** (see Activities & tours, page 131).

The Bay of Mont St-Michel

After Cancale, the geography of the Bay of Mont St-Michel is soon apparent. To one side the bay,

Mont St-Michel.

Mont St-Michel

This World Heritage Site lies just over Brittany's border in Normandy. It is a magnet for visitors from all over the world and busy at any time of year. The shape and situation of the rock, looming from the misty bay, lends to its mystique, but the real marvel is the feat of labour that achieved the monumental abbey buildings. Every single piece of stone had to be carried over and hoisted to its destined place. The result is sublime, both sturdy and intricate, endless stone stairs below and vaulting above.

Visit the delicate cloister almost overhanging the sea, the crypt supported by massive pillars and the inspiring Romanesque abbey church.

It's a fact...

A notable first – oysters from the Bay of Mont St-Michel have been granted the coveted AOC guarantee of quality.

vastly exposed to sand-yachts and gatherers at low tide, to the other a flat area of *polder* (reclaimed marshland), with dykes, marsh, water channels and sturdy stone windmills. The tide here is

phenomenal – it recedes for up to 16 km and then rushes in at breakneck speed, taking the unwary by surprise. If you want to walk out on the flats, it is best to join an organized excursion (see Activities & tours, page 131). The visitor car parks below the Mont are only uncovered at certain times. Silting up of the bay is a constant problem, and the question of whether land should be reclaimed for agricultural activity or whether the Mont should be restored to a proper island are still environmental issues.

Mont Dol

2 km north of Dol-de-Bretagne.

This natural hill rising from the marshy environs was one of Brittany's most prolific Paleolithic sites with finds of mammoth and rhinoceros bones. It's tamer now, and you can drive up to the summit to find a windmill and two towering religious memorials. The views are superb, across the *polders* to the bay or inland to Dol-de-Bretagne and its cathedral. The little chapel has a window, visible through a grill in the door, commemorating the First World War. In the village below, there's an interesting church with frescoes.

Dol-de-Bretagne

Via the N176, 24 km southeast of St-Malo.

This little town is well worth a visit. It contains the oldest houses in Brittany, one with three beautiful arches dating from the 12th century (now a flower shop), at No 17 in the main street, Grand'Rue des Stuarts. This name recalls that the Scottish dynasty was descended from a Breton *seneschal* (stewart in English) of Dol, who was given lands in Scotland after fighting in the Battle of Hastings. Medieval half-timbered and porch houses also line the continuation Rue LeJamptel.

The Rue Ceinte behind is interesting for the many different facings and types of modernization, and an octagonal stair-turret at No 16. The Promenade des Douves offers a rampart walk on the old walls, giving a sense of the height of the town above the surrounding marshland.

Dol was first made an Episcopal centre by Judual, king of Domnonée in the sixth century. It played a significant role in the ninth-century emergence of Brittany as a distinct entity. Some claim that Nominoë was actually crowned king here, but what is sure is that he elevated the bishopric of Dol to the status of Metropolitan see, making Breton bishops independent of Tours across the border.

Cathédrale St-Samson (21 rue Ceinte, open every day). The exterior is rather austere, apart from the south side which has an exuberant doorway from the 14th century (with 19th-century panels added) and a more restrained smaller, earlier porch. A former building was destroyed by King John's army in 1203, and one tower of the new cathedral was never completed for lack of funds. You enter under

Medievalys, Dol-de-Bretagne.

the organ loft to an impressive interior by virtue of its height and length, with a series of cross-vaults leading the eye to the amazing ancient window in the distance, one of the earliest in Brittany.

In the north transept is the unusual Renaissance-style tomb of Bishop Thomas James, produced by Italian craftsmen in the 15th century before the style was much known here. The choir stalls are remarkable but sadly not easy to view.

Medievalys (4 Place de la Cathédrale, T02 99 48 35 30, medievalys.com, 1000-1900, Jul and Aug until 2000, Nov-Mar until 1800, €7.50, €4.90). Next to the

tourist office, this large exhibition features the themes of castles and cathedrals, and looks at many aspects of medieval life. There is also a section on the Knights Templar. Special events and performances are arranged in summer months, and audio-guides for the town and cathedral are also available here.

Menhir de Champ Dolent On the edge of Dol is this huge menhir (10 m), now rather scaled down by a neat enclosure with hedges and picnic tables. According to legend, the Devil threw a great stone at St-Samson's cathedral, which knocked part of the tower off, then landed in a field. A more curious story tells of two brothers fighting to the death, when suddenly separated by the stone coming up from the earth.

Dinard

8 km west of St-Malo, 18 km north of Dinan.

The town has long-standing British connections. A plaque on the Promenade de la Lune (also called the Promenade Anglaise) commemorates the arrival of the first British residents in 1836. The popularity soon spread and Dinard developed into a famous coastal resort, complete with casino, spa, yacht club and golf course.

The statue of Alfred Hitchcock, with birds, reflects the story that he based the house in *Pyscho* on one here.

Dinard is the perfect place to swim, relax on the beaches, stroll on the prom and admire the distinctive 19th-century villas all around.

Grand'Rue des Stuarts, Dol-De-Bretagne.

The Marches of Brittany

This is a flourishing, rich agricultural region, the main cattle-rearing area of Brittany. Many of its festivals revolve around food and drink with products of the land like the apple and the chestnut at the forefront. The beautiful beech forest of Fougères is perfect for relaxing walks or more strenuous pursuits.

The area's distinctive legacy as the border country between France and Brittany is symbolized by the awesome castles of Fougères and Vitré. It is an area steeped in history, from Nominoë's great triumph at Ballon (Bains-sur-Oust) in AD 845, to the final battle of Breton independence lost at St-Aubin-du-Cormier.

Fougères old town.

St-Aubin-du-Cormier

23 km northeast of Rennes, on the A84 motorway.

Famous as the site of the battle in 1488 that brought Breton independence to an end, this little town has an attractive central square and a ruined château by a large lake with a walking circuit. Built by Duc Pierre I in the 13th century, the castle was subject to symbolic destruction by Charles VIII after his victory over the Bretons, "as if cut in half by the sword of Roland", as the historian Ducrest wrote.

Between the old houses in the **Place Veillard**, the rather striking tower (1764) is all that's left of an earlier church. The current church dates from 1902 and is in typically Byzantine style but with curious carved capitals in the nave. There is a modern **memorial** for those who died in the Battle of St-Aubin-du-Cormier, just outside the town. It records that 500 English archers died for Brittany. This refers to the contingent of 440 men brought by Sir Edward Woodville from the Isle of Wight. Only one survived.

Fougères

"Fabuleux château de Fougères" runs the advertising slogan, and it's true. You won't find a better castle than this, and in fact the town is pretty fabulous all round. Allow at least a day to see the château, the medieval town nearby (often neglected by visitors) and the largely 18th-century 'high town' above. Yes, above, because the amazing castle is not built on the top of the hill – the Church of St Leonard now looms well above it, which makes the position even more striking.

Lovers of history and literature will enjoy Fougères. The **tourist office** (2 rue Nationale, T02 99 94 12 20) has an excellent document on the literary connections of the town, including writers Balzac, Victor Hugo and Chateaubriand (the latter grew up in the Château du Combourg, which is 50 km west). After the Revolution, the town's renewal came with an explosive economic growth thanks to the newly established shoe-making industry – by the 1920s, there were 100 factories in Fougères.

Tip...

To find the memorial, take the Combourg road out of the town and about 1 km after crossing the motorway, you'll find it on the right.

St-Aubin-du-Cormier.

Château de Fougères

Jul and Aug daily 1000-1900, May, Jun, Sep daily 1000-1300, 1400-1900, Oct-Apr 1000-1230, 1400-1730 (closed Mon out of school holidays), Jan closed. €7.50/€4.50, family pass €19.50, audio tour in English available.

Built on a great outcrop of rock in the marshes around the Nançon river, the château's earliest structure is the Gobelins Tower, at the highest point. Duke François II built two towers, Raoul and Surienne, in the 15th century, in the new horseshoe shape, as he was facing increasingly powerful artillery. In fact, it was too late, as the château, like the rest of Brittany, soon after passed into the hands of the King of France, and its defensive purpose was redundant.

This is a château in three parts – a defensive outer court protecting the entry (which could be flooded

Fairy-built?

The Mélusine tower is named after the fairy said to have been responsible for many medieval buildings. If caught in the act, she left the work unfinished, which explains all those missing bits… She was the patron of the Lusignan family, who took over Fougères in 1256.

in case of attack), then a contained area of 2 ha, once housing the lord's living quarters, and place of refuge for the town population, and finally, the ultimate defensive position in the far triangular corner. Here you can see what might be the stone foundations of the original wooden tower that Henry II razed in 1166. Walking the curtain walls provides views of both the high and low towns outside.

The special value of this château is that distinct elements from different periods of building remain

Below: Château de Fougères. Opposite: The statue of the Marquis de la Rouerie in Place Aristide-Briand.

intact, so it provides a clear lesson in the development of military architecture from the 12th to the 15th century. The site is exceptionally well presented, with often dramatic audio-visual material in three of the towers. The contrast between the ancient stones and the sophisticated modern presentation works well and heightens the experience of a visit.

Medieval quarter

Enter the network of little streets at the foot of the château walls through the massive medieval town gate, La Porte Notre-Dame. Here you'll find a secret world of half-timbered houses, including the **Maison de Savigny** with its painted wooden balconies, now a venue for exhibitions. Extensive old *lavoirs* line the pretty stream of the Nançon, with a scenic backdrop of red quarry faces. This area was once the workplace of tanners, cloth-makers and dyers. The **Place du Marchix** has an atmosphere of long-gone times, as well as a bar, bakery and one of the best crêperies around in a delightful *maison à pans de bois*.

The Flamboyant-Gothic **Eglise St-Sulpice** contains the famous statue of Our Lady of the Marsh, said to have been found here in the 13th century; but what really makes an impression is the 18th-century panelled nave and marble statuary. The graceful exterior is decorated with many gargoyles and what one local guidebook calls 'rather naughty figures'.

High town

The best things to see here are all conveniently lined up in one street, the **Rue Nationale**. This has particular connections with the writer Chateaubriand – two of his sisters lived here (at No 18 and No 32) and the great man often visited. Five fires in the 18th century saw this area almost completely rebuilt in contemporary style.

Start at the **Théâtre Victor Hugo** (1886) and pass along to the **Beffroi**, a free-standing bell tower, said to be the oldest (1397) in Brittany, built by proud (and rich) local merchants, with the

octagonal tower later remodelled. The bell still chimes out across the town.

Fougères was a commercial portal to Brittany in medieval times, with the transit of goods as important as local markets and industries. The cloth trade was extremely important here, as were all aspects of leather-working. Paper and pewter (or *pintery* – hence the Rue de la Pinterie leading to the castle) were later products.

There are two museums on Rue Nationale. Firstly, the **Atelier et Musée de l'Horlogerie** (daily mid-Jun to mid-Sep, otherwise Tue-Sat), is good for those interested in time-keeping in many forms. You can also see Alain Le Floch repairing clocks and watches when passing his workshop to reach

The Chouans

Balzac's novel *The Chouans* was set in Fougères. He spent a month here soaking up the atmosphere in 1828 and the book was published a year later. In 1831 he decided to stand for election as a deputy for the town, but a friend persuaded him that a Parisian was not likely to be the most popular choice.

This was a major centre for the Chouan movement at an aristocratic level thanks to the Marquis de la Rouërie, Armand Tuffin, whose statue is in Place Aristide-Briand.

Vitré.

the museum area, which includes many exhibits on the measurement of time. Secondly, the **Musée Emmanuel de La Villéon** (Wed-Sun 1000-1200, 1400-1700, free), in the only remaining *maison à porche,* displays paintings by a local post-impressionist artist.

In the mainly neo-Gothic **Eglise St-Leonard** you can see some of the oldest stained glass in Brittany (chapel on left as you enter), showing St-Benedict. The 15th-century nave has a multiple-gabled façade, a style favoured in this region. If the tower is open, you can go up for the best views over the town. If not, to the side of the church is a gate leading to extensive beautiful gardens with large terraces down the hillside and stunning views over the château (go in the evening for a view of the château lit up).

Forêt de Fougères

On the edge of the town you immediately plunge into this huge 1700-ha forest. (It is not well signed from the centre, so follow the direction of Louvigné-du-Désert.) This was once the regular haunt of salt-smugglers, who could make a fortune across the border when the salt-tax (from which Brittany was exempt) was very high. Bloody battles with customs' officers were frequent here.

There are many kilometres of walking, cycling and riding trails. The activity centre **La Ferme de Chênedet** (chenedet-loisirs.com) can arrange, advise on and even provide accommodation (see

Sleeping, see page 121). Otherwise, park by **Le Cordon de Druides** (actually a Neolithic alignment of menhirs) and wander at will.

Vitré

If you're arriving by car from the direction of Rennes, it's worth stopping at the Tertres Noirs viewpoint before the town for a superb view of the splendid château.

Vitré has an incredibly well-preserved medieval quarter dense with architectural detail. The **tourist office** (T02 99 75 04 46, ot-vitre.fr) presents a very good exhibition on many aspects of the development of the town and its distinctive heritage. The 15th and 16th centuries saw commercial prosperity on a grand scale, particularly as a result of exporting local rough canvas cloth to Holland and the towns of the Hanseatic league. This success came from a commercial organization called the Marchands d'Outre-mer, founded in 1472. They were basically middlemen in the buying and selling of canvas, and they became very wealthy. It is their elaborately ornate houses that survive in remarkable numbers here.

Château du Vitré

May-Sep 1000-1245, 1400-1800, Oct-Apr 1000-1215, 1400-1730. €4. A special deal for entry to Vitré's château, the nearby Château des Rochers and two other museums is available.

The present château overlooking the Vilaine valley dates from the 13th century, but a Romanesque-style gate of an earlier structure can still be seen. The triangular design surviving today was developed and maintained under the ownership of the Lavals, one of Brittany's leading noble families, who were Protestants. Because of this many Huguenot workers were employed here, and the château was besieged by Leaguers during the Wars of Religion.

You enter by the tower called Le Châtelet into a huge interior courtyard with the current town hall rather oddly in what was formerly the old seigneurial quarters to the right. The château itself is rather more captivating than the exhibition in the towers, which was set up in 1877 by the famous Breton historian Arthur de la Borderie. This includes a collection of religious objects and a room displaying a 'cabinet of curiosities' in the spirit of the late 19th century, with an array of stuffed birds and some amusing samples, such as the fighting frogs.

Medieval quarter

It's not hard to imagine these narrow streets teeming with noise and activity 500 years ago, around the former market halls. The best areas from which to admire the medieval architecture are the Rue d'En Bas, leading up from the Auberge du Château restaurant (notice especially the tower of No 10 and the stone monkeys of No 20), and Rue Baudrarie (meaning a place of leather-workers). In the latter, the Renaissance style is predominant – No 5 has a fine outdoor staircase, and there's interesting sculptural detail at No 7.

The **Eglise Notre-Dame** at the top dates from the 15th-17th centuries, with hints of an earlier Romanesque phase. The church has the Flamboyant-Gothic style multiple-gables called 'saw-tooth', which are characteristic of this area. On the south face is a beautiful outdoor pulpit, with a three-faced representation of the Trinity that would be more suitable for the three faces of Eve.

Château du Vitré.

Forêt de Paimpont

This forest has been associated from medieval times with Arthurian Brocéliande. A distinct strand of tales involving primarily Merlin and Lancelot attributed to locations here shows the link between legend and landscape. When and how these entered the Breton tradition is unclear, but such stories now vivify this magical setting, from the home of the Lady of the Lake at the Château de Comper to the Valley of No Return and an Arthurian-themed church at Tréhorenteuc. It is certainly an enchanting environment for relaxing strolls or challenging walks, with delightfully romantic destinations like the Spring of Eternal Youth.

Merlin's tomb.

Paimpont

One of the main centres for exploring the forest, this is an attractive village set around the ancient abbey and 75-ha lake, with picnic areas and walks by the waterside. In the high street there are shops to satisfy even the greatest craving for fairies, magical apparatus and colourful medieval-style clothes. The hairdresser is rather wittily called 'The Enchanted Scissors'.

L'Abbaye de Paimpont There's some fine statuary here, including a 15th-century representation of Dark Age King Judicaël, founder of the original abbey. The wood-vaulted nave is the oldest part of the church, but the lower panelling, with its carved heads, is 400 years younger. Typical of the region is the elaborate baroque canopy of the high altar. Considerably more moving and still a focus of popular worship is the beautiful medieval statue of Notre-Dame de Paimpont in a side niche. A peep into the atmospheric little Chapel of the Holy Sacrament (reserved for silent prayer) shows the religious banners carried in procession. In high season, the Treasury, with many valuable pieces of statuary and silver, is open every day.

Château de Comper

Centre de l'Imaginaire Arthurien, Concoret, 7 km northwest of Paimpont, T02 97 22 79 96, centre-arthurien-broceliande.com.
End Mar to mid-Oct 1000-1730 (Tue groups only, closed Wed), Jul and Aug 1000-1900, closed Wed. €5.50.

This red schist lakeside château is a fitting setting for a celebration of the romantic Arthurian tradition. Fans of Excalibur and the Sword in the Stone will have a field day here, with extravagant costumed tableaux (shame about the wigs) and magical artefacts. Most of the information is presented on illustrated panels with a reasonable mix of imaginative speculation and historical research. There are many artistic interpretations of Merlin and fairies, and even a space with crayons

Tip...

A Pass Brocéliande, available from tourist offices, gives reduced entry to a number of attractions.

where you can colour in knights and dragons. The emphasis is on the complex personage of Merlin, and his uneasy combination of wise counsel and sorcery. His relationship with Viviane gets lots of attention – after all, this is her place, and from the windows you can have a good look for the Lady of the Lake. Burne-Jones' *Beguiling of Merlin* with the lurid eyes is the key iconograph. You really do get a sense here of the power legend can still exert over modern minds. The inside of the building is interesting in its own right, with the exhibition covering two floors. Once you have a ticket, you can also walk in the park with its lakeside and woodland trails.

Château de Trécesson

Off D40 near Campénéac

This must be one of the most picturesque châteaux in Brittany, dating from the end of the 15th century. Although it is not usually open to the

Inside Paimpont Abbey.

Chêne à Guillotin

It's worth a little drive to see this remarkable oak tree near Concoret. It's said to be over 1000 years old and is still flourishing.

public, it is certainly worth a short diversion to see the immensely impressive and evocative deep red façade and causeway across the lake, and have a peep into the courtyard.

Tréhorenteuc

This small village with a year-round friendly **tourist office** (T02 97 93 05 12, broceliande.valsansretour. com), is the starting point for walks in the Valley of No Return. The delightful 17th-century church was given a revamp in the 1950s by Abbé Gillard, who developed the theme of the Holy Grail and the Arthurian legends in the church's decor. Here you will find paintings of the Round Table, a frieze of the White Stag and a window showing the Grail Chalice. It all works surprisingly well.

Val sans Retour

This is the highlight of a visit to the Forest of Brocéliande, the perfect setting for an atmospheric walk. It is called the Valley of No Return in legend because Morgane, half-sister of Arthur, was betrayed by her beloved Guyomard and so set out to trap all false lovers here. Only Lancelot, who was true to Guinevere, survived.

Reality is less romantic – another valley was first identified as the Val sans Retour, but the building of a factory in the mid-19th century rather spoiled the image, so this one took over. It does have all the right ingredients – deep forest, stark stone heights, a placid pool for the Fairies' Mirror and bright red stream water.

After an outbreak of forest fires in 1990, the Arbre d'Or (Golden Tree), which was the work of François Davin, was placed here, symbolically among burnt remains, as a reminder of nature's powers of regeneration, and 30,000 new trees were planted. The shape of the sculpture suggests the horns of the stag, which is so important in Celtic religion.

There are three starting-point car parks, with a choice of circular or linear routes. From No 3 you come to the Arbre d'Or and Le Miroir aux Fées (fairies' mirror) after 300 m.

Jardin des Moines

It's worth seeking out this less well-known site. Although it's doomed to semi-obscurity by its lack of Arthurian connections, its own tale of debauched monks being turned to stone is just as good. Dating from about 3000 BC, this is a Neolithic burial site, although there is no actual chamber. A rough trapezoid of stones – with contrast between greyish quartzite and the red of local schist – was originally divided into three 'rooms'.

L'Hôtié de Viviane

Actually a Neolithic burial chamber rather than the house of Viviane, although you could argue it proves fairies were small. The tomb is unusual in that it consisted of a single chamber originally covered by a cairn of small stones, as old photos of the excavation show. Its high location provides wide views over the forest, with an attractive walk from the parking at La Touche Guérin.

Tombeau du Géant

This is one of those sites reached from its parking area by a pleasant 1-km walk along open tracks, then into woodland. It's a high, lonely site on the same plateau as the Hôtié de Viviane. A set of Neolithic menhirs have been used by later generations in the Bronze Age to construct a tomb, originally covered by an earth mound.

Merlin's Tomb & the Fontaine de Jouvence

At the other end of the forest are the slight remains of a megalith, long ruined by treasure-seekers, today known as Merlin's Tomb. It is little more than two stones and a holly tree, but recognizable by the votive offerings left by modern pagans. The footpath leads on for a few hundred metres to the Fountain of Youth, a circular enclosure of stones around a rather sluggish spring. The origin of the legend that the water restored a youthful appearance is obscure. Have a look opposite in the quarry at some modern stone sculpture.

Tip…

The forest is mostly private, so stay near the popular sites during the hunting season, which runs from October to March.

Tombeau des Anglais

This larger megalith is further along the same road: turn left at Brousses Noires, its other name. The English connection probably came from their 14th-century presence during the Wars of Succession. A battle was fought at nearby Mauron in 1352, hence the association with a grave. In fact the alley grave, which was disturbed from its original shape by treasure-seekers, dates back to about 3000 BC.

Fontaine de Barenton

The beautiful trail of a little over 1 km leading up to the *fontaine* starts from a car park in the hamlet of Folles Pensées (or Mad Thoughts) – whether the spring water gave you these or cured you of them is uncertain. This idyllic location was where Merlin met and fell in love with Viviane, to the extent he taught her all he knew of magic, despite recognizing that she was dangerous. As a result, Viviane later imprisoned him in nine circles of air.

Château de Trécesson.

Pays de Redon

This may not be a very well-known area for a holiday destination, but it has much to offer in terms of sights and activities, especially if you are interested in river or canal sailing. The Vilaine is a majestic waterway, connecting Rennes with its former staging port of Redon, which also sits on the Nantes–Brest canal. La Gacilly makes good use of the pretty River Aff, which provides a backdrop for some of the gigantic outdoor exhibitions of this very arty town, where the streets are full of craft studios and workshops. One of the best megalithic sites in Brittany can be found nearby at St-Just, where lines of stones and burial chambers are spread over the moors of a high granite plateau, the Landes de Cojoux.

Route de Vilaine.

The busy market town of Redon sits at a historically strategic point: the confluence of the Vilaine and the Oust rivers. Today it has a large pleasure port and a famous canal museum, for the Nantes–Brest Canal crosses the Vilaine here. For a long time Redon was the port for Rennes, as the tidal waters of the Vilaine permitted the harbourage of large three-masted sea-going ships. Goods were unloaded and then taken by barge upriver to the capital. But what really put the town on the map originally was the foundation of an abbey here in AD 832 by the monk Conwoïon, and this religious centre was to become an important stopping-place on the Compostela trail, as the Quai St-Jacques indicates today.

In the 15th century it was a regular meeting place for the Breton Parliament, in what is appropriately called the Rue des Etats. The gourmet restaurant La Bogue (see Eating, page 128) now occupies the relevant building near the abbey church. Grand'Rue preserves many half-timbered houses, with many ghastly clashing modern shop fronts below the colourful ancient façades.

The Old Port & the Vilaine

Situated behind the current pleasure port, on the banks of the wide Vilaine, the old commercial port has many merchants' houses from the 17th and 18th centuries – some have iron balconies on the upper floors where the living quarters were, with the ground floor acting as warehousing. The Passage de Saulniers (salt-dealers) points to the history of one of the most valuable commodities, especially that from the marshes to the east around Guérande. Wine, fish, building materials and linen also passed in and out of Redon. The 18th-century English blockades disrupted trade to an alarming degree, but the town continued to flourish as a market centre for the whole area, and so it remains.

To the north, across the canal, the Vilaine runs beneath the medieval ramparts of the town, where there is a little monument recording this stage of the Compostela trail. Pilgrims came to Redon overland and by water, before continuing their journey towards Nantes. A plaque on the actual walls is a tribute to Nominoë, founding father of the Breton state. The date is significant – in 1932 nationalism was a European issue, and this tribute to an independent spirit came from the right-wing group, L'Union Régionaliste Bretonne.

L'Abbaye de St-Sauveur

Place St-Sauveur.
Open every day.

The political significance of this abbey was important in the birth of the ninth-century Breton state. Nominoë backed the monk Conwoïon's plan in AD 834, when Louis the Pious, King of Franks, was stalling, and the project went ahead. The Romanesque tower is one of the finest relics of this period of architecture in Brittany, best viewed from the cloister, which dates from Cardinal Richelieu's time as commendatory abbot. It's now full of

Redon house.

Route de Vilaine

This well-signed tourist driving route runs between Redon and Rennes, using quiet roads much of the time and passing scenic sites. You could easily while away a day following the trail, which is marked by brown signs in each direction.

If you feel like a riverside walk or picnic not far from Redon, the little quay at Brain-sur-Vilaine provides an idyllic location. Don't miss the Chapelle Ste-Agathe at Langon.

students from the enclosed *lycée*, but you can walk around, past some highly ornate baroque doorways. The great Gothic tower that now stands alone was separated by a devastating fire – its partner was never built. The interior of the church is an uneasy contrast between a dark Romanesque nave with carved capitals and a bright Gothic altar.

Musée de la Batellerie de l'Ouest (Inland Waterways Museum)

12 quai Jean Bart, T02 99 72 30 95.
Daily mid-Jun to mid-Sep, 1000-1200, 1500-1800, out of season Sat, Sun, Mon, Wed 1400-1800, closed Nov-Mar. €2, children €1.

Set on the quayside of the pleasure port, this museum gives a genuine insight into the lost way of life of canal folk, and the heritage of the inland waterways of Brittany. There's an evocative film (English version) to set the scene and afterwards you can browse a collection of old photographs and artefacts, including La Bricole, the harness used by men (or sometimes women) to pull their own boats when they had no horse. Also on display are old engines, and implements used by the bargemen, including an eel trap and special scissors for grabbing the captives. There's an interesting relief model of the Armorican peninsula, showing the obstacles canal builders had to surmount in connecting the various river basins, and an English commentary through headphones explains the construction of the extraordinary Rigole de Hilvern, which brought water to feed an artificial section of the canal from more than 60 km away. An automated model offers you the chance to bring a boat through a miniature lock yourself.

Art and flowers in La Gacilly.

La Gacilly

14 km north of Redon.

Renowned as a town of artists and artisans, La Gacilly has also won awards for its flower displays, with every street a blaze of varied colour. Each summer a vast and impressive photographic exhibition, often on ecological themes, is set up all around the town, lining the main pedestrian areas. By the river enormous paintings are displayed on buildings and bridges in a natural setting. The **tourist office** (T02 99 08 10 18, paysdelagacilly.com) near the bridge can provide a leaflet on all the studios and galleries with creations from leaf art to glass-blowing. The town is also famous as the home of Yves Rocher, founder of a beauty-from natural-products empire which still dominates the place today. There is a *halt nautique* with facilities for boat owners at the Port de la Gacilly, and you can also hire boats here (see Activities & tours, page 131) for a day or longer on the peaceful Aff or Oust rivers.

St-Just

18 km northeast of Redon.

It was heartbreaking to see the fire damage in September 2009 to this outstanding Neolithic site, and sadly it's not the first time in recent memory that flames have ravaged the high plateau of the Landes de Cojoux. The stones cover over 1 km of heath, and often you will have them all to yourself.

From the parking areas you go right through the impressive Alignements du Moulin, and further on pass the Demoiselles de Cojoux, to the left. This group has two raised stones (young women

Tip...

Avoid Mondays out of season in La Gacilly, when most of the artisans' shops and restaurants and the tourist office are closed.

The natural art of beauty

In the 1960s Yves Rocher decided to generate new energy in his declining native town by starting an enterprise to provide local employment. His natural products are now a byword in the world of beauty and cosmetics. The factory remains in La Gacilly, together with its shop (see Shopping, page 130) and botanical gardens. He also endowed a new museum, the Vegetarium, focusing on the plant world. In 2009 the Yves Rocher ecological hotel development (see Sleeping, page 122) opened on the hill above the town. Yves Rocher died on 26 December 2009.

petrified) and two smaller ones lying down (often referred to as a mother and baby). Two intriguing burial sites, Le Château Bû, a Neolithic dolmen reworked in the Bronze Age, and Le Croix St-Pierre, a corridor grave from c 4500 BC, follow. Even more interesting is the Tribunal: a semi-circle (once 15, now with some missing) facing a single stone, as if sitting in judgement. It may be an early form of a calendar.

It's possible to continue on the path right across the *landes* to reach a steep descent to the lake Etang de Val. If you want a real challenge, some of the rock faces here are kitted out for climbing (*escalade*), with ropes and holds, and have open access, at the responsibility of the individual. (To drive to the bottom, follow signs from the village to the Etang.)

The **Maison Nature et Megaliths** (T02 99 72 69 25, landes-de-cojoux.com, Jul and Aug daily, May, Jun, Sep, Oct Wed-Sun 1400-1800, Nov-Apr Sun 1400-1800, €5) in St-Just presents the relationship between man and the landscape, in Neolithic times and the present day.

Megaliths of Monteneuf

If you're interested in megaliths, this site is in easy range of Redon. It has an outdoor educational section (with open access), visually demonstrating the answers to questions such as: what did Stone Age houses look like? How did they make pottery? How were the menhirs raised?

The Nantes–Brest canal

The canal is a fantastic leisure resource, providing scenic walking or cycling along more than 350 km of towpath, and an inland waterway for sailing or canoeing. Not all sections are navigable, and Lac de Guerlédan (see page 163) effectively divides the route into two. To the east you can hire a boat in Nort-sur-Erdre or Sucé-sur-Erdre (bretagne-fluviale.com) or Redon and sail as far as Pontivy. To the west, the whole 81-km stretch of Finistère is open, plus a short section in Côtes d'Armor. Boats can be hired at Châteauneuf-du-Faou (aulneloisirs.com).

The canal was built in the first half of the 19th century to provide a secure internal supply route at a time when English ships were blockading the Breton coasts. Napoleon particularly wanted to link the arsenals at Brest, Nantes and Lorient, so that the equipment of fleets could be maintained. In fact, by the time the canal was finished, its prime purpose became the transport of goods. Today the canal also has a symbolic significance: it runs right across historic Brittany, linking the territory of Nantes and Loire-Atlantique which were severed from the region of Brittany during the Second World War.

Originally there were 237 locks along the full length. The canal consists mostly of harnessed rivers and beautiful waterways like the Oust, the Blavet and the Aulne. Less than 20% is made up of straight, artificial channels, dug out laboriously through hillsides to join up the river valleys. The Grande Tranchée, near Glomel in Côtes d'Armor, is more than 3 km long and took a decade to construct, using prison labour from Brest. These sections had to be fed with water, often brought long distances across the contours of the land. The Rigole d'Hilvern, constructed in the 1830s, took an astonishing 63 km to reach the canal from a reservoir at Bosméléac.

Lac de Guerlédan with its barrage and hydroelectric station was created in the 1920s, when the heyday of the canal had passed in the face of better roads and faster train systems. The Blavet valley was flooded, losing 400 ha of woodland and 17 locks of the canal, which still stand underwater with their keepers' houses. A proposal to build a ladder of locks and keep the passage open for barges was too expensive to fulfil.

Along the route of the canal, you'll discover many spots of exceptional natural beauty and also of historical interest. It passes through the towns of Redon, Malestroit, Josselin and Pontivy, and flows past the ruined Abbey of Bon Repos.

Tip...

If you're planning a trip on the canal, check for periods of chomage, when sections of the canal are drained for maintenance. September and October are commonly affected. Boat hire firms and tourist offices will be able to help you find out.

Useful websites for the canal are canaux-bretons. net and smatah.fr.

Listings
Sleeping

Rennes

Hôtel Anne de Bretagne   €€€
12 rue Tronjolly, T02 99 31 49 49, hotel-rennes.com.
Map: Rennes, C5, p88.
Cécile Legendre has made this three-star establishment a very pleasant, welcoming place to stay. Well-equipped rooms all have bath with shower, and separate toilet. The road outside is busy; rooms at the back are quieter. A big advantage is a few private parking places. There's a cosy residents' bar tucked away behind reception, and an attractive breakfast room.

Symphonie des Sens   €€€
3 rue du Chapitre, T02 99 79 30 30, symphoniedessens.com.
Map: Rennes, B3, p88.
Perfect for a luxurious treat, these rooms are in a fabulous 17th-century house near the tourist office. A shop on the ground floor sells the same sort of sumptuous fabrics and decor found in the bedrooms. Breakfast can be taken on a pretty outdoor terrace between two half-timbered walls on the first floor.

Mercure Centre Parlement €€€-€€
1 rue Paul Louis Courier, T02 99 78 82 20, mercure.com.
Map: Rennes, D4, p88.
In an interesting former industrial building, this large three-star

hotel enjoys a relatively quiet yet central location. Comfortable rooms with minibar, satellite TV and Wi-Fi. Bar and breakfast room, but no restaurant, and room service oddly does not operate on Fri and Sat, when rooms are cheaper.

Hôtel de Nemours   €€
5 rue de Nemours, T02 99 78 26 26, hotelnemours.com.
Map: Rennes, C4, p88.
This popular hotel is in a stylish building just south of the river, handy for the Champs Libres, metro and indoor market. Rooms with individual and tastefully understated decor vary in size (and price), but you do usually need to book in advance, even out of season. There's a good buffet breakfast to set you up for the day.

Hôtel des Lices   €€
7 Place des Lices, T02 99 79 14 81, hotel-des-lices.com.
Map: Rennes, B2, p88.
Recommended for a stay in the heart of the medieval town, this pleasant hotel is surrounded by atmospheric bars and restaurants, and has an underground car park right next door. Spacious rooms, with free Wi-Fi and good bathrooms. There's a lively nightlife to hand – this is not for lovers of silence – and the best market (Saturday) is just outside the door.

St-Malo

Hôtel Elizabeth   €€€-€€
2 rue des Cordiers, T02 99 56 24 98, st-malo-hotel-elizabeth.
This warmly inviting three-star hotel brings a distinctive historical style to a building dating back to the early 17th century. The lovely rooms are spacious, attractively decorated in period fashion, and have the welcome extra of hot-drink facilities. The basement breakfast room (buffet of fresh products) is really delightful.

Hôtel San Pedro   €€
1 rue Ste-Anne, T02 99 40 88 57, sanpedro-hotel.com.
Mireille Morice's personality has much to do with the success of the San Pedro. Everything is on a small scale here, but it only adds to the exceptional charm and style of this appealing hotel. Bonuses are a sea view on the top floor and special breakfast treats. Located in a quiet part of the Intra-Muros, the ramparts and swimming pool are on the doorstep. Highly recommended.

Hôtel Le Nautilus   €€-€
9 rue de la Corne de Cerf, T02 99 40 42 27, lenautilus.com.
A popular and very friendly hotel near the busy heart of the Intra-Muros. It's a colourful sort of place in many ways – there are pleasant bedrooms over several

floors with bright furnishings and en suite showers, and lively artwork adorning the little breakfast room and bar, with an 'on board' theme. Good value for money in a central location.

Hôtel de la Vallée €€€
6 Avenue George V, Dinard, T02 99 46 94 00, hoteldelavallee.com.
A highly desirable position for this very individual designer-styled hotel – it's apart from the crowds, but within easy walking distance to the main beach. The decor manages to be very contemporary while still conjuring up a belle époque image fitting for the town. Ask for a sea view as the building backs onto a cliff face – as a perspex wall in the toilets shows!

Les Champs de Roz €
8 Grand'Rue, Roz Landrieux, Dol-de-Bretagne, T02 99 48 25 19, monsite.wanadoo.fr/leschamps.deroz/.
This old farmhouse is part of the *Bienvenue à la ferme* scheme, and Mme Mainsard is a very welcoming host. There are five attractive rooms, including a family room and a mini-apartment with kitchenette on the ground floor. Look forward to a delicious breakfast with freshly made crêpes and *craquelins*, a local speciality.

Hôtel Balzac €
15 rue Nationale, Fougères, T02 99 99 42 46, balzac-hotel.fr.
Well situated in the main street of the high town, this is the best place to stay centrally. Guests get a warm welcome from Danielle Carlini, whose English is very good, and information is readily offered. There's a rather suitably old-fashioned feel to the decor and furnishings in the 18th-century building, and the comfortable rooms have bright art prints.

Hôtel du Château €
5 rue Rallon, Vitré, T02 99 74 58 59, perso.orange.fr/hotel-du-chateau.
A tardis of a hotel with 23 good-sized rooms (including one with disabled access) off a winding staircase. Superior rooms have a sitting area and spacious bathrooms – those at the top have the best views to the château. There's also a sweet interior courtyard with fountain. An excellent base for exploring medieval Vitré.

La Lanterne €
110 rue de la Pinterie, Fougères, T02 99 99 58 80, lalanternefougeres.com.
A *gîte urbain* a few paces from the château and the medieval quarter. Frédéric Guérin has renovated an ancient townhouse with style. The four bedrooms have exposed stone walling, chic decoration and colourful shower rooms. The kitchen, where breakfast is served, is also available for guests to cook if they wish, and there's a garden.

Self-catering
Chênedet Loisirs
Forêt de Fougères, T02 99 97 35 46, chenedet-loisirs.com.
For something completely different, you can rent a yurt with a pretty painted door at this activity centre deep in the forest of Fougères, or camp by the lake. The yurts are set in a group, quite close together.

La Résidence des Bas Rochers
Route d'Argentré du Plessis, T02 99 96 52 52, vitre-golf.com.
Superb studios to rent in a renovated house on this golf-course estate. Each spacious unit has a little kitchen area and a shower room, all stylishly decorated. There are also two tiny and seriously romantic beamed cottages, let through Gîtes de France. It's not essential to be golfers. The club has a bar/restaurant/terrace, in the former stables of the Château des Rochers. From one night (€65-95) to a week (€330-450).

Forêt de Paimpont

Le Relais de Brocéliande
€€€-€€
5 rue des Forges, Paimpont, T02 99 07 84 94, relais-de-broceliande.fr.
This Logis de France is a perfect base for exploring the area, situated near the lake and abbey in Paimpont. Rooms in the older building or garden annexe are spacious, extremely comfortable and well equipped. The decor is stylishly plain, with subtly coordinated furnishings. Welcoming staff and a good restaurant too.

La Maison du Graal €
21b rue du Général de Gaulle, Paimpont, T02 99 07 83 82, lamaisondugraal.net.
Ideally placed for the lake and abbey, this B&B in the main village street has two letting rooms of good size, with parquet floors, wrought-iron beds and private bathrooms, plus the sort of decorative details that fit the atmosphere of the Brocéliande experience. Romantics should opt for 'Merlin and Viviane'.

Self-catering
Le Val sans Retour
5 rue de Brocéliande, Tréhorenteuc, T02 97 93 08 08, rando.abri.free.fr.
Closed Jan.
A great base for walkers, cyclists and horse riders, this cheerful *gîte d'étape* (accredited Rando Accueil) is right in the village of Tréhorenteuc, near the famous Valley of No Return. Breakfast, evening meal, picnic lunch, kitchen facilities and bike hire available. Provision can be made for horses. About €16 a night.

Camping
Camping de Barenton
Folle Pensée, Paimpont, T02 97 22 68 87, pagesperso-orange.fr/souriez.com/barenton.htm.
Open all year.
If you really want to get away from it all and make the most of the enchanted forest, this is the place to do it. Great location, great site adorned with spiritually frescoed caravans (to rent), and great for walkers with its *gîte d'étape* providing 22 places.

Pays de Redon

La Grée des Landes (Eco-Hotel Spa Yves Rocher) €€€
La Gacilly, T02 99 08 50 50, lagreedeslandes.com.
An innovative hotel just outside La Gacilly, with environmentally sensitive and harmonious architecture. In the spacious interior all is wood, slate and natural fabrics, creating a suitably 'zen' atmosphere for all those relaxing treatments in the spa. Bedrooms on the ground floor have private little terraces, good light and restful decor.

Hôtel Asther €
14 rue des Douves, Redon, T02 99 71 10 91, asther-hotel.com.
Conveniently situated near the abbey and railway station, this is good value, with friendly staff and pleasant rooms. A few parking spaces are available through a narrow entrance. Rooms at the back are near the station, but have double glazing. No restaurant, just a reasonably priced supper-tray service.

Eating out in Vitré.

Hôtel Le France €
30 rue du Guesclin, Redon, T02 99 71 06 11, hotel-lefrance-redon.com.
One of the Citôtel group, this hotel is situated right by the Nantes–Brest canal and is handy for the Musée de la Batellerie. The rooms are fairly standard but pleasant enough, with free Wi-Fi. Those at the front have views over the canal and pleasure port. You can also rent bikes here and set off along the towpath.

Chambres d'hôtes/ Self-catering

Le Clos du Tay €€
Le Tay, T06 65 55 36 58, closdutay. com.
This is a lovely, tranquil place in rural surroundings. The house has quite a history – Didier will be happy to tell you the story of the fireplace and its symbols. He and his wife Caroline are committed to ecological principles and they hold a 'Clef Verte' award. The B&B rooms (one suitable for disabled use) are spacious and very comfortably furnished, with tea-making facilities. The three gîtes sleep two to six with prices from €250-470 for a week. For donkey riding, see Activities & tours, page 131.

Eating & drinking

Rennes

Auberge du Chat Pitre €€
18 rue du Chapitre, T02 99 30 36 36, auberge-du-chat-pitre.com.
Mon-Sat, 2000-2300.
Map: Rennes, B3, p88.
A medieval restaurant in one of the most attractive houses of this ancient street. Costumed waiting staff, musical entertainment and robust dishes (ragout of lamb with honey and almonds, gingered pork and sausage). The food is fine, but that's not really the point. You need to book.

Le Cours des Lices €€
18 Place des Lices, T02 99 30 25 25.
Mon-Sat 1200-1400, 1900-2200.
Map: Rennes, B2, p88.
A first-class restaurant for food, service and gastronomical atmosphere. The daily lunch option at under €20 for three courses is excellent value. On the main menu there's a memorable *millefeuille* of foie gras with artichokes and truffle oil. If the pear crumble is offered, it's divine. Excellent wine list.

Au Goût des Hôtes €€-€
8 rue Rallier du Baty, T02 99 79 20 36.
Mon-Sat 1200-1400, 1930-2300,
Sun (Jul and Aug) 1200-1400,
1930-2300.
Map: Rennes, B2, p88.
Our pick of a string of restaurants in this popular eating square.

Typical bistro-style fare – chicken crumble, bream *en croute* – with some good combinations of flavours and textures. The set menu at €15 for three courses at lunch is very good value. There's an attractive upstairs room too or outdoor terrace.

Auberge Saint-Sauveur €€-€
6 rue St-Sauveur, T02 99 79 32 56.
Tue-Fri 1200-1500, 1900-2300,
Mon, Sat 1900-2300, closed Sun.
Map: Rennes, B3, p88.
In one of the ancient timber-framed houses of the old quarter, you will find traditional dishes lovingly cooked, charming service, rather eclectic decor, and a good range of fish and meat options. The scallop *flan* and grilled salmon are recommended.

Crêperie Saint-George €€-€
11 rue du Chapitre, T02 99 38 87 04.
Tue-Sat 1200-1400, 1900-2230.
Map: Rennes, B3, p88.
Something original – a non-rustic crêperie, shamelessly contemporary in appearance and sophisticated in menu. Love or hate the decor, you have to admire the sense of style. The downstairs room is sober compared with the two funky options above – and don't miss the TV in the toilet. Crispy crêpes are pretty good too; give George Harrison a try.

Cafés & bars
Place des Lices and Rue St-Michel (Rennes' 'street of thirst'), are both full of bars and restaurants. They are *the* places to sit outside with an aperitif; later in the evening, bars around Place Ste-Anne and Rue St-Malo hot up.

Café Babylone
12 rue des Dames, T02 99 85 82 99.
Closed Sun.
Map: Rennes, A3, p88.
This cheerful café is a handy breakfast or coffee stop right next to the cathedral. It has an outdoor terrace, and also operates as a bistro-type restaurant later in the day.

Le Daniel
19 rue Jules Simon, T02 99 78 85 82.
Closed Sun afternoon and Mon morning.
Map: Rennes, C5, p88.
A peaceful place for tea or coffee, luscious cakes or a hearty quiche and salad lunch. This patisserie by the indoor market also has a range of chocolate to die for.

St-Malo

Restaurant Delaunay €€€€
6 rue Ste-Barbe, T02 99 40 92 46.
From 1830, closed Sun (and Mon outside Jul and Aug).
A highly respected gourmet venue, with booking advised for a gastronomic treat of excellent food and general atmosphere of bonhomie. It's funny to see the

words 'granny-smith' appear on such a menu, but they combine well with crab for a starter, and the turbot with chestnuts is recommended.

La Bouche en Folie €€€-€€
14 rue de Boyer, T06 72 49 08 89. Open 1200-1400, 1900-2200, closed Mon and Tue out of season.
This is a lovely restaurant with a genial atmosphere, in a quiet street. The menu is creative, with an innovative slant on well-known dishes such as a risotto of red mullet with mushrooms, and crème brûlée of pear and ginger. Great-value three-course menu for €15 for those on a budget. Highly recommended.

Le Bistro de Jean €€-€
6 rue de la Corne de Cerf, T02 99 40 98 68. Open 1200-1400, 1900-2230, closed Sat lunch and Wed and Sun.
An archetypically French eating experience awaits in this bistro adorned by ancient sporting equipment. No menu, just a blackboard or two with regular dishes and the day's specials. Imaginative cooking, friendly service and good wines (by the glass too). Recommended.

La Bisquine €€
21 rue Jacques Cartier, T02 99 40 97 40. Open 1200-1400, 1900-2200, closed Thu.

In a long row of eateries, but recognizable for its boat-effect terrace frontage, this restaurant has two pretty dining rooms. The set menus (lunch €15, dinner €20-36) are good value, with an emphasis on fish and shellfish, but plenty of other choices.

Crêperie Chantal €
2 place aux Herbes, T02 99 40 93 97. Apr-Sep 1130-2230, Oct-Mar 1130-1500, 1830-2130, closed Mon (except school holidays).
If you want to get away from the madding crowd, try what is actually the oldest crêperie in St-Malo, dating back to 1955, in a quiet spot. The two-level dining area, with an unusual upstairs kitchen, is bright and cheerful, service is swift and the crêpes are excellent.

La Brigantine €
13 rue de Dinan, T02 99 56 82 82. Open 1200-2200, closed Tue and Wed Oct-Jun.
It's easy to miss the narrow façade of this crêperie – look for the wooden ship plaque – and the unassuming interior, but it's a very popular choice with locals and visitors for the sheer quality of its crêpes, made from organic *blé noir* flour and fine ingredients.

Around St-Malo

Hôtel de la Vallée €€€€-€€€
6 avenue George V, Dinard, T02 99 46 94 00, hoteldelavallee.com. The attractive dining room and

outdoor terrace of this hotel are waterside. There are no set menus – so it's on the pricey side – but the *carte* has a wide selection of shellfish, their speciality. There are other fish and meat options, and truly yummy desserts, like chocolate fondant or rhubarb tiramisu. Worth it for a treat.

La Pointe du Grouin Hôtel/ Restaurant €€€-€€
Pointe du Grouin, T02 99 89 60 55, hotelpointedugrouin.com. Apr-Nov 1200-1400, 1900-2200, restaurant closed Tue (and Thu lunch outside Jul and Aug).
What a lovely experience to eat delicious food with close views of the Ile de Landes and Mont St-Michel in the distance! Any dish here will be good, and accompanied by imaginative vegetables. Good wine list. Menus from €20 up to the *gastronomique* at €78.

Cancale
Oysters are the speciality. The best thing is to buy them fresh from the market, lemons provided, get a takeaway glass of wine from the nearest restaurant and sit on the beach. But if you want to eat in, here are some recommendations:

Au Pied d'Cheval
10 quai Gambetta.
You can buy fresh oysters/ mussels outside or eat in. Omelettes for the non-fish

fanciers. Why 'horse's hoof'? It's the name of a large oyster.

Au Rocher de Cancale
5 quai Administrateur Thomas.
€12.50 for nine oysters, up to €79 for oysters, a platter of *fruits de mer* and wine for two people.

Au Vieux Safran
2 quai Gambetta.
A popular traditional restaurant specializing in *fruits de mer* (€26), but plenty of other options too.

La Maison Blanche
2 quai Administrateur Thomas.
Overlooking the oyster area, with a large heated terrace and every manner of shellfish, or fresh catch of the day.

Le Surcouf
7 quai Gambetta.
An excellent rich fish soup, and a fricassée of the sought-after Breton (blue) lobster for €48.

There are two local dishes to look out for around Vitré: the *Roulade Sévigné* (rolled stuffed guinea-fowl) and *Le Vitréais*, a scrumptious almond and caramelized apple layer dessert. The tourist office has recipes if you want to try them out.

Auberge du Château €€-€
34 rue d'En Bas, Vitré, T02 99 75 01 83, aubergeduchateauvitre.com.

Open 1200-1400, 1900-2200, Apr- Sep closed Mon and Wed evening, Oct-Mar closed Sun and Mon.
The restaurant is situated in an ancient and irresistibly attractive building in a great location (with outdoor terrace) by the château. A good range of crêpes – they have the Crêperies gourmandes quality mark – and plenty of grilled dishes and daily specials too in typical brasserie fashion.

Crêperie Grill I e Raoul II €
3 place Raoul II, Fougères, T02 99 99 31 97.
Daily 1200-1430, 1900-2230.
This is one of several eateries in the square overlooking the château, ideal if you want a cheap, filling feed to get up your strength for all those tower stairs. The menu is basic but varied, with slightly stodgy crêpes, salads and tasty omelettes, grills (sausage, steak, chicken) and *moules frites*.

La Gourmandise Creperie €
26 rue d'En-Bas, Vitré, T02 99 75 02 12.
Tue evening-Sun 1200-1400, 1900-2200, closed Mon, and Tue lunch.
A little strip of a restaurant in the medieval town, where the huge fireplace takes up much of one wall. The food here is incredibly good value – a daily special like veal escalope in a creamy mushroom sauce, followed by

crème brûlée costs as little as €8. Crêpes are good too, substantial and tasty. The bill comes (with sweets) in a little wooden chest.

Le P'tit Bouchon €
13 bis rue Chateaubriand, Fougères, T02 99 99 75 98.
Open 1200-1400, 1900-2200, closed Sun.
This is a lovely familial place to eat, with Eric greeting and Isabelle producing traditional dishes in the kitchen. The interior is all ancient wood and stone, with charmingly eclectic decor from large bookcases to a fish tank. The food is good – starters of hot salads and terrines and daily specials that might include roast pork with apple or rabbit in mustard sauce.

Tivabro €
13 place de Marchix, Fougères, T02 99 17 20 90.
Open 1200-1400 and 1900-2130, closed Mon (also Wed and Sun evening outside Jul and Aug).
The best crêperie in town (Crêperies gourmandes mark) in a fine half-timbered house in the medieval quarter. *Galettes* and crêpes are made from organic flour, with many locally sourced products for ingredients, and a wide choice of fillings. The ice creams are delicious. They also serve a large range of top-quality ciders.

Forêt de Paimpont

Hôtel Le Relais de Brocéliande Restaurant-Bistrot €€€-€€
5 rue des Forges, Paimpont, T02 99 07 84 94.
The dining room with high-back chairs is almost austere, but the kitchen turns out a reliably good menu in set formulas (€21-35) or à la carte. Sesame-flavoured roast cod with beans works well, and the unusual crème brûlée with orange and sechuan pepper is good. The bistro menu is cheaper.

Bar de l'Abbaye €€-€
Ave Chevalier Ponthus, Paimpont, T02 99 07 81 12.
Apr-end Sep 1200-1400, 1700-2230, closed Mon in Sep.
The outdoor terrace here overlooking the lake has a large open grill in the centre. You need to like the taste and smell of meat to enjoy this, but if you do, the food is delicious. (The bar is also a butcher's shop.) A generous turkey *brochette* (kebab) comes dangling over the plate of chips and salad on a metal stand.

Au Temps des Moines Crêperie €
16 Ave Chevalier Ponthus, Paimpont, T02 99 07 89 63.
Open 1200-1400, 1900-2200, closed Mon and Tue, irregular opening Nov-Apr.

A pretty garden setting on the lakeside. Eat in the enclosed veranda or outside. The menu is simple, but with some unusual savoury fillings – try the tomato and anchovy. Very good value.

Pays de Redon

La Bogue €€€€-€€€
3 rue des Etats, Redon, T02 99 71 12 95.
Open 1215-1330, 1915-2100, closed Sun evening and Mon.
Eat in the historic building where the Breton Parliament once met. This gastronomic restaurant has a fine wine list and a wide-ranging seasonal menu. Interesting combinations include stuffed rabbit with beetroot *coulis*, and rhubarb finding a natural partner in almond for dessert. (The name, incidentally, means 'husk of the chestnut'.)

L'Abri Cotier €€-€
39 rue des Douves, Redon, T02 99 71 13 42.
Open 1200-1400, 1900-2200, closed Wed.
A very welcoming eatery with nautical decor. The Tricot menu at under €20 is excellent value with a buffet of starters (meat, fish, salad), and a good selection for other courses. Pork in cider sauce is delicious, and a pistachio, strawberry and salted caramel dessert sounds alarming

but actually works well. Straightforward good food and good value.

Crêperie L'Akène €
10 rue du Jeu de Paume, Redon, T02 99 71 25 15.
Open 1200-1400, 1830-2200, closed Wed.
Attractive interior with frescoes of a Breton family eating their daily *soupe*. Here you may find a special of thick local sausage and caramelized onions wrapped in a buckwheat blanket, or try the dessert crêpe filled with rich, sweet chestnut cream. A very good selection of Breton beers is available.

Les Enfants Gat'thés €
24 rue Lafayette, La Gacilly, T02 99 08 23 01, lesenfantsgatthes.com.
Open 1215-1430, closed Wed. Salon du thé 1530-1830.
The name of the restaurant/café is a play on words (spoilt children and tea). The chef here, Caroline Douaron, is from Le Clos du Tay (see Sleeping, page 123). The food is organic, with salads memorable for their dressings and the edible-flower content. A €15 set menu includes a delicious nettle tart starter and *clafoutis* dessert. Try the cheese!

Entertainment

Rennes

Bars & clubs

Popular spots for drinks and music include **Le 1929** (13 rue St-Michel), Celtic sounds at **Ty Anna Tavarn** (19 Place Ste-Anne) and **Mondo Bizarro** (264 ave General Patton). If you want a late night and a young crowd, try **Le P'tit Velo** (8 Place St-Michel, open Wed-Sun 1100-0300) or **La Banque** (5 allée Rallier-du-Baty, Sat 1800-0300), which was a prison in the 18th century.

Festivals & events

Les Tombées de la Nuit (tdn.fr) in July has all manner of musical and other performances in various venues, and a lively atmosphere in the streets.

In early December the **Transmusicales** (lestrans.com) covers mainly rock music. Tickets from €10-28, with free events at the Champs Libres.

Théâtre National de Bretagne

1 rue St-Helier, T02 99 31 12 31, t-n-b.fr.
Closed Jul-Aug.
Top-quality European theatre performances, from Feydeau to Faulty Optic, and an important stage for new and established choreographers in the contemporary dance programme.

St-Malo

Festivals & events

Etonnants Voyageurs
etonnants-voyageurs.com.
May.
A wide-ranging celebration of travel writing, this event draws a huge international crowd of armchair travellers and true adventurers in a very convivial atmosphere.

Music

La Route du Rock
laroutedurock.com.
Feb and Aug.
St-Malo is renowned for one of France's top rock events.

Dinard

Cinema

British Film Festival
festivaldufilm-dinard.fr.
Oct.
This festival has been held here for the last 20 years. Dozens of films are shown at five different venues for €5.50 a performance, (or a *carte pass*, €60, covers everything).

Festivals & events

La Promenade au Clair de Lune
Every late evening from Jul to mid-Sep, this wonderful walkway along the seafront is lit up, and musicians provide a convivial ambience.

Pays de Redon

Festivals & events

During Jul and Aug, every Thursday night (2100-2300) is dancing night – Breton dancing! Here's an opportunity to learn some basic steps and join in the fun as local groups give a free introduction. Venue details from the tourist office (T02 99 71 06 04, tourisme-pays-redon.com).

Le Mois de Marron: Foire Teillouse and the Bogue d'Or
Oct.
A whole month of celebration, loosely based on the chestnut harvest. It's a massive event embracing food tastings, culinary and musical competitions (Breton instruments), and children's entertainment. Many of the activities are free or under €5.

Shopping

Rennes

Art & crafts
Aux Artisans Créateurs
*1 rue des Francs Bourgeois,
T02 99 79 18 10.*
Open 1030-1230, 1400-1900,
closed Wed and Fri morning.
All manner of original and
interesting works of art for sale.

Flea Market
Every Thursday at the Halles
Centrales (0730-1300).

Food & drink
Les Halles Centrales, Place
Honoré Commeurec, are open
every day (Mon-Sat 0700-1900,
Sun 0930-1230) for fresh food
stuffs, and don't miss the huge
Saturday-morning market in the

Place des Lices with the best
produce from all around.

Around St-Malo

Food & drink
Cancale is famous for its oysters.
The port La Houle has a little
daily outdoor market of stalls
selling oysters and other
shellfish. Perfect for your picnic
– they really don't come fresher
than this.

L'Epicier Breton
3 quai Thomas, Cancale.
Open most days 1000-1800.
An emporium of Breton
products, especially beer, cider
and whisky, biscuits and cakes,
Quimper pottery, nice cider
boules and – not surprisingly –
oyster knives.

Forêt de Paimpont

Au Pays de Merlin
*28 rue du Général de Gaulle,
Paimpont, T02 99 07 80 23.*
Open all year, closed Mon and
Tue out of main season.
Everything for aspiring medieval
knights, magicians, witches and
Arthurian souvenir hunters.
Books and clothes too. This is
also the only place for bike hire
in the village.

Pays de Redon

Arts & crafts
La Gacilly is full of artists and
artisans, and you can find
anything from pottery to
metalwork, jewellery, hand-
blown glass, wood sculpture and
soap, as well as original artwork.
The workshops welcome visitors
to watch or talk about processes,
as well as purchase. The tourist
office has a leaflet with map
listing all the artisans. Many are
closed on Mondays outside July
and August.

Beauty products
Yves Rocher factory and shop
La Croix des Archers, La Gacilly.
Mon-Sat 1000-1800.
The home base store of this
famous range of natural beauty
products. Everything beautifully
presented, and with many
special offers.

Activities & tours

Cultural
The tourist office (T02 99 67 11 66) has details of guided tours of the city. Telephone-style audio guides (€5) in English are available, enabling you to see what you want at your own pace with commentary. You must book here in advance, for the best of all – the Breton Parliament building (€6.80).

Around St-Malo

Food & wine
La Ferme Marine
Cancale, T02 99 89 69 99, ferme-marine.com.
In English every afternoon Jul to mid-Sep at 1400, or in French Feb-Oct at 1500; mid-Sep to Jun Mon-Fri only.
A chance to find out everything there is to know about oysters. This active business has a large exhibition centre and guided visits to see how oysters are grown and processed.

Maison de la Baie
Vivier-sur-Mer, maison-baie.com.
Open all year.
This centre offers walks and tractor-pulled rides out onto the bay to find out about the tides and marine life here, as well as the production of oysters and especially *moules de bouchot* (grown on posts), which are

St-Malo.

famous here. Tours (€12.50) are in French but some of the guides will also give explanations in English– ask in advance.

The Marches of Brittany

Outdoor actvities
La ferme de Chênedet
chenedet-loisirs.com.
A centre of activities in the heart of the Forêt de Fougères for forest riding, walking and cycling. There's also a lake for canoes or kayaks. The centre will help to arrange a programme for a day or a week to suit your needs. The sylvan location is hard to beat for a combination of peace and activity.

Pays de Redon

Boat trips
Hire a boat and enjoy a leisurely spell on Brittany's inland waterways. At La Gacilly (T02 99 08 05 02, day-boats.com) boats without a licence (for six) are available by the hour (€25) or the day (€115) for the rivers Aff and Oust.

At Redon you can hire boats for two-12 persons for a weekend or a week from **Cris'boat Crosières** (T02 99 71 08 05, crisboat.com). Different types of craft are available, with a sample price of €683-1240 for a boat for four to six people for a week.

Donkey treks
Le Clos du Tay (see Sleeping, page 123, closdutay.com) offers treks from a couple of hours to a week, with a donkey for transporting tents and another for a child to ride. This can be combined with staying in a Sioux tepee camp nearby.

Contents

Côtes d'Armor

Cormorants, Cap Fréhel.

Introduction

Côtes d'Armor contains one of the most famous littoral regions in France – the Pink Granite Coast, with its fantastically shaped rock formations. Wild Cap Fréhel is another memorable location on a coastline that provides the very best in beaches, the highest cliffs in Brittany and plenty of traditional fishing ports. This maritime heritage was encapsulated in the 1990s name change from Côtes du Nord to Côtes d'Armor – Land of the Sea. It's the least populated of Brittany's four departments, but visitor numbers soar in summer around family resorts such as Perros-Guirec.

Dramatically placed Fort La Latte is one of the most visited sights in Brittany, and Dinan with its lively nightlife also has an unforgettable ensemble of medieval ramparts and half-timbered houses. Guingamp, St-Brieuc and telecommunications centre Lannion also offer modern facilities against comely historic backdrops.

The interior Argoat is a quieter world, where tiny villages boast lovely chapels and sculpted calvaries, lofty castles such as Tonquédec and Roch Jagu watch over river valleys, and megaliths crown the high granite heaths above the ruined abbey of Bon Repos. For those in search of energetic holidays, the coast and Lac de Guerlédan, the largest lake in Brittany, provide a wealth of water sports, while walkers, cyclists and riders cannot fail to be enticed by the incredible variety of unspoilt landscape.

Lighthouse and the Pink Granite Coast, Ploumanac'h.

What to see in...

...one day
Visit **St-Brieuc**, then enjoy a picnic and swimming at Palus Plage. Take a boat to the **Ile de Bréhat** or a lunch cruise on **Lac de Guerlédan**. Soak up the medieval sights and irresistible shops of **Dinan**, walk along the estuary from **Lannion** to the lovely village of **Le Yaudet**, or play knights in the Château de Tonquédec.

...a weekend or more
Take a drive around the Trégor, exploring **Lannion** and **Tréguier**, and discover the wonders of the Pink Granite Coast on foot, maybe with a birdwatching trip to the **Sept-Iles**. If you can tear yourself away from Dinan, visit the **National Stud** at Lamballe, then head on up to **Cap Fréhel** and dramatic **Fort La Latte**, or cycle along the **Green Ways** before taking a boat on the **Rance**.

St-Brieuc & the Côte de Goëlo

St-Brieuc sits at the base of a vast bay with one of the largest tidal ranges in the world, causing the seascape to appear remarkably different throughout the day. The Côte de Goëlo is a glorious series of beaches, coves and headlands, where ports and resorts retain a traditional holiday atmosphere. Today, this distinguished, yet often harsh, maritime heritage is celebrated in a series of feasts and festivals.

Walking the coastal path alongside this magnificent bay provides constant visual entertainment, with the most sensational viewing points on the high cliffs around Plouha.

St-Brieuc.

St-Brieuc, the administrative capital of Côtes d'Armor, is a labyrinthine old town in two deep valleys of the Gouët and Goëdic. Flying past on the expressway viaducts through an industrial sprawl, there is little sense of what lies below, where the narrow medieval streets are interspersed by lavish 19th-century civic buildings and the brooding presence of a fortress-style **cathedral**. According to legend, St-Brieuc, one of the founding saints of Brittany, arrived here in the fifth century: the site of his earliest settlement is marked by a *fontaine* at the Chapelle Notre-Dame-de-la-Fontaine.

To the north of cathedral lie the best examples of the colourful half-timbered houses. In the Place au Lin, the ornate **Maison Le Ribeault** now houses a restaurant, for dining in cramped historic splendour. Further up the Rue Fardel are fine examples of 16th-century dwellings. No 15, known as the **Hôtel du Chapeau Rouge** or Hôtel des Ducs de Bretagne, is decorated with Renaissance-style sculptures and, at roof-level, a griffon, which became the town's symbol.

In July and August, Les Nocturnes festival livens up the central area, and you can enjoy the spectacle from many bars and restaurants in the heart of the city.

Cathédrale de St-Etienne

Open 1000-1800.
Map: St-Brieuc, p138.

This sober cathedral still has marks where little shops were once built up against its walls. The high arrow-slits and massive towers, more defensive than aesthetic, are a reminder that the building was besieged during the Wars of Succession. Statues and altarpieces were destroyed at the time of the Revolution, when the cathedral was used as stabling, but the interior is still an impressive sight. The fine altar of St-Sacrament (c 1750), by Yves Corlay, was saved and stands in the south aisle of the nave. In its own little chapel is the tomb of Guillaume Pinchon, the first Breton to be canonized

Essentials

❶ Getting around St-Brieuc centre is small enough to explore on foot. Buses do cover the Côte de Goëlo route, but less frequently outside summer. A car is needed for sight-hopping.

❷ Bus station The Gare Urbaine is in Boulevard Clemenceau (tubinfo.fr). Tickets €1 or 10 for €8.70. A three-hour ticket for combined town and district buses is €2. For regional bus travel, see page 274.

❸ Train station St-Brieuc station (Paris–Brest route) is at Place F Mitterand. Guingamp and Lannion also have train links. For regional train travel, see page 274.

❾ ATMs 3 rue de Rohan.

⊕ ✚ Hospital and pharmacy Rue des Capucins, T02 96 78 46 00.

⤷ Post office Place de la Résistance.

❶ Tourist information 7 rue St-Gouéno, T08 25 00 22 22, baiedesaintbrieuc.com, Monday-Saturday 0930-1230, 1330-1800, July and August 0930-1900, Sunday 1000-1300. Côtes d'Armor region: cotesarmor.com.

Tip...

For something a bit more unusual, visit the site of a Viking camp at Péran, 7 km from St-Brieuc.

by the church in Rome in 1247. His skull is among the collection of reliquaries of saints nearby.

Le Musée d'Art et d'Histoire

Cours Francis Renard, rue des Lycéens Martyrs. Tue-Sat 0930-1145, 1330-1745, Sun 1330-1745. Free. Map: St-Brieuc, p138.

This is a well-organized town museum. On three floors, the main facets of the 19th-century world of the area are revealed, with maritime replicas and objects at ground level, a well-explained analysis of cloth production with looms and spinning implements on the first floor, and evidence of daily life such as furniture and costumes, including many *coiffes* (distinctive Breton lace headdresses) above. Temporary exhibitions also cover a range of arts and crafts.

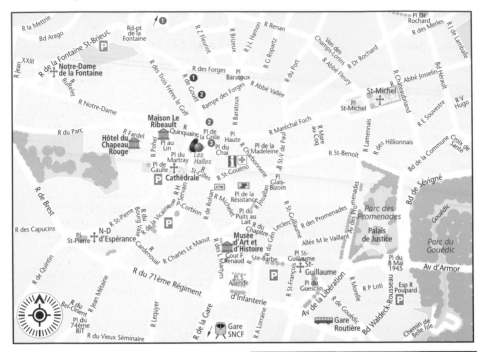

St-Brieuc listings

❶ Sleeping

1 Hôtel de Clisson *36-38 rue du Gouët*
2 Hôtel Ker Izel *20 rue du Gouët*

❶ Eating & drinking

1 Aux Pesked *59 rue du Légué (off map)*
2 L'Air du Temps *4 rue du Gouët*
3 La Cuisine du Marché *4-6 rue des Trois Frères Merlin*

St-Brieuc.

Pointe du Roselier

6 km northwest of St-Brieuc.

Not far from St-Brieuc is this stunning viewpoint for the Côte de Goëlo. There's an orientation table and the *four à boulets*, an elaborate oven where soldiers heated cannonballs to send flying in the direction of English ships prowling the coast below.

Binic

14 km northwest of St-Brieuc.

From the quay of this charming little port you can watch pleasure boats on one side of the jetty and families enjoying the beach on the other. The town has a 'Family Plus' quality mark for its facilities, entertainment and welcoming atmosphere, designed to appeal to all ages. There are many organized events, or you could take a boat up the Goëlo coast to the Ile de Bréhat in summer. There's a festival to celebrate the cod-fishing tradition in May, with nautical songs and dancing, but now the marine emphasis is on shellfish. The **Museum of Popular Traditions** (Apr-end Sep, 1430-1800, closed Tue except in Jul and Aug, €3.50) is packed with artefacts and models that illuminate the economic and everyday life of the old days.

St-Quay Portrieux

22 km northwest of St-Brieuc.

Visitors today are welcomed a good deal more cordially than Saint Ké, see right. St-Quay prides itself on being the Coquille St-Jacques (scallop) capital of Brittany, with a festival on that theme in May. There are plenty of eateries to try them at in this family holiday resort (Family Plus mark), with good beaches and summer entertainments. The town blossomed into a popular tourist resort after two ladies from Guingamp tried the curative powers of the seawater baths in 1841, starting a trend which led to rapid development when the

Cod fishing in the New World

From the 16th century boats from Binic, St-Quay Portrieux and Paimpol made the incredible year-long return journey to Newfoundland in search of cod. Some 300 years later the scene moved to Iceland. The harsh toil of these bleak voyages and constant risk of death was described in Pierre Loti's famous novel *Pêcheur d'Islande*. The churchyard in Ploubazlanec has a commemorative wall for those lost at sea.

railway brought Parisian visitors. A carefully constructed deep-water port, rare on this northern coastline with its tidal peculiarities, keeps this maritime tradition alive. There is a seawater swimming pool on the Plage du Casino for those long low tide times, and the busy Friday market provides another chance to sample fresh local produce.

Palus Plage

28 km northwest of St-Brieuc.

Don't miss a small sign off the D786 to the simple and unspoilt Palus Plage. Green-clad hills enclose a pebble and sandy crescent, perfect for swimming or just lazing. For the more energetic, the coastal path snakes steeply uphill to the north, giving

The strange story of Saint Ké

Saint-Ké, a holy man from Wales, arrived on the shores of Brittany in the sixth century. Suspicious local washerwomen attacked and beat him with gorse branches, leaving Ké bleeding. The Virgin Mary came to his rescue, causing a spring of healing water to gush out of the ground. This is still to be seen, now covered by a later *fontaine*, near the Grève d'Isnain. Saint-Ké is sometimes identified with Sir Kay of Arthurian legend, and another version of his name lives on in St-Quay Portrieux.

For rainy days...

If the weather is against beachcombing, two unusual sights are not far from Plouha. The chapel at **Kermaria**, open every day in July and August, contains the famous fresco of the *Danse Macabre* or Dance of Death. Human figures hand in hand with skeletons symbolize that death comes to all regardless of estate.

Remains of an 11th-century circular temple at **Lanleff** are a curiosity. Once assumed to be Romano-Celtic, it now seems more likely that a local lord returning from the first crusade modelled this place of worship on the church of St-Sepulchre in Jerusalem. It's an exercise of the imagination to decipher the subject of carvings on the capitals – animal, vegetable or human?

wonderful views across the bay. There is also a children's playground here and parking for camper vans. Refreshments include a beachside bar in high season, and restaurants by the slipway.

Cliffs of Plouha & Gwin Zegal

Said to be the highest cliffs in Brittany, these undulating verdant hills provide some of the best coastal walking in Côtes d'Armor, with the GR34 footpath running all the way up the Côte de Goëlo. Start from Palus Plage and walk north to Plage Bonaparte, passing many fine viewpoints such as the Point de Plouha (104 m), an up-and-down route of about 8 km. On the way, admire the little harbour of **Gwin Zegal**, where boats are moored to cut-off trunks of trees once planted in the sand with weighted roots. This gave rise to the legend that

The cliffs at Plouha.

robbers used to be tied up there and left to the mercy of the tides. Plouha tourist office, T02 96 20 24 73, has a leaflet pack of circular walks in the area.

Plage Bonaparte

4 km from Plouha.

This was the scene of Operation Bonaparte during 1944, when 135 allied airmen were safely evacuated thanks to a local resistance network, the Réseau Shelburne. *'Bonjour tout le monde à la maison d'Alphonse'* was the coded message for these operations. Brought secretly to a nearby house, the men were then taken to the beach and rowed out to a waiting boat by night. The 'Maison d'Alphonse' was later burnt down by the Germans: its site is marked by a memorial and can be reached by the Sentier Shelburne, a footpath off the coast path. La Stèle is a cliff-top memorial to all those involved in this dangerous enterprise. The beach itself is reached through a rocky arch, past another commemorative plaque. It's a popular place for swimming, especially with teenagers in school holidays.

Paimpol

16.5 km northwest of Plouha.

The modern and rather unattractive port here is now devoted to pleasure craft. The streets of **Vieux Paimpol** branching out from the Place du Martray give a softer impression of the town. The little towered house in the square is where author Pierre Loti used to stay. Rue de l'Eglise leads up to the Vieille Tour (1760), the lonely bell tower of the former parish church. No 5 is an attractive half-timbered house, but even older is 6 Rue des Huit Patriotes, dating from the 15th century, which has been an ironmonger's for more than 100 years.

The town is extremely busy in July and August, when the little **Musée du Costume** (1030-1230, 1400-1830, €3) with Breton furniture and costumes is open, in Rue Raymond Pellier near the tourist office. The **Musée de la Mer** (mid-Jun to end Aug 1100-1230, 1400-1830, Apr to mid-Jun and Sep

1400-1800, €5) is an exhibition underlining the achievements and sacrifices of Paimpol's maritime history, displayed in a former factory with a brick chimney. The town's international sea-shanty festival is in early August.

The best view of the town and bay is from the Tour de Kerroc'h just to the north.

Abbaye de Beauport

Kérity, Paimpol, T02 96 55 18 58, abbaye-beauport.com.
Mid-Jun to mid-Sep 1000-1900, Oct-May 1000-1200, 1400-1700. €5.

The particular quality of this romantic ancient abbey comes from the combination of architecture and environment. Built in a position to profit from natural resources, trade and pilgrimage, it is also scenically a beautiful spot hugging the shore just south of Paimpol. Sudden glimpses of the bay and islands appear through stone arches as you wander around the remains and beautiful gardens.

The monks of this Augustine foundation, dating back to the 12th century, later acquired a reputation for dissolute behaviour, hence the saying: *Il n'est de moine à Beauport/ Qui n'ait de femme à Kérity* (There's no monk at Beaufort who hasn't got a woman in Kérity). The size of the church reflects that this was the first continental stopping point for many pilgrims from Britain on the Compostela trail, who were welcomed in the magnificent Salle du Duc. In later centuries it had industrial uses, including cider-making, with a small hydraulic canal, still to be seen under a grating outside. Grouped around the cloister are the refectory, chapter house, functional rooms and a skeletal remnant of the church.

Ile de Bréhat

Regular daily sailings from the Pointe d'Accourest give easy access – a 10-minute crossing – to this appealing island with its mild climate and glowing local stone. There are no cars, so families can enjoy touring on hired bikes (but no cycling is allowed on the coastal path). Details at vedettesdebrehat.com.

The Trégor

The world-renowned Pink Granite Coast is rightfully the jewel in the crown of this northwest area of Côtes d'Armor, but the sheer range of experiences on offer here, from megaliths to hi-tech exhibitions, is another powerful attraction. The busy coast around Perros-Guirec is balanced by the quieter green heart of the interior with its fine castles and handsome villages of warm yellow stone. The two main towns – bustling Lannion and dignified Tréguier – provide yet another contrast of pace and atmosphere.

Plage St-Guirec.

Lannion

Lannion is a busy and prosperous place, its success based on the telecommunications industry, with the research and development centre CNET based here since the 1960s. All that remains of the medieval château are a few glimpses of old ramparts, but many ancient houses still line the streets and flowery squares. The town flourished as a port in the 18th and 19th century, and the river Léguer is part of the centre's attraction. The friendly tourist office (T02 96 46 41 00, ot-lannion.fr, Jul-Aug 0900-1900, Sun 1000-1300, Sep-Jun 0930-1230, 1400-1800) is on the Quai d'Aiguillon.

The Quays

Visiting the town to take the waters as a cure, the Duc d'Aiguillon, Commander-in-Chief of Brittany, saw the commercial potential of developing an inland port on the Léguer. He laid the first stone of the quays in 1762. The impressive building dominating the left bank of the river is the former Monastery of Ste-Anne, which now houses a *médiathèque* alongside the chapel. The adjoining park makes a good picnic spot by the river.

Place du Général Leclerc

Some very modern shopfronts and signs on one side of this square don't spoil the medieval feel of the other side. Among these half-timbered houses from the 15th and 16th centuries, which once belonged to rich merchants, note the incredibly narrow Café Lannionais at No 31. Just to the east of the square, the Rue Cie Roger de Barbe also contains a row of ancient dwellings, and on the corner a plaque commemorates the Chevalier de Pont-Blanc, who fought heroically against the English here during the Wars of Succession.

Tip...

Use car parks on the left bank and walk across the bridge to the old town. Parking is free on Mondays.

Eglise de Brélévenez

A mini-pilgrimage up 140 steps leads to the lofty church of Brélévenez, which in part dates back to the 12th century. The church was possibly a foundation of the Knights Templar in the days of the crusades.

The oldest sculpture is the little group of the Ascension scene above the door of the sacristy. In the crypt, accessed by very narrow steps, is a graphic Entombment scene with life-size figures. Note also the holy-water stoop in the south aisle, which began life as a market measure for a bushel of wheat.

Around Lannion

Le Yaudet

5 km west of Lannion.

This delightful little hamlet on a natural defensive spur overlooking the entrance to the Léguer estuary is an important archaeological site, with excavations revealing Iron Age and Roman fortifications. A marked discovery path leads to impressive rock forms, coastguards' huts and an isolated *fontaine*, with constant flashes of view over the bay. (An informative leaflet is available from the Mairie in nearby Ploulec'h.) Don't miss the **Eglise Notre-Dame de Yaudet** and its intriguing oddity of a main altarpiece showing the Virgin lying in bed – literally – with the baby after the birth of Jesus. This is the perfect spot for a scenic picnic and an up-and-down walk, with steps leading to the water's edge. Or try the unpretentious *restaurant de terroir*, **Ar Vro** (see Eating, page 170).

Pleumeur-Bodou

7 km northwest of Lannion.

Cité de Télécommunications (T02 96 46 63 80, cite-telecoms.com, Apr-Sep and school holidays 1000-1800, Sat and Sun 1400-1800, €7, €19.60 family). This large site is devoted to describing how telecommunications have developed over the decades. The father-founders Morse and Marconi have their place here, together with exhibits of

Procession of St-Yves, patron saint of lawyers.

equipment and interactive exercises. You can also speculate about the future: for example, will cars drive themselves in 20 years' time? Inside the adjoining Radôme is the antenna built in 1961-1962 to receive the first live television pictures from America via Telstar. It's a good place for young people, but if you tire of telecommunications, an excellent Planetarium (planetarium-bretagne.fr) and a Gaulish village (levillagegaulois.free.fr) reconstruction for Asterix fans are nearby.

Menhir de St-Uzec This giant standing-stone is one of the best examples in Brittany of a Christianized menhir. The stone dates from Neolithic times but was elaborately engraved with symbols of Christ's passion in the 17th century, following the missions of Père Maunoir (see page 33) to root out paganism.

Château de Tonquédec

11 km south of Lannion, Tonquédec, T02 96 54 60 70, chateau-tonquedec.com.
Apr, Jun, Sep 1500-1900, Jul and Aug 1000-2000, Oct Sat and Sun 1400-1800. €5/€2.50.

This is an impressive location for this fascinating château, situated on a spur overlooking the Léguer river. With drawbridges, turret stairs and dank cellars, it has all those elements essential to make a castle visit fun for all ages. Earliest parts date back to the 13th century, but most was rebuilt after being partly destroyed for supporting Charles de Blois in the Wars of Succession. The castle is now the property of the Le Rougé family, who are related to its original owners. As it's in private hands, the structure is less manicured than many, which adds to the sense of authenticity when scrambling about amid long grass and piles of rubble. Tonquédec was essentially a fortress rather than a home but domestic details remain in the tracery of chapel windows, fireplaces in former tower rooms and some fine latrines. You can also have a competition to see who can spot the most masons' marks on the stonework.

Tip...

From the castle, the well-signed 10-km walking circuit of Tonquédec takes in the Château of Kergrist and several chapels and *fontaines* as well as a beautiful river valley.

Perros-Guirec

9.5 km north of Lannion.

Perros-Guirec is an attractive resort town, with all the traditional seaside attractions. The Centre Ville is on the hill-top above the two main beaches and busy pleasure port. The Port Minature is a boating lake for family fun, and nearby there is a local museum (open Apr-Sep) with a collection of *coiffes* (lace headdresses) and exhibitions of Breton history, including the Atlantic Wall defences used in this area in the Second World War. The casino provides more active entertainment or, as a contrast, try the thalassotherapy centre for the languid sensations of a salt-water spa. From the Gare Maritime near the Plage de Trestaou, you can take a boat to the Sept-Iles or reach the starting point for a walk along the famous Pink Granite Coast.

Tréguier

20 km east of Lannion.

Tréguier is a most appealing town, with its glorious cathedral, half-timbered houses, cafés, restaurants and waterside spaces. The tourist office is situated in a tower building by the River Jaudy, the port area in the commercial heyday. The old houses in the town reflect this same 16th-century prosperity, mostly based on the cloth trade. A large Neolithic reconstruction sits nearby unobtrusively, by the easiest parking area. Stroll up the colourful Rue Renan, which honours the writer and philosopher Ernest Renan, whose work, such as *Life of Jesus*, often challenged the accepted tenets of Catholicism. His statue keeps an ironic eye on the cathedral and the house where he was born in 1823 contains a museum dedicated to the great man.

Around the Place du Martray are many twisty streets with a vibrant variety of architectural detail from different periods. The Rue Colvestre has half-timbered houses of the 16th century and the earlier Maison du Duc Jean V, which now contains a bookshop. Further up, only the Flamboyant-Gothic doorway remains of the Vieil Evêché, built in 1430.

In Place du Général Leclerc is a memorial to 500 years of printing in Tréguier, which saw Jehan Calvez produce the first French/Latin/Breton dictionary in 1499. Off the Boulevard Anatole Le Braz ahead, the Bois du Poète is an appealingly unkempt park beside the river. It contains a simple stele to Anatole Le Braz, one of the most famous native writers, whose collections of oral testimony have done so much to preserve Breton traditions.

Cathédrale St-Tugdual This glorious structure is on the spot of the foundation of Welsh monk St-Tugdual, one of the founding saints of Brittany, but today it is the home of St-Yves. Largely a fine Gothic remodelling, the north transept retains hints of the earlier Romanesque architecture. At the Revolution it was sacked by soldiers, so the impressive tomb of St-Yves, originally ordered by Duke Jean V, is an identical copy. The precious relic of his skull is also proudly on display. In a side-chapel is the tomb of the duke himself, whose long reign (1399-1442) brought a period of stability after the Wars of Succession. The greyhound symbolizing Brittany lies at his feet.

Tip...

Don't miss the cloister here, for its own sake and for the best views of the two towers and later spire.

St Yves

Yves Hélory de Kermartin, patron saint of Brittany, was born in 1253 at a manor house near Tréguier. He studied law in Paris before returning to Brittany as an ecclesiastical judge, gaining a reputation for fairness regardless of the social class of petitioners. After his death in 1303, many miracles were attested at his tomb, and he was canonized in 1347. Saint Yves' iconography usually shows him between two men, one rich, one poor, to symbolize impartiality. The pardon on the third Sunday in May is often attended by more than 20,000 people, with lawyers from all over the world paying respects to their patron.

Pink Granite Coast

Perros-Guirec is the best starting point to admire the wonders of the Pink Granite Coast, following Le Sentier des Douaniers, the Customs' Officers Path, along the coast to Ploumanac'h, a distance of about 3 km. Prepare for some awesome and amusing sights among the extraordinary variety of shapes and textures on view. Granite is a volcanic rock in origin, pushed up from the centre of the earth to the surface by the expanding heat of magma, then cooling and falling prey to erosion over millions of years. The granite here is a mixture of black mica, greyish quartz and rose-coloured feldspar; its pink tinge becomes more pronounced in certain lights. The rocks along this stretch of coastline have been transformed by the power of the tides and winds into all manner of fantastic shapes. The outer sections crumbled away into sand, leaving hard cores to tumble and settle into the kaleidoscope of forms now on show. Many

have been given names, like The Tortoise, Death's Head and Napoleon's Hat – there is certainly plenty of scope for using your imagination to the full.

Access to the path begins above the Plage de Trestraou behind the Gare Maritime. The islands visible offshore are the Sept-Iles, an important nature reserve with thousands of seabirds. The way is fairly level and easygoing and after 800 m you can see large formations looming ahead. The first elaborate conglomeration is known as the Devil's Castle, for obvious reasons. Round the point of the Skevell, the path passes a little Custom Officers' lookout (guérite) used for watching for smugglers, and a powder store close by, before reaching the cove of Pors Kamor. This is the remnant of an ancient river valley, a scenic spot today where the light-blue water contrasts strikingly with the glow of the rocks. Continue past the lifeboat station and lighthouse, and you soon

reach the **Maison du Littoral** (summer Mon-Sat 1000-1300, 1400-1800, school holidays Mon-Fri 1400-1700) which has displays about nature and geology in this unique environment.

Rounding the next point to the Plage St-Guirec brings yet another wonder with this bay, a rock-strewn jumble at low tide. This is the beach where Saint Guirec landed in Brittany in the sixth century, according to legend, in a stone boat. Just by the stone cross is a plaque commemorating the code message 'Is Napoleon's hat still at Perros-Guirec?' transmitted to the Breton resistance by the BBC from London in 1944.

The prominent island château of Costaérès at the mouth of the bay dates from the 1890s. Here Polish author Henri Sienkiewicz finished writing his famous novel *Quo Vadis*. On the beach is the raised oratory of Saint Guirec, lapped by waves at high tide. Legend has it that sticking a pin in the saint's

nose would ensure marriage within a year. This is why the granite statue here now was needed to replace an earlier wooden one that lost its nose from repeated assaults. But even granite can't stand up against determination, as you can see.

The rocky spectacle comes to an end as you continue up past the nearby chapel and round the rocks to come out at the port of Ploumanac'h, where a dam with tide-mill crosses the estuary. You can either retrace your steps or take a detour through the Vallée des Traïouero. The name actually means the 'Valley of the Valleys' thanks to a French cartographer's misunderstanding of Breton in the 18th century. It can feel like a lost world to explore the many paths, caves and wild vegetation around the lake and feeder streams. This place provides a welcome, shady refuge from the coast on a hot day, and the greenery can come as a relief after all those gleaming rocks.

Dinan & Northeast Côtes d'Armor

The stark beauty of Cap Fréhel and nearby Fort La Latte is a welcome change from busier coastal areas. Here, the famous GR34 footpath offers a world of dramatically changing seascapes and natural rock art. Inland, if small places like Corseul with its Roman remains and the sporting centre of Jugon-les-Lacs provide exercise for mind and body, the beautiful face of Dinan is an atmospheric feast for the eyes and the soul. Here, a medieval heart still beats to the lively rhythm of modern life.

Dinan port.

Dinan is a small town with a big heritage, an ancient centre with a modern buzz, somewhere to get your head swivelling from side to side as one gem follows another, from the impressive ramparts to an extraordinary variety of medieval houses. It is one of those places that is actually enhanced by the people filling its streets, creating a gregarious ambience.

William the Conqueror, before his invasion of England, drove Conan, duke of Brittany, out of Dinan castle – an event recorded on the Bayeux Tapestry, which shows a wooden tower building and Conan sliding down an escape rope.

Some 200 years later the town became part of ducal possessions in Brittany and stout ramparts were constructed. During the Wars of Succession, Dinan was unsuccessfully besieged by the English supporters of Jean de Montfort. The most famous soldier of the age, Bertrand du Guesclin, was involved in this conflict, the best-known incident in Dinan's history.

The Montforts were victorious in the war and Jean de Montfort became Duke Jean IV. The château was built under his auspices in 1380. Today this and the Tour de Coëtquen form the museum, which is well worth a visit.

Musée du Château de Dinan

T02 96 39 45 20.
Jun-Sep 1000-1830, Oct-May 1330-1730, closed Jan. €4.25.

Entry is through the chapel, where the duke had his own little private niche with a fireplace. On the way down to the gloomy kitchen, there are examples of Roman remains from the area, including a second-century plaque with a fish-tailed Triton fighting a hippocamp. Upper rooms with huge fireplaces house temporary exhibitions, and there is access to the walkway at the top for fine views over the town. In the tower of Coëtquen the highlight is the Salle des Gisants, a murky deep basement where the uneven floor formed from the rock is often partly underwater,

Tip...

Allow a full day for visiting the town. Parking outside the ramparts is easiest, as everything is then accessible on foot. You can drive down to the port to avoid a steep hill. The Tourist Office is at 9 rue du Château, T02 96 87 69 76, dinan-tourisme.com.

Thursday is market day in the Place du Guesclin. For railway enthusiasts the Musée du Rail at the train station is a must (T02 96 39 81 33, museedurail-dinan.com, Jun to mid-Sep 1400-1800).

Bertrand du Guesclin

Bertrand du Guesclin (1320-1380) grew up near Dinan at Broons. He was a staunch supporter of the Penthièvres' claim to the dukedom of Brittany. His prowess in armed contest was remarkable, and the king of France grew to rely on du Guesclin's achievements. At Dinan, his younger brother was taken prisoner by an English knight, Thomas of Canterbury, during a truce. Du Guesclin complained to the commander of the enemy forces, the Duke of Lancaster, who agreed that a duel should decide the issue. Du Guesclin won, as an unobtrusive stele notes in the Place du Champs where the fight took place, not far from du Guesclin's fine equestrian statue. He went on to become French Commander-in-Chief. On his death his bones were taken to St-Denis in Paris for burial alongside those of kings, but his heart came back to Dinan, and is now in the Church of St-Sauveur.

and greening effigies of medieval knights lie heedless of their spooky resting place under a finely vaulted ceiling.

Rampart walk

After the Wars of Religion, when Dinan was for a time a Catholic stronghold, the need for town defences was over and the ramparts fell into disuse. They were later threatened by development plans and the Gate of Brest was destroyed in 1881. Public reaction soon led to their classification as a historic monument. Now there is a fine walk (at a

Around the region

distance of just under 3 km) around the ramparts. Some of it goes along the summit and some of it around the foot. Look out for the arrow-slits converted for cannon in the Tour Penthièvre, and admire the view over the port from the Tour Ste-Catherine. A leaflet from the tourist office outlines this path.

Medieval centre

It's easy to lose yourself in the mass of narrow streets, but the clock tower in the Rue d'Horloge is a good point for orientation. It is actually an ancient **bell tower**, given its finest bell by Anne de Bretagne in 1507. For a small fee you can climb to the top (Apr-May 1400-1800, Jun-Sep 1000-1830) to look down on thronging crowds and enjoy the best views of the town. Superb half-timbered houses can be found in Rue de l'Horloge below: No 6 **Hôtel Kératry** (1559), which now contains a

Celtic harp centre, No 13 with its stone effigy outside and No 33, in a rather more faded state. In the nearby Place des Merciers and Rue de la Mitterie (or mint, where coins were once produced) are many other fine examples. Cafés and restaurants are everywhere, punctuated by chic shops and craft studios. There is a leaflet detailing the latter on a plan of the town, so you can easily find some modern creative work to your taste, and talk to the artists in their workplace. Many of these are in the **Rue Jerzual** and **Rue du Petit Fort**, the most attractive of all Dinan's old streets, which lead down to the port, but don't get too carried away by the shops and scenic details – the way is steep and uneven.

Eglise St-Malo

The religious architecture of Dinan is rich and varied, with convents of the Franciscans

Eglise St-Malo, Dinan.

Five of the best

Things to see in Dinan

❶ **Hôtel Kératry,** 6 rue de l'Horloge.

❷ **Salle des Gisants,** Tour Coëtquen.

❸ **Eglise St-Sauveur.**

❹ Equestrian statue of **du Guesclin.**

❺ View of the port from the **Jardin Anglais.**

Dinan.

(Cordeliers), Jacobins, Dominicans and Benedictines. There are also two fine churches that derserve investigation. The Eglise St-Malo (with a magnificent magnolia tree outside) dates from the late 15th century, in mainly Gothic style. A wonderful horned devil holds up the holy water stoop near the entrance. Striking stained-glass windows from the 1920s depict scenes from the town's history such as Geoffrey of Dinan on return from the crusades and the visit of Anne de Bretagne, resplendent in a blue and red dress.

Eglise St-Sauveur

According to one story, the Eglise St-Sauveur was built as the result of a promise made during the crusades by Dinan knight Rivallon le Roux. Certainly the three entrance arches from the 12th century have eastern motifs, and be sure on entering the church to look behind the door to the left for a couple of camels topping a column. The church has a strange mixture of architectural styles, Romanesque on one side of the nave, Flamboyant Gothic on the other from a later extension during the church's long development. Du Guesclin's heart is in the north transept, behind a 14th-century tombstone. It was brought here from the Dominican monastery, closed at the time of the Revolution – the transfer is shown in the stained-glass window beside it. Less-than-Christian images in the side chapels mingle with the traditional here – look out for the man eating leaves.

If you wonder why there is a parasol in the altar area, it symbolizes the status of basilica, granted to St-Sauveur in the 20th century. Behind the church,

the Jardin Anglais provides a restful spot away from the crowds and fine views over the port.

Northeast Côtes d'Armor

Port of Dinan

Below the viaduct, the port of Dinan clusters around an attractive old stone bridge. Cafés and restaurants line the waterside, for people- and boat-watching. You can hire a boat, a canoe or a kayak here, or take an organized cruise down to Léhon. On the opposite bank is the **Maison de la Rance** (Apr-Nov Tue-Sun 1400-1800, Jul and Aug 1000-1900), with an exhibition presenting many

Around the region

aspects of fluvial life through displays, a diaporama and interactive puzzles for all the senses, including smells. An interesting feature explains how tides work in accordance with moon phases.

Léhon

2 km south of Dinan.

Just upriver from Dinan lies one of Brittany's least well-known 'little towns of character'. Beautiful stone houses decorated with bright flowers cluster around the **Abbey of St-Magloire** on the banks of the Rance. The church contains the effigies of Jehan de Beaumanoir, famous for his role in the Battle of the Thirty (see page 253) and his wife. It also has a remarkable 12th-century granite font. Vikings destroyed the first building, and the abbey today dates from the 13th to 17th centuries. In July and August (1000-1200, 1400-1800) you can visit the former refectory and monks' dormitory as well as the attics with their upturned boat-style roof timbers.

There is free access to the remains of the **château**, which lays claim to being the oldest hill-top fortress in Brittany. It was besieged by Henry II in 1168 and destroyed, then rebuilt. From the squat towers, the flag flying from the château at Dinan is clearly visible.

Menhir de St-Samson

4 km from Dinan. Park on the main road (D57) by the blue heritage site sign.

The engravings on this leaning Neolithic site have weathered badly, so try to go on a bright day when sunlight brings out traces of its patterns. Asterix fans can have fun taking photos of each other with a 'menhir on the back', Obelix-style.

Druids Cemetery

12 km north of Dinan.

The so-called Druids Cemetry at Preslin-Trigavou, set in a grove of young oak, is an alignment of 65 quartz stones in rough lines. The Druid allusion is not founded on any evidence – the site is late

Corseul.

Neolithic (c 2000 BC), although one legend says that it came into being after weary fairies dropped the stones they were carrying to build Mont St-Michel. The July live-music Festival of the Megaliths began here in 2009.

Corseul

10 km northwest of Dinan.

Roman remains of any scale are not common in Brittany, but the essence of a street with half columns and building foundations is preserved at Corseul, which was once the main centre of the Coriosolites tribe, on a major Roman road to the west. The street would have been part of a commercial area, lined by shops and a basilica used by merchants. There are good explanations and reconstruction drawings on the site.

Nearby at Haut-Bécherel are the remains of a huge octagonal temple to the god of war, called Fanum Martis or the shrine of Mars, the largest sanctuary in the Armorican peninsula. The lone ruined fragment of the **Temple of Mars** is impressive enough, but it was once integrated in the vast surrounding complex.

A reconstructed model of the site in the excellent little **Musée de Corseul** (upstairs in the Mairie, Mon-Fri 1000-1200, 1430-1730, Sat morning only) comes as quite a surprise. Other artefacts are well laid out, giving enough information to conjure up many aspects of life in the area under Roman rule from 50 BC-AD 300.

St-Cast

35 km northwest of Dinan.

This headland forms a traditional seaside resort of seven golden beaches and a long promenade with plenty of places to buy ice creams or fishing nets. It is a favourite spot for families with young children and for older strollers. A famous incident in Breton history is commemorated here with a column. In 1758, during the Seven Years War, English troops who had threatened St-Malo were now trying to re-embark from the Grande Plage at St-Cast. They were first attacked by locals and then the army of the Duke of Aiguillon. Some 2000 English were killed against 149 Breton/French; the latter are buried in the 'Heroes' Cemetry'. A hundred years later, on Napoleon III's instructions, the memorial was erected; on the top, the greyhound of Brittany triumphs over the leopard of England.

Jugon-les-Lacs

21 km west of Dinan.

Nestling in the valley of the Arguenon below the expressway, Jugon-les-Lacs is a small picturesque old town at the head of a lake of 70 ha. It has many historic buildings, such as Hôtel de Sevoy, an elaborate *manoir* of 1634, and the Maison de L'Escu, which now houses a restaurant in the main square. But it's water that dominates the scene: some houses have their own little bridges over fast-flowing streams, and flowery *lavoirs* strike a nostalgic note.

The lake is an excellent base for outdoor activities of all sorts and there are several sources of cheerful help and advice about how to get going – the tourist office in the main square, the VTT station and the Centre Nautique by the lake, and the **Maison de la Pêche** (maisondelapeche22.com). The latter has an interesting exhibition about fish, and a dramatic eel ladder in the water rushing below the building, visible through glass.

Cap Fréhel

42 km northwest of Dinan.

Cap Fréhel remains a wild clifftop of *landes* or heathland, studded with the bright colours of heathers and gorse. Even the crowds of visitors don't spoil this image. Parking areas are set back behind the lighthouse, and once past this only the little lookout tower on the promontory stands between you and the vastness of the sea. Views are sensational, with the craggy outline of Fort La Latte to the right, and the sandy beaches of the Côte d'Emeraude stretching away to the left. The striations of rock colour are striking, with pink sandstone and grey schist, interspersed with the greenery of coastal vegetation. At the end of the promontory, curious rock stacks have been carved out by the forces of erosion. To the right, below the restaurant of the same name, is the rock formation known as La Fauconnerie (falconry), usually covered with seabirds. You may see gulls, guillemots, pied oyster catchers, puffins and shags here.

If you're feeling energetic, try a walk along the coastal path with sensational views at every step – allow an hour and a half to reach Fort La Latte.

Fort La Latte.

Tip...

Get to Fort La Latte early, before the school parties or tourist groups arrive.

Fort La Latte

Fréhel, T02 99 30 38 84, castlelalatte.com.
Apr-Sep 1000-1200, 1400-1800, Jul and Aug
1000-1900, out of season Sat, Sun, school
holidays 1400-1800. €4.90/€2.60.

There is a palpable sense of excitement in crossing the first drawbridge into this fort, and not only because it was used as a film set for *The Vikings* (1958), with Kirk Douglas and Tony Curtis. A second majestic entrance with portcullis leads into the inner courtyard. Building began in the 14th century, with improvements up to the Wars of Religion when it was besieged and taken, later falling into disuse. It was revamped as part of Louis XIV's coastal defence system in the early 18th century.

The location itself is striking, not least in the moulding of the fort to the contours of the land, and it has all those typical castle features that stir the imagination. One of the first sensations is simply nausea in looking down into the alarming oubliette near the gatehouse, and imagining the reality of being imprisoned in such a space. Passing the residential quarters now inhabited by the owners of the castle, the best part is exploring the fortifications and bulk of the imposing keep. Look for the apostles' symbols on the outer wall here. Not surprisingly, the fort was never taken by sea.

Coming out on top of the tower gives panoramic views, but if you really want to test your nerve, continue up into the lookout point by the flag pole, but do cling on to the rope provided in high wind! Another point of interest is the cannon-ball oven, one of those ideas that sounds good but is hopelessly impractical – it took two hours to make the missiles red-hot, by which time the enemy ships had probably moved off! There is also an exhibition showing the restoration of the fort in more recent times.

Château de la Hunaudaye

Le Chêne au Loup, Plédéliac, T02 96 34 82 10, chateau-hunaudaye.perso.neuf.fr.
Apr to mid-Jun and mid-Sep to early Nov, Wed, Sun, public holidays 1430-1800, Jun-Sep daily 1030-1830, closed Nov-Easter. €4.50/€3.50.

The originally 13th-century château was finally burnt and sacked as a Chouan refuge by Republicans in 1793. The ruins have recently been well restored, but make this a somewhat sanitized version of a genuine ruin like the Château de Tonquédec (see page 144). It's still fun for castle-lovers of all ages, with plenty to explore. If the château is closed, a path leads right around the outside by the moat for good views of the sturdy towers. It's a fine setting for the medieval performances each summer. There are some peculiarities to be seen inside – the Chapel Tower is a room with religious carvings around the door, in fact most probably made by a secluded prisoner. The Seigneurial Tower has exhibition space on each floor, culminating in a room strangely containing an old-fashioned television set.

Right by the château is a lake with picnic tables and a crêperie *à la ferme* open for drinks and ice creams in the summer.

40 km via motorway or 44 km by D768 west of Dinan.

Lamballe is famous as the former main stronghold of the Penthièvres, bitterest opponents of the dukes of Brittany. For that reason it no longer has a castle, but there are some lovely medieval houses. On the central hill there's an unusual table of orientation highlighting the development of this historic town in response to the demands of the 20th century.

Haras (National Stud)

Place du Champ de Foire, T02 96 50 06 98, haraspatrimoine.com.
Tue-Sun, guided visit at 1500. €5.50/€3.

This is a great family-outing venue, housed in a former château, so the horses live in fine style. Guided tours (in English in summer months) enable visitors to see every aspect of how the horses are raised. An impressive display is put on every Thursday in summer.

Maison de Bourreau – Musée Mathurin Méheut

Place du Martray, T02 96 31 19 99.
Apr 1000-1200, 1430-1700, Jun-Sep 1000-1200, 1430-1800, closed Sun, May, Oct-Dec 1430-1700 Wed, Fri, Sat. €3.

The Executioner's house (the reasons for its name are unknown) contains an exhibition dedicated to the Lamballe-born painter Mathurin Méheut. Despite living in Paris for most of his life, his distinctive work remains one of the finest evocations of traditional Breton life in the fields, by the sea or at worship. Adjacent is the **Museum of Popular Traditions** (Jun-Sep Tue-Sat 1000-1200, 1430-1800) with costumes, photographs and items from everyday life.

Guingamp & the Argoat

Guingamp is an agreeable small town, lately boosted by a famous sporting triumph that has upped the energy levels considerably. To the south, central Brittany remains sparsely populated, despite a great number of British property owners settling here in recent years. It's a quiet, rural area of undulating landscape punctuated by gorges, rivers and lakes. Twisting roads amid granite boulders trace a route through isolated settlements, past sacred springs and wayside calvaries, with chapel spires apt to appear at any moment. Loc-Envel and Bulat-Pestivien are wonderful examples of simple country villages with exquisite churches.

Eglise de Notre-Dame de Bon-Secours.

Guingamp is very much on the map these days thanks to the triumph of their relatively lowly football team in the French Cup final in 2009. The town was an important centre of the cloth trade with England in medieval times, and its name is probably the origin of the word 'gingham'.

The town hall, which is in an old Augustinian monastery, is worth a look: you can see a few large paintings by Paul Sérusier of the Pont-Aven school (see page 47) in the former cloister area. A public reception room still has the fireplace and bread oven of the monks' kitchen.

The Place du Centre has many fine medieval half-timbered houses (Nos 31 and 33 especially) and later granite ones. Peep through the archway of No 42 to see the finest Renaissance-style doorway of them all. The elaborate fountain is named **La Plombée** thanks to its lead basins, and is decorated with dragons and mermaids.

An unusual feature of the interesting **Eglise de Notre-Dame de Bon-Secours** is the cult of the Black Madonna, whose statue is in the entrance porch, overlooked by some anodyne apostles. Inside the eye is drawn constantly upwards to where all the action takes place in a mêlée of vaulting and buttresses. The church is very much a match of two halves, divided across the nave between the Gothic and the Renaissance.

Continue up the hill to see the former château site, where one tower remains in good shape and remnants of the stout ramparts can be seen via the Venelle de St-Jacques.

Around Guingamp

Menez Bré

10 km west of Guingamp.

From the expressway, the **Chapelle St-Hervé** on top of this hill is visible. The saint is said to have performed a miracle here in striking water from the rock.

The current chapel dates from the 16th to 17th centuries, but look inside the porch at a door that

reflects much earlier foundations. This is a superb viewpoint, with an orientation table pointing out places in the Trégor and Pink Granite Coast to the north. Picnic with Côtes d'Armor at your feet!

A momentous meeting is said to have taken place up here in the mid-sixth century. The cruel tyrant Conomor, historically ruler of a wide area and in legend a Breton Bluebeard, was called to account for his actions by a council of bishops and holy men, including the blind St-Hervé. He was excommunicated; a stained-glass window in the nearby church of Pédernec records this event.

Belle-Isle-en-Terre

16 km west of Guingamp.

This very attractive village gets the name 'island' from the embrace of its two rivers, the Gouic and the Guer. There was once a large paper-making industry in the valley just to the north, now transformed into a natural site with walks and discovery trails. Every July a festival of l e Gouren or Breton wrestling and other games is held here. Details from the tourist office (T02 96 43 01 71, ot-belle-isle-en-terre.com).

Evidence of Lady Mond's (see page 158) bounty remains – she funded the building of the post office and the Mairie, which lies next door to her last château. This had to be knocked down as soon as it was finished and rebuilt because it was too close to the road. It now houses a centre for

Chapelle St-Hervé, Menez Bré.

Lady Mond

The eerie emptiness of Lady Mond's former château at Loc-Envel contrasts with the glamour and richness of her extraordinary life. She was born in 1869 at nearby Belle-Isle-en-Terre, a miller's daughter, named Mai Le Manac'h. After going to Paris to seek her fortune and acquiring a certain notoriety for flamboyant behaviour, she married and moved to London. After her husband died, Mai became the mistress of the Infant of Spain, Antoine d'Orléans. This brought her into high society and in 1910 she met the 'nickel king' industrialist millionaire Robert Mond, at the Savoy Hotel. They wed in 1922 and he was knighted by George V in 1932.

As Lady Mond, Mai remained close to her roots. Her husband bought the château that remains in semi-ruined condition on the edge of the Wood of the Night and they divided their time between this country retreat and fashionable Dinard.

Many famous people were entertained here before the war. Widowed in 1938, Lady Mond was imprisoned in Guingamp for a while during German occupation, and afterwards decided to build a smaller château on the site of her father's former mill in Belle-Isle-en-Terre, where she had already funded many public buildings. She died in 1949 and is buried with Sir Robert in a large mausoleum at the chapel of Locmaria, 2 km north of Belle-Isle.

Stained-glass window in Loc-Envel's fascinating church.

information about rivers and an aquarium. There are pretty gardens along the Guer behind the building.

Loc-Envel

19 km west of Guingamp.

The château, once the home of Lady Mond, is at the end of a long, tree-lined track, a pleasant 1-km walk from the village car park. A strange atmosphere lurks around this vast, grandiose ruin that once echoed to the laughter and music of high-society parties and cultural gatherings. It is on the edge of the Wood of the Night (Coat Noz), where there is a botanical walk.

Loc-Envel has an exceptionally interesting church with a superb wooden rood screen from the 16th century, an 18th-century pit and pendulum clock, and many amusing carvings of humans and animals on the horizontal beams.

The Argoat

Enjoy a gentle day exploring the simple charms of the Argoat (land of the woods) by car. This is the quintessential Brittany of quiet country roads, church spires peeping over undulating hills, rough fields strewn with giant granite boulders, wayside crosses and tiny hamlets. The religious heritage of the area and the landscape of this granite plateau are equally memorable.

From Guingamp head south via St-Péver to **St-Fiacre**, where the church's little ossuary building still has boxes containing skulls on display. In the porch, the carvings of animals and even a 'Green Man' show that Breton Christianity had many touches of earlier paganism.

It's worth stopping to see the calvary at **Senven-Léhart** by Roland Doré, a 17th-century sculptor. Some of the figures are missing, but those remaining show a great sensitivity of expression, especially those mourning the body of Christ. Just ahead is the *lavoir* and *fontaine* of St-Connan.

A few kilometres away is the village of **Lanrivain**, with its characterful bar next to the bakery in the huge central square. The ossuary by the church retains piles of neatly sorted bones and skulls, and the churchyard has a vivid calvary.

Continuing west on the D87, don't blink or you'll miss the hamlet of **St-Antoine**. Here, ancient buildings are being restored as part of a *chanvrière*, where hemp is grown and then transformed into a range of products. The owners also serve drinks and ice cream in their little café/shop. Gorgeous clothes in glowing colours, bags, soaps, oils and even chocolate are made from this versatile plant. Ask to see the chapel and you'll be given the key.

Some 400 m further on is a forest parking area on the right with a track leading up to the barrage on the Blavet river. On the other side of the main road just over the bridge, a footpath (fork left almost at once) leads through woodland to the **Gorges de Toul Goulic**, a little-known example of the granite 'chaos' phenomenon. Erosion has caused boulders of all shapes and sizes to tumble down the riverbed, here creating a magically secret atmosphere. Allow around half an hour to walk there and back.

Opposite and above: Lanrivain.

To the north via Peumerit-Quintin is the lake of Kerne-Huel, which is perfect if you're looking for a beautiful picnic spot near water. Near the barrage there is a centre nautique where you can hire boats and kayaks.

Continue towards Maël-Pestivien on the D50. You will pass the tiny chapel of St-Gildas in the hamlet of Coat Maël and about 1 km later you'll need to look out for a blue sign on the left to the **Bois de Kerohou** and **Chaire des Druides**. Go to the end of this little road and park.

The stones are just above in the wood. Don't miss this site for a chance to let your imagination run riot. A hilly grove of oaks conceals all manner of granite boulders in strange configurations. Legend has it as a place of Druid sacrifice and there is indeed a rather eerie, claustrophobic atmosphere under the leafy canopy. One stone appears to have the form of a human body on it, but in fact this is over 2 m long and seems to have had a helping human hand in the shaping of its curvatures. The

site is now managed by Bretagne Vivante and has a colony of crows that are called *culottés* (or 'trousered') because of their feathered-covered legs.

Continue into the wild country towards **Bulat-Pestivien**, with granite boulders appearing on each side in the fields. Every year a three-day pardon complete with horse festival is held here in September. You'll also find one of the finest churches in the area, where you can climb up a tiny winding staircase to the viewing platform below the tallest spire in Côtes d'Armor. Opposite the church is the little **Maison du Granite** (Jul to mid-Sep, Tue-Sun 1430-1830), which gives an interesting perspective on the countryside of this tour. Nearby **Pestivien** has an unusual calvary.

Return to Guingamp via **Bourbriac**, where the church has the tomb of St-Briac and a stone container behind said to have been the saint's original coffin. There's also an atmospheric three-room crypt with simple pillars dating back to the 12th century.

Lac de Guerlédan

Right in the centre of Brittany and accessed off the N164 expressway, this vast lake is the ideal place for activity holidays, with interesting options for non-sporty types too. It is a very beautiful, peaceful environment with its serpentine form and densely wooded surrounds. Created in the 1920s when a barrage to generate electricity was constructed, Lac de Guerlédan effectively cut the Nantes–Brest canal in half and put an end to through traffic. Some 400 ha of land and 12 km of the Blavet river were flooded for this, submerging 17 locks and all the lock-keepers' cottages. Today there are swimming beaches, walking trails and places to enjoy waterside refreshment.

Lac de Guerlédan

The main points of access to Lac de Guerlédan are on the north at Beau Rivage (via Caurel), at the eastern end at the Rond-Point (via Mur-de-Bretagne) and to the south, via the Anse de Sordan. There are bathing beaches at each of these. Cruises, including lunch and dinner options, start from Beau Rivage. The Anse de Landroannec, also near Mur-de-Bretagne, is quieter, with a large picnic area overlooking the water, and a little beach. Bon Repos is at the western extremity, after Lock 137 of the Nantes–Brest canal.

On the water There are centres for hiring boats at the Rond-Point (T02 96 67 12 22, base-plein-air-guerledan.com). Canoes, kayaks and pedaloes are also available there and at Beau Rivage (L'Embarcadère, T02 96 28 52 64) or the Anse de Sourdan (Restaurant Merlin, T02 97 27 52 36). For waterskiing, the **Ecole de Ski Nautique** (T06 09 38 03 26, May-Sep) is based at Beau Rivage, where tuition and equipment are available. A 10-minute run costs €25 for non-members, less for a group of more than five if booked in advance.

Cycling Cyclists can enjoy 300 km of marked routes, graded according to difficulty. The **Station VTT** (T02 96 67 12 22) at the Rond-Point has maps, bikes, helmets and baby-carriers for hire. This works in conjunction with the **Base Départmentale de Plein Air de Guerlédan** next door, which organizes accompanied outings (take a look at base-plein-air-guerledan.com).

Opposite and below: family fun and bicycles at Lac de Guerlédan.

Around the region

The Green Way from Mur-de-Bretagne to Bon Repos via Caurel provides uncomplicated riding. Tourist offices have details of 24 circular routes using this old railway line as a starting point.

Walking It is possible to walk right around the lake, crossing at the lock near Bon Repos, a distance of just over 50 km. There are plenty of options for camping if you want to make a weekend of it. As part of a journey along the Nantes–Brest canal, walkers can choose to pass along the north or south side of the lake. Both have easy and challenging parts, although generally the south side through the Forêt de Quénécan (GR341S) is more up and down. During the hunting season, which runs from October to February, certain parts of the routes will be closed and marked alternatives must be followed. There is also the easier option of following an old railway line, now a Green Way, above the lake from Mur-de-Bretagne to Bon Repos. In addition there are four separate walking routes (ranging from 4 to 11 km) in the beautiful Forêt de Quénécan, starting from Bon Repos. The tourist office in Mur-de-Bretagne has details, or get advice at the Rond-Point.

Horse riding The equestrian centre at Treffaut, near Mur-de-Bretagne, is open all year. It is best to phone or email beforehand to make arrangements (T02 96 26 02 02, centre-equestre-guerledan.com). Equibreizh (equibreizh.com, see page 77) has marked tracks for riding on the south side of the lake.

Fishing There are many suitable points for fishing in the lake, which contains pike and perch. Permits and advice can be obtained from the **Relais du Lac** at Caurel, the **Café de l'Abbaye** at Bon Repos and the **Société de Pêche** (T02 96 26 35 37) at Mur-de-Bretagne. The latter can also tell you about available fishing lessons and courses.

Around Lac de Guerlédan

Abbaye de Bon Repos

Bon Repos, 5 km west of Lac de Guerlédan,
T02 96 24 82 20, bon-repos.com.
Mar to mid-Jun, mid-Sep to Oct 1400-1800, mid-Jun to mid-Sep 1100-1900. €3.50.

This is a delightful spot for a picnic, a stroll or simply a break to sit by the water of the Nantes–Brest canal, looking across at the ruined abbey. This Cistercian foundation was established as the result of a dream by Alain de Rohan in 1184, as he rested after hunting here. After the French Revolution, when abbeys ceased to function, it became a clothing factory until damaged by Chouan attacks, and later provided housing for engineers of the Nantes–Brest canal. A famous annual Son et Lumière show is held here (see Entertainment, page 175).

Forge des Salles

3 km from Bon Repos , T02 96 24 90 12,
lesforgesdessalles.info.
Easter-end Oct weekends 1400-1830, every day Jul and Aug 1400-1830. €5.

A very interesting social history is enshrined in this former forge-workers' village from the 18th to 19th centuries. As well as the rough remains of working areas, where iron was smelted and shaped, you can see the chapel (unusually a Protestant one, following the faith of the noble Rohan family who initiated the enterprise), a school room, an accounts office and workers' cottages. Period objects, such as beds and washing utensils in the latter, illustrate daily life in the heyday of the village. The grand house, with its terraced gardens, not surprisingly belonged to the master of the forge. A little stream running through the site is the boundary between Morbihan and Côtes d'Armor, so you will be in two departments on your visit.

Musée de l'Electricité

St-Aignan, 3.5 km southwest of Mur-de-Bretagne, T02 97 27 51 39.
Mid-Jun to mid-Sep, 0930-1230 and 1430-1830, closed Sun morning. €3.50.

Not far from the barrage, this unusual and very enjoyable little museum is organized by those passionate about electricity and all its uses and applications. Barn-like buildings (complete with nesting swifts) house old railway signalling devices and early hydroelectric machinery – ask for a demonstration. Upstairs is a room devoted to interactive models showing how electricity works, and a fascinating collection of utensils and domestic items – a washing machine and toaster from 1935, for example. One room and an interesting film of scenes from the 1920s onwards illustrate the building of the Barrage de Guerlédan. This is a good place for older children and adults. While you're here, visit the church, opposite, which has a famous Tree of Jesse altarpiece.

Mur-de-Bretagne

1.5 km off the N164 expressway.

This is a good base for enjoying active holidays. The tourist office (T02 96 28 51 41, guerledan.fr) by the church is the main source of information for Lac de Guerlédan. In summer there's a market every Friday evening (1800-2030), with musical entertainment. In July and August the Cap Armor initiative, which encourages participation in sporting and cultural activities, opens an office in the centre, if you want to sign up for organized events, such as Breton games, riding or waterskiing. Also, take a look at the **Chapelle Ste-Suzanne** (Jul and Aug, 1000-1200, 1500-1800) at the top of the town to see the fine

18th-century painted ceiling and unusual double-arched entrance below an elegant tower.

Each September a well-attended Foire Biologique (Organic Fair) is held here.

Musée de l'Electricité.

Allées couvertes de Liscuis

Just to the north of Bon Repos are three Neolithic alley graves, c 3000 BC, on a hillside with fantastic views. It's a lovely walk for a sunny day...

Listings
Sleeping

St-Brieuc

Hôtel de Clisson €€
36-38 rue de Gouët, T02 96 62 19 29, hoteldeclisson.com.
Map St-Brieuc, p138.
This hotel is well situated in the old centre near the cathedral. There are different categories of rooms – it's a good choice for single travellers – but all are comfortable and good value. Ask for one overlooking the pretty garden, where you can have breakfast in good weather. No restaurant, but a bar for guests' use only. There are also some private parking spaces, which is very useful in St-Brieuc.

Hôtel Ker Izel €
20 rue de Gouët, T02 96 33 46 29, hotel-kerizel.com.
Map St-Brieuc, p138.
A well-priced hotel in an old house near the cathedral, with garden terrace and heated outdoor pool (summer only). Rooms are on the small size – in No 4 you might have to choose which bit of your body to put in the bathroom at one time – but they're comfortable enough and suitably equipped. A few car parking spaces are available in a garage along the street.

Côte de Goëlo

Hôtel des Agapanthes €€-€
1 rue Adrien Rebours, Ploubazlanec, T02 96 55 89 06, hotel-les-agapanthes.com.

Well situated near the coast between Paimpol and the ferry to Bréhat, this smart, comfortable hotel has pleasant rooms (some small) in two buildings, some with sea views and little terraces or balconies. Everything here is beautifully presented – reception, bedrooms, even the lavish breakfast buffet – in a modern chic style, with lots of attention to detail.

Chambres d'hôtes/gîtes

Char à Bancs Ferme-Auberge €€
Plélo, T02 96 79 51 25, aucharabanc.com.
This is a really special place to stay, in a fantastic setting. There's a restaurant (in which they make their own cider) and a boating area in the bottom of the Leff valley. The delightful gîtes/ chambres d'hôtes rooms are up a pretty track. The decor is sophisticated rural-chic, a fascinating blend of ancient and ultra modern, in a series of delightful little cottages. Gîtes cost up to €500 a week. A highly recommended choice.

La Maison du Phare €€
93 rue de la Tour, Plérin, T02 96 33 34 65, maisonphare.com.
A stylish green-shuttered, half-timbered B&B in a former merchant's house just past the port. Excellent designer-styled rooms, some with balcony/

terrace, and one on the ground floor. Good sea views and well-placed for St-Brieuc centre or the coastal resorts, with easy parking and a bus route passing the door.

Le Palus €€-€
Plage du Palus, Plouha, T02 96 70 38 26, le-palus.com.
The chambres d'hôtes option is a recent venture for this long-established restaurant (see Eating, page 170). It has a superb location right by the lovely beach Palus Plage, with sand-castling, swimming and a coastal path on its doorstep. The bright and simply furnished rooms are above the bar area, with sea or beach and cliff views. Good-value double or family rooms, and buffet breakfast.

The Trégor

Hôtel Aigue Marine €€€
Port de Plaissance, Tréguier, T02 96 92 97 00, aiguemarine-hotel.com.
Situated on the waterfront, a short uphill walk to the town centre, this bright, comfortable hotel has large, well-equipped rooms with balconies overlooking the river. Very friendly service, and a modern restaurant where chef Yoann Peron's fish dishes are reliably excellent. The breakfast buffet is a treat in itself. The hotel also has

a garden with an outdoor swimming pool, and gym/sauna.

Manoir du Sphinx €€€
Chemin de la Messe, Perros-Guirec, T02 96 23 25 42, lemanoirdusphinx.com.
An attractive cliff-top villa, well placed for the facilities of the town, yet in a peaceful spot. It also offers superb views over the Sept-Iles. Rooms are comfortable and well equipped, and some have full-glass bay windows to make the most of the location. Try some gourmet seafood in the chandeliered dining room.

Ar Vro €€
Le Yaudet, T02 96 46 48 80, restaurant-ar-vro.com.
Spend a night in this tranquil and beautiful village near Lannion and the coast. Of the five pleasant rooms at Ar Vro, one (No 7) has a view over the bay. A stay here is on the basis of demi-pension, so you can take advantage of the excellent restaurant with *produits du terroir* (see Eating, page 170). About €60 per person (based on two sharing) including bed, breakfast and dinner, is good value.

Villa Cyrnos €€
10 rue du Sergent l'Héveder, Perros-Guirec, T02 96 91 13 36, monsite.orange.fr/villacyrnos22/.
On the way down to the port, this large house in well-kept

gardens has five bedrooms, including two adjoining, suitable for families. Old family photos create a homely feel, and Roger Guyon is an obliging host. Ask for a room with a sea view; if there isn't one available, at the very least you can enjoy a panoramic perspective from the breakfast room.

Chambres d'hôtes de Scavet €
10 rue Ker Coz, Tréguier, T02 96 92 94 18, chambresdescavet.fr.
This house of pink granite is very conveniently placed near the cathedral. It offers two good-sized bedrooms, each en suite, separated by a large kitchen/dining/sitting area where guests can prepare their own meals. This communal space is pleasant and eclectically decorated, giving the feel of staying in a friend's house. Gaëlle Huon-Tregros serves delicious breads and home-made jam for breakfast.

Kerlilou €
3 Calvary, Plouguiel, T02 96 92 24 06, kerlilou.fr.
Well located for town and coast, this is a lovely old house with garden setting, a positive haven for those seeking quality accommodation in a tranquil location. The large, beautifully decorated rooms with period furniture also have spacious bathrooms, hot drinks trays and

internet access. The welcoming hosts can provide dinner every night except Sunday. A useful stop for walkers, as the GR34 coastal path passes the property.

Tara B&B €
31 rue Ernest Renan, Tréguier, T02 96 92 15 28, chambrestaratreguier.com.
An almost secret location in an ancient house behind the owner's shop, yet right in the centre of town. There are five en suite rooms (one suitable for the disabled), each with its own Irish title. The name Tara (home of the early kings of Ireland) reflects Guy Arhant's ancestry: he and his wife Malou, who speak English, happily share their enthusiasm for Celtic traditions in a real Breton home. A corner kitchen is available for guests to prepare their own evening meals, which can then be enjoyed outside in the enticing gardens.

Gîtes
Gîtes-en-Trégor
Guergillès Guirec, Ploubezre, T02 96 47 17 86, gites-en-tregor.com.
Three lovely gîtes in a quiet location near the Chapelle de Kerfons, well placed for visiting the Trégor. Clara and Martin Cronin are helpful on-site hosts, and can advise on walking (the GR34A is nearby) and sightseeing. Families are welcome, with the possibility

of using two adjoining houses for larger groups. Le Grange is suitable for disabled visitors. Smaller gîtes (sleeping four) from €250, larger (for eight) from €500.

Camping

Camping de Traou-Mélédern
Pontrieux, T02 96 95 69 27, campingpontrieux.free.fr.
An excellent position for this quiet site by the Trieux river, with spacious pitches for tents and caravans, and accommodation to rent. Regulars of many nationalities appreciate the helpful owners and clean facilities. You can rent a gîte (two or five person) or mobile home from €200-380 a week. Camping for two people is about €10 per night. Open all year.

Dinan

Hôtel Le d'Avaugour €€€
1 place du Champ, T02 96 39 07 49, avaugourhotel.com.
Overlooking the busy Place du Champ, this is a very comfortable and well-furnished hotel. Even the bathrooms have telephones. Bedrooms are double-glazed, but ask for a room at the back, overlooking the lovely garden. It's surprisingly large and has the bonus of a rampart terrace with a view of the château. The hotel

has a lift, a bar and charming breakfast room. Staff give visitors a very warm welcome.

Hôtel Arvor €€
5 rue Auguste Pavie, T02 96 39 21 22, hotelarvordinan.com.
A friendly hotel right in the heart of the medieval centre by the Jacobins Theatre and near the famous clock tower. The building is 18th century, a fact that can be appreciated in the attractive sitting room, but it's well-modernized in terms of facilities, and has a lift. Private parking is available – a big plus in Dinan.

Northeast Côtes d'Armor

Manoir de la Pichardais €€
Créhen, T02 96 41 09 96, manoirdelapichardais.com.
In a quiet location, this delightful manor house has been in the de Courville family since the 17th century. There are two large period bedrooms, one Renaissance-style, the other an airy mix of blues, with a smaller room adjacent suitable for children. All rooms are finely proportioned, with some exquisite monumental fireplaces. The manoir has an interesting history: the English burnt down part of the estate in 1758. But, if you are English, you are

nevertheless assured of a very warm welcome from Madame de Courville!

Lamballe

Le Manoir des Portes €€
La Poterie, Lamballe, T02 96 31 13 62, manoirdesportes.com.
Just outside the town, this stylishly decorated hotel has an international clientele, with Hervé Jamin and his team creating an atmosphere of calm competence and comfort. Bright, tastefully furnished bedrooms, an excellent restaurant with menus created daily, and pleasant grounds furnished for relaxation add up to the ideal venue for a real treat.

Guingamp

La Demeure €€€-€€
5 rue du Général de Gaulle, T02 96 44 28 53, demeure-vb.com.
Proprietor Carinne Solo's passion is decor, and each room, whether in the new wing or original building, has a different style and feel. You can even buy items of decoration that take your fancy. The overall tone is smart and chic. One suite has a corner kitchen and rooftop terrace for sipping your evening drinks. The breakfast room overlooks a pretty walled garden.

Eating & drinking

Lac de Guerlédan

Auberge Grand Maison €€
1 rue Léon Le Cerf, Mur-de-Bretagne, T02 96 28 51 10, auberge-grand-maison.com.
A very reasonably priced choice for staying in comfort and in pleasant surroundings. Rooms are of a good size with individual decor and well-equipped bathrooms. Another powerful motive is the acquisition of a first Michelin star for Christophe Le Fur's restaurant (see Eating, page 174). He and his wife Mireille warmly welcome guests, and nothing is too much trouble. Highly recommended.

Les Jardins de l'Abbaye €
Bon Repos, St-Gelven, T02 96 24 95 77, abbaye.jardin.free.fr.
Five recently refurbished bedrooms in attractive old buildings next to the ancient abbey, with views towards the Nantes–Brest canal. No 4 is the best, with a large window; others have smaller 'portholes'. This is the best place to stay for the August Son et Lumière spectacle (see Entertainment, page 175) – you can stroll across to bed at 0100 while others scrabble about in the packed car park.

Pear Blossom House €
14 rue de la Résistance, Mur-de-Bretagne, T02 96 26 05 79, pearblossomhouse.com.
Carol and Harvey Partridge have created an attractive, friendly guesthouse, with two bedrooms, one on the ground floor with its own entrance. Both are en suite with tea/coffee facilities. A copious breakfast (full English is extra if required), is brought to your room. Guests can enjoy a secluded shelter in the garden and use the BBQ to cook an evening meal. Good value.

Camping

Nautic International Camping-Caravanning
Beau Rivage, Caurel, T02 96 28 57 94, campingnautic.fr.st.
This site on the lakeside at Beau Rivage is spacious and nicely landscaped, with facilities such as a large swimming pool, tennis and badminton. Handy for all sporting options on the lake, it's also close to restaurants and places of interest. Renting a mobile home for a week ranges from €272 in the off-season to €610 in August.

St-Brieuc

L'Air du Temps €€
4 rue de Gouët, T02 96 68 58 40, airdutemps.fr.
Tue-Sat 1200-1400, 1900-2130.
There's funky chic-trad decor In this restaurant, which is in an old house with a huge fireplace and beams. Specialities are fish and meat dishes *en cocotte* (casserole), with imaginative starters such as goat's cheese and Serrano ham with rhubarb compote. Vegetarian dishes if required. A three-course dinner with limited choice is under €20.

Aux Pesked €€
59 rue du Légué, T02 96 33 34 65, auxpesked.com.
Tue-Fri 1200-1400, 1900-2300, Sat 1900-2300, Sun 1200-1400.
On the way to the Port de Légué, complete with large fish sculpture outside. A true gastronomic delight for fish-fanciers, from a *menu du pêcheur*, depending on the catch of the day, to the superlative chef's *menu de dégustation* at €68. Two- or three-course lunches for under €25 is a good-value treat.

La Cuisine du Marché €€-€
4/6 rue des Trois Frères Merlin, T02 96 61 70 94, lacuisinedumarche.net.
Open 1200-1400, 1900-2200, closed Sun evening and Mon.
There's a good atmosphere in this bright, busy restaurant,

equally popular with locals and visitors. There's lots of choice on the menu, with daily blackboard specials. The Breton sausage with light mustard sauce and creamy mashed potatoes is recommended, as is the café gourmand – a terrific selection of desserts plus strong coffee.

Côte de Goëlo

La Ferme de Kerroc'h €€-€
*Route de Bréhat,
Ploubazlanec,
T02 96 55 81 75.*
Apr-Oct Wed-Sun and daily Jul and Aug 1200-1400, 1900-2130.

On the main road to the Bréhat ferry, this grill/crêperie offers a high standard of country cooking in a gorgeous old house with very fine stone doorways. Simple dishes – such as chicken in white wine sauce with rice – are full of flavour and attractively presented. Recommended.

Le Palus/Restaurant La Homardine €€-€
*Palus Plage, Plouha,
T02 96 70 38 26, lepalus.com.*
Daily Apr-Oct, closed Tue in winter.
A varied choice with a brasserie/crêperie and a restaurant in this large establishment with upper and lower dining rooms, both overlooking the beach and sea. Seafood – *moules de bouchot à la crème*, oysters, langoustines – is the speciality, but there are steaks and crêpes too. Set menus from €20-30.

Fleur de Blé Noir Crêperie €
*9 rue du Commandant,
Malbert, St-Quay Portrieux,
T02 96 70 31 55.*
Open 1200-1400, 1900-2200, closed Wed, Thu lunch and Sun dinner out of season, also closed Nov and Dec.
Opposite the casino and beach, this little crêperie has an upper with some good sea views and an outdoor terrace. They serve very tasty savoury and sweet crêpes made with quality products. Give La Bisquine a try if you like caramel sauce and ice cream. The service is very friendly and there's a pleasant atmosphere.

The Trégor

Ar Vro €€
*Le Yaudet, T02 96 46 48 80,
restaurant-ar-vro.com.*
Every day Jul and Aug, closed Mon and Tue out of season, 1230-1330 and 1930-2100 (but hours do vary).
This restaurant with rooms has a reputation for chef André Minne's fine cooking. The emphasis is on local products of

Tréguier.

quality, with fish figuring strongly on the menu. The €25 *menu du terroir* might include a starter of *foie gras* presented in the form of a crème brûlée. Filet of monkfish with fennel and creamed quinoa is recommended.

Auberge du Trégor €€-€
3 rue St-Yves, Tréguier,
T02 96 92 32 34,
aubergedutregor.com.
Tue-Sat 1200-1400, 1900-2100, Sun 1200-1330.
Near the cathedral, this beautiful old stone house has a pretty dining room. Christian Turpault works wonders in the kitchen, while his wife welcomes diners with good-value set menus and a tempting *carte*. Goat's cheese with bacon and apples, followed by scallops and prawn with artichokes in a vanilla sauce might leave room for an apricot version of Breton *far*.

Le Moulin Vert €
15 rue Duguesclin, Lannion,
T02 96 37 91 20.
Daily 1200-1400 and from 1830.
You can't miss the green windmill signs outside this attractively decorated corner restaurant. Menus decorated with local scenes, bright tablecloths and plants all contribute to a pleasant atmosphere. The simple food

is excellent, focusing on salads, *galettes* or pasta dishes – try a warm salad with Breton sausage. Very popular with both locals and tourists.

Cafés & bars
Le Lannionais
31 place du Général Leclerc, Lannion.
Squeeze into the very welcoming atmosphere of this ancient half-timbered building. The small bar area inside has a superb beamed ceiling, but it's nicer to sit outside and enjoy the bustle of the main square.

Le Manoir Elfique (Manoir de Kerloas)
Ploulec'h, signed off the main Lannion/Morlaix road, T02 96 46 36 64, manoirelfique.fr.
Mon, Wed-Fri 1700-0100, Sat and Sun 1200-1500, 1800-0100.
A new cultural venture in a fine 15th-century château, with a café/bar offering food ranging from tapas to boeuf bourguinon. The events programme includes exhibitions, concerts and storytellers.

Dinan

Auberge des Terres-Neuvas €€-€
25 rue du Quai, T02 96 39 86 45.
Closed Sun and Wed evening, except in Jul and Aug, lunch only Oct-Mar.
Cécile and Grégory Correaux keep a very stylish dining room

and outdoor terrace down at the port. A few meaty options, but fish is *the* dish here: from whelks to oysters and prawns to salmon, or try one of the various casseroles (*en cocotte*). The two-course lunch menu is excellent value at €12.

La Cale de Mordreuc €€
22690 Pleudihen-sur-Rance,
T02 96 83 20 43,
lacaledemordreuc.com.
Closed Mon evening and Tue.
Drive out from Dinan on a pleasant evening to eat outside with lovely views over the Rance estuary. If the tide is up you may see a regular visiting seal in the water or taking a turn up the jetty. The restaurant has even adopted her as their logo. Reliably good meat and fish dishes here, and for dessert there might be a delicious peach soup.

La Petite Cantine €
17 rue de l'Apport,
T02 96 87 56 75.
Open 1200-1400, 1900-2200, closed Mon evening out of season.
Handy, cheap and cheerful crêperie/grill right in the old centre with surprisingly imaginative specials. Good crêpes, but also grills, omelettes and home-made burgers, so something for all the family. The tarte tatin made in-house is delicious.

La Fauconnière €€
Cap Fréhel,
T02 96 41 54 20.
Easter-15 Jun, 1215-1430 (closed Wed), daily 15 Jun-Nov.
This restaurant (and *salon du thé* until 1800) is on a cliff top with panoramic ocean views. It can only be reached on foot, and you can enjoy the changing hues of sea and sky from every table. It's not cheap, but fish dishes are reliably excellent, and the chef enjoys presentation with panache. It's popular with families in the summer, especially with a bargain *menu du jour* on weekdays.

La Bretannière €
Place du Martray, Jugon-les-Lacs, T02 96 31 63 32.
Apr-Jun, Wed-Sat lunch and dinner, Jul and Aug daily 1200-2130, closed Sep-Mar.
This standard-looking crêperie/pizzeria with a small dining room and large outdoor terrace in fact has very tasty dark *galettes* with generous fillings such as scallops and creamed leeks, or omelettes and pizzas. It's an excellent budget choice.

Cafés & bars
La Kabane
Next to Fort La Latte parking.
Apr-Sep.
This charming little cabin bar with deckchairs and garden tables is a good stop for hot and cold drinks, such as the Breton beer Coreff. Cool music plays in the background and service is super-friendly.

Lamballe

Chez Camille et Margaux €
44 rue Charles Carte, T02 96 31 05 35.
Mon-Sat lunch, Thu-Sat dinner.
An individual little restaurant with an imaginative menu (try the salmon crumble of spiced bread with pine nuts), specializing in savoury tarts of many flavours and using locally sourced products. Welcoming and friendly service. They also have a range of speciality teas.

Ty Coz €
35 place Champ de Foire, T02 96 31 03 58.
Open 1200-1400, 1900-2100, closed Wed, Sun lunch out of season and Tue evening in winter.
Near the stud, this highly recommended crêperie is very popular with locals. The name means 'old house' in Breton, and the atmospheric dining room has exposed beams and a fireplace. Ty Coz holds a Crêperie Gourmande label, which means you can be sure of quality local produce in your pancakes. The house cider is excellent too.

Guingamp

La Boissière €€€ (€ set lunch)
90 rue de l'Yser, T02 96 21 06 35, restaurant-la-boissiere.com.
Tue-Fri 1200-1330, 1915-2100, Sat 1915-2100, Sun 1200-1330.
Excellent service of superb food in a dining room that manages to feel both elegant and cosy. Chef Thomas Montfort changes the menu regularly, offering a very reasonable no-choice three-course lunch on weekdays (maybe mussels, salmon with black olive sauce and Breton *far*) and à la carte in the evening. Attention to detail is evident – from the 1950s-style washroom to a blissful plate of home-made sweets with coffee.

Le Crêperie du Roy €
4 rue aux Blés,
T02 96 43 75 36.
Closed Tue evening and Sun.
Delicious *galettes* of all sorts here: try the ham, cheese and onion stuffed 'Guingampaise' with a potato on top. There are also hot salads and a cheap daily dish such as *blanquette de veau*. This place is popular with local workers.

Lac de Guerlédan

Auberge Grand Maison €€€-€€
1 rue Léon Le Cerf, Mur-de-Bretagne, T02 9628 5110, auberge-grand-maison.com.
Not so much a meal as an eating experience! Christophe Le Fur has been awarded a Michelin star for his skilful and inventive menus. Delights include a *navarin* of lobster, *brochette* of monkfish and mini beef tournedos. The lunch menu *Retour du Marché* at €25 is an incredible three-course bargain, accompanied by freshly baked rolls. Desserts are all drool-worthy. The beautifully laid dining room is in the capable hands of a very young team, who combine professionalism with natural charm.

Auberge du Guerlédan €€-€
35 rue Roc'Hell, Caurel, T02 96 26 35 16.
Daily mid-Jul and Aug, otherwise closed Tue and Wed.
This charming and popular *auberge* has good-value three-course menus. Traditional dishes include the very Breton grilled *andouillette* (tripe sausage) or a meltingly tender pork filet with mushrooms. There are also snails on offer, an uncommon occurrence in Brittany restaurants.

Café de l'Abbaye €
Bon Repos, T02 96 24 91 06.
Apr-Nov 0830-2130, Nov-Apr 1000-2000.
This busy café/brasserie, highly popular with tourists, has a basic menu of sandwiches, omelettes and quiches. The daily specials, such as *moules frites,* are warmly recommended by locals. Or just have an ice cream in the delightful location, sitting on the terrace across the water from the abbey ruins, and watch the world go by.

Crêperie de Bon Repos €
Bon Repos, St-Gelven, T02 96 24 86 56.
Open all year, closed Mon except holidays.
This crêperie gets very busy, especially with locals, and as everything is freshly and carefully cooked, be prepared for a wait. There are no frills and fancies on the menu, but the *blé noir* crêpes are excellent, with an unusual light and delicately crisp texture. Fillings are generous.

Cafés & bars
Thématique
Place de l'Eglise, Mur-de-Bretagne, T02 96 26 01 35, thematique.net.
Open 0900-1800, closed Wed, Sun 1100-1400.
Very pleasant English-owned café and *salon du thé*, with bookshop and internet access. You can have drinks and sandwiches or salads inside or on the terrace overlooking the little market square.

Lac de Guerlédan.

Entertainment

St-Brieuc

Each Thursday and Friday evening in July and August, **Les Nocturnes** bring music and theatre to the streets. From punk and garage to clowns and puppets, there's something for every taste and age.

Côte de Goëlo

Festival du Chant Marin, Paimpol, see page 141.

Dinan

Bars & clubs
The Rue de la Chaux in the old town is locally known as the 'rue de la soif' (street of thirst) as it's *the* place to enjoy evening drinks. Together with the nearby Rue du Cordonnerie, Rue de la Mittric and Rue du Petit Pain you should be able to find music every evening, summer and winter. For the atmosphere of a club, there's the **Le Rive Gauche** (T02 96 87 56 77, 1800-0500) at 4 and 6 rue du Port. More upmarket is **Le Patio** (T02 96 39 84 87, lepatiobar. fr, open every day 1100-0100, Sun from 1700) at 9 place du Champs-Clos, with music every weekend in summer and themed nights about once a month otherwise.

Lamballe

Each Thursday at 1730 in July and August, the Haras (National Stud)

puts on an equestrian spectacle, showing off the paces of horses and riders.

Lac de Guerlédan

Bon Repos Son et Lumière
pays-conomor.com.
Every August there are five performances of this extraordinarily elaborate show, which begins as darkness falls. A huge audience watches energetically performed excerpts from Breton history against the façade of the ruined abbey, cleverly lit as a changing backdrop. An Iron Age village, galloping horses and packs of hounds add to the drama. Good fun for all ages.

Shopping

St-Brieuc

Food & drink
Patisserie du Theatre
3 rue Michelet, T02 96 33 41 68.
0845-1915, closed Mon and Sun afternoon.
Tiny shop with delicious cakes and coffee, also chocolate and sweets that would be suitable for presents, attractively gift-wrapped if required.

Terre de Terroirs
5 rue St-Gilles, T02 96 33 02 01.
Tue-Fri 0900-1300, 1530-1900, Sat 0800-1300, 1500-1900, Sun 1000-1200.
Delicatessen of minimalist decor selling superb regional products such as cheeses, cold meat, foie gras and smoked salmon, for a superior picnic.

The Trégor

Clothing
La Goélette
135 rue de Saint-Guirec, Ploumanac'h, T02 96 91 40 90.
Feb to mid-Nov daily 0930-1930 (except Sat and Sun morning).
A treasure trove of marine fashion Breton-style, this store is packed with all the well-known makes, such as Le Glazik and Armor-Lux, for men, women and children.

Activities & tours

Food & drink
Au Fournil Gourmand
16 place du Général Leclerc, Lannion.
Tues-Sat 0730-1930, Sun 0730-1300.
Despite changing from its famous wood-fired oven to gas for baking, the quality here is still excellent. Pizzas and fruit tarts are delicious, or try their Flûte Gana speciality bread.

Dinan

Arts & crafts
Maurice and Evelyne Roinel
Artistes Verriers, *66 rue du Petit Fort, T02 96 39 93 31.*
Easter-end Sep 1000-1300, 1430-2000, otherwise 1000-1200, 1400-1800.
Imaginative jewellery, mirrors, ornaments and sculptures, most attractively displayed, from these specialists in glass and ceramics. Pick up an original present, from as little as €5.

Food & drink
Barnabé
82 rue du Petit Fort, T02 96 85 03 12.
Daily 0800-2000.
This baker's shop at the bottom of Rue du Petit Fort has delicious cakes made to traditional Breton recipes, as well as salted caramels and excellent cider to take home.

Market
If you're in Dinan on Thursday morning for the market, make a beeline for the stall of Erika Hicks, a local cheesemaker who produces superb organic Cheddar (yes, in France) and also the French cheese *tome*.

Guingamp & the Argoat

Art & clothing
Chanvrière St-Antoine
Nr Lanrivain, T02 96 36 57 12, lchanvre.com.
Jun-Sep daily 0900-1900, Oct-May Mon-Fri 0900-1200, 1400-1800.
Surprising range of products derived from hemp. Lovely clothes and bags, fabric, soap and body scrub, oils and chocolate. Drinks available while you browse.

Lac de Guerlédan

Souvenirs
Les Mineraux de l'Abbaye
Abbaye de Bon Repos, St-Gelven, T02 96 24 80 41, mineraux-abbaye.com.
Jul and Aug every day 1100-1230 and 1430-1900, Sun all year.
A shop full of gorgeous things in an old abbey building. Quality jewellery, crystals of every shape and colour, and a selection of Breton minerals such as *staurotides*.

Côte de Goëlo

Boat trips
Vedettes de Bréhat
T02 96 55 79 50, vedettesdebrehat.com.
Ferries to the Ile de Bréhat from the Pointe de l'Arcouest, a trip of 10 minutes (return journey, adults €8.50, children over four €7). On certain days they also offer four-hour sailings up the Trieux estuary, with a long stop at the Château de Roch Jagu (€18/12.50). Booking is advised in summer.

Train trips
La Vapeur du Trieux
Av Général de Gaulle, Paimpol, T08 92 39 14 27, vapeurdutrieux.com.
This steam train runs along the Trieux valley between Pontrieux and Paimpol, stopping at the Maison de Traou-Nez, once the centre of a famous mystery murder. Sample local products served by costumed waitresses and listen to Breton musicians. Return trip, adults €22, children €11. Advance booking is recommended.

The Trégor

Boat trips
Vedettes de Perros-Guirec
Gare Maritime, T02 96 91 10 10, armor-decouverte.fr
A boat trip around the Sept-Iles is a must for bird lovers. Various options are available – a

two-hour trip including the islands and Pink Granite Coast is €16 for an adult, €10 for children. Some trips make a short landing on the Ile aux Moines.

Flights
Aéro-Club de la Côte de Granite
T02 96 48 47 42, accg.asso.fr.
From Lannion, you can take a flight over the Pink Granite Coast lasting 15 minutes (€65 for two people), or go further afield to the Côtes des Ajoncs or above the Manoirs of the Léguer valley, with 30 minutes at €105.

Waterparks
Armoripark
Bégard, T02 96 45 36 36, armoripark.com.
Apr-Sep, 1100-1800 (1900 in summer). €7-11.

Children will love a visit to this aquatic park, where there are many fun pools, bumper boats, trampolines, playgrounds (including one for toddlers only) and farm animals.

Dinan

Cultural tours
Jaman IV
Port de Dinan, T02 96 39 28 41, vedettejamaniv.com.
This cruiser provides a one-hour trip on the Rance with commentary (English for groups of six-plus) through the lock at Léhon. Boats leave the Port de Dinan every day in July and August, and every day except Monday April to June, September to October. €11/7.

Lac de Guerlédan

Boat trips
Vedettes de Guerlédan
Beau Rivage, Caurel, T02 96 28 52 64, guerledan.com.
Apr-Oct.
Take a tour on the lake with a cruise of 1½ hours, daily at 1500 in July and August, adults €7.50, children €4.50. Or enjoy a dining cruise – €37-59 depending on the chosen menu.

Cycling
VTT/Cycling
Lakes and their hilly surrounds provide a great variety of attractive cycling for all levels. At Jugon-les-Lacs, the Station VTT Arguenon-Hunaudaye (T02 96 31 70 75) by the lake has details of more than 200 km of well-marked cycling circuits, from 10-30 km. See also page 163.

Ile de Bréhat ferry.

Contents

International Festival of the Sea, Brest.

Introduction

Finistère is the most Breton part of Brittany, the starting point for the defence of Breton language and custom, proudly upheld in festivals such as the magnificent Festival de Cornouaille in beautiful Quimper, the departmental capital. Brest, a visually modern city, proclaims its effervescent maritime identity every four years (next time in 2012) in the Fête Maritime Internationale, attracting thousands of boats and hundreds of thousands of visitors. Smaller towns like Morlaix and Douarnenez add further layers of character to the dense history of an area full of contrasting experiences.

The End of the World is fittingly a place of extremes – the highest hills in Brittany, the tallest standing stone in France and the biggest waves, Atlantic breakers storming onto the superlative coastline of the Crozon Peninsula and Pointe du Raz. There's also a stunning landscape in the wild heather-covered moors and peat-bogs of the Monts d'Arrée. It's a place of legend and strong beliefs, a fitting context for one of the finest religious displays in Brittany in the parish closes.

What to see in...

...one day
There are plenty of options – laze on a quiet beach on the **Crozon Peninsula**; take a tour of the parish closes; visit **Brest** for the shops, then sail on the **Rade**; have a cultural day in **Quimper**'s excellent museums; walk or ride in the **Monts d'Arrée**, or visit the boat museum at **Douarnenez**.

...a weekend or more
Combine a trip to **Quimper** with a tour of **Pays Bigouden**, enjoy the open spaces and eco-museums of the **Monts d'Arrée**, visit **Océanopolis**, then take a boat to **Ouessant** and **Molène**.

Flower market at the foot of the ramparts of St-Corentin Cathedral, Quimper.

Quimper & Pays Bigouden

Quimper is a wonderful city, administrative capital of Finistère, and home to the famous Festival de Cornouaille each July. Smart modern shops line streets of bright medieval houses around the stunning cathedral and River Odet. To the southwest, Pays Bigouden is a bastion of distinctive customs and traditions, with two museums offering a taster of the very essence of Breton life in Pont l'Abbé and Le Guilvinec, an archetypal fishing port. The extraordinary coastlines around Penmarc'h and St-Guenolé admirably reflect the dangers and pleasures of the coast of Brittany.

Quimper.

Quimper is a busy place, historic and highly cultural, but with the successful aura of a small capital city. The word means 'confluence' (*kemper* in Breton), as the Steir and Frout meet the wide Odet here. Unusually the settlement was the domain of the bishop, and ducal authority only began across the Pont Médard near the Place Terre-au-Duc. The cathedral and the bishop's palace, now the Departmental Museum, dominate the ancient heart with its narrow cobbled streets. The oldest house, which dates back to the early 15th century, is to be found in Rue Treuz.

A town tour

Start in the Rue du Parc opposite the impressive Prefecture building on the quay. This was rebuilt after the Germans burnt it on being driven out by the Resistance.

Continue along the river past the *passerelles* (footbridges), a legacy of the south bank being lined by individual grand houses with their own personal bridges. The distinctive wrought-iron modern one is dedicated to Max Jacob; if the water is low you can see his portrait etched on the pillar below. This Quimper artist died in a concentration camp; an ironic twist is that the Ouest-France building across the river, in 'steamboat' style, was the design of Olier Mordrel, architect, Breton nationalist and German collaborator.

Go through the wall doorway by the pretty garden to the cathedral and the **Bishop's Palace**. The latter is mostly 17th century, renewed after fires during the Wars of Religion. The entrance hall of the superb Departmental Museum here is in the original kitchen of 1645, complete with well and bread ovens.

Stand opposite the cathedral's main entrance, at the end of the Rue de Kéréon, to look up at the spires and statue of King Gradlon on horseback; surprisingly both are 19th-century additions. The square here, Place St-Corentin, was the scene of the burning of statues of saints after the revolution.

Essentials

❶ Getting around Parking is easiest on the quay past the tourist office; the centre is small enough to walk around.

❷ Bus station For the local bus network, T02 98 95 26 27, qub.fr. For regional bus travel, see page 274.

❸ Train station Place Louis Armand. TGV links to Brest (1¼ hrs) and Paris (about 5 hrs). For regional train travel, see page 274.

❸ ATMs Crédit Agricole, 10 rue René Madec.

⊕ Hospital Avenue Yves Thépot, T02 98 52 60 60.

✚ Pharmacy 15 rue St-François.

➲ Post office Boulevard Amiral de Kerguelen.

❶ Tourist information Place de la Résistance, T02 98 53 04 05, quimper-tourisme.com, July and August 0900-1900, otherwise 0930-1230, 1330-1830. Finistère region: finisteretourisme.com.

The **Cathedral of St-Corentin** is famous for its crooked nave, achieved when work restarted after a long break because of the disruption of the Wars of Succession and 14th-century outbreaks of plague. The strange angle may have been because the newly adjoined bishop's palace forced this, or possibly because of problems with earlier foundations or the proximity of the river. More fancifully, some suggest it mirrors the incline of Jesus' head on the cross. An extra half-chapel inside on the south compensates for the angle.

In the south aisle the bronze tomb of Bishop Du Parc with a frieze of the seven Founding Saints of Brittany (see page 40) has attracted the custom of performing a mini Tro Breizh pilgrimage here, by walking around the tomb, touching seven points of the bishop's effigy. You can see which ones…

Tip…

Ask at the tourist office about the Pass Quimper, which gives a reduction on entry fees to main attractions if you visit four (€10).

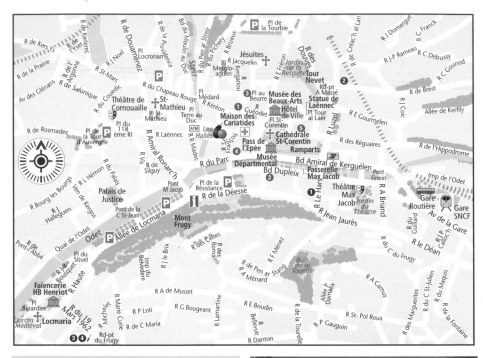

Quimper listings

❶ Sleeping

1 **Escale Oceania** *6 rue Théodore Le Hars*
2 **Hôtel Gradlon** *30 rue de Brest*
3 **Hôtel Oceania** *17 rue du Poher (off map)*
4 **Orangerie de Lanniron** *Allée de Lanniron (off map)*

❶ Eating

1 **Bistrot à lire** *18 rue des Boucheries*
2 **Café des Arts** *4 rue Ste-Catherine*
3 **Crêperie du Sallé** *6 rue du Sallé*
4 **L'Epée** *14 rue du Parc*
5 **Le Saint Co** *20 rue du Frout*

Locmaria, Quimper.

On the wall at the east end is the statue and skull of Santig Du, the Little Black Saint, a Franciscan who helped the poor in Quimper and died during the plague of 1349. For 500 years he has been invoked to help find lost items – many today continue this custom, placing loaves of bread on the table below in thanks.

In the north aisle a painting shows Père Maunoir receiving the gift of the Breton tongue from an angel (see page 33). He came from eastern Brittany and therefore did not speak Breton when he was called to succeed Michel Le Nobletz in missionary work in Basse Bretagne. A miracle or clever 17th-century marketing?

It's worth looking at the Chapel of St-Corentin – the stained-glass window shows an early crêpe pan!

Continue along the Rue de Frout behind the cathedral and then left past the former ramparts. You can see the only tower remaining, the **Tour de Nevet**. Go up the steps just beyond into the **Jardin de la Retraite**, a beautiful refuge, overlooked by the huge Jesuit chapel.

Exit at the other end of the garden and turn left then second right to view old houses in **Place du beurre** and **Rue du Sallé**. A restaurant adorned by caryatid sculptures is in the nearby **Rue du Guéodet**. Turn down to the **indoor market** (Les Halles) in Rue St-François, where you can stock up for lunch with all manner of enticing food, or perhaps have a crêpe made freshly to order. Then continue to the Pont Médard via Rue de Kéréon with its fashionable shops.

Cross the bridge over the Steir, then go left through the square and along **Rue René Madec**. The painted panel at No 5 records this man's extraordinary achievement. Born in Quimper in

Max Jacob

Max Jacob (1876-1944) was a poet, essayist and painter, living in Paris amongst the artists of Montmartre as the Cubist movement developed. He was a friend of Picasso, Modigliani, Cocteau and British painter Kit Wood.

Born a Jew in Quimper, he converted to Catholicism at the age of 40, after seeing visions of Christ. He began to write and paint on religious subjects, and retired to the abbey at St-Benoît-sur-Loire. He was arrested by the Nazis in 1944 and taken to Drancy where he died two weeks later.

1736 of humble origins, he went to sea, and served in India for the Compagnie des Indes. He later entered the private army of the Grand Mogul, and was made a nabob. Continue ahead to return to the Odet and tourist office below **Mount Frugy**, which is a good place for a pause or a climb for views over the city. A cult of the Goddess Reason was set up here at the time of the Revolution.

After lunch, take a peaceful stroll along the Odet to **Locmaria**, the oldest settlement. Pottery was a tradition here even in Roman times and it was revived as a major industry in 1690 by Jean-Baptiste Bousquet. The works of Henriot are still operational today – there is a large shop selling all kinds of pottery with the famous colourful naïf designs. You can also take a tour of the factory to see how the pieces are made. If eating is more appealing, there's a lovely biscuit shop too.

The church of **Notre Dame de Locmaria** is a thrilling example of Romanesque architecture, with remains of the 12th-century cloister through a side door. The **medieval gardens** opposite by the river are a delightful place to take a rest.

Musée Départemental Breton

1 rue du Roi Gradlon, T02 98 95 21 60.
Jun-Sep daily 0900-1800, Oct-May 0900-1200, 1400-1700 (closed Mon, Sun morning and public holidays). €4.
Map: Quimper, p184.

Did you know…?

The little round markers with the date 2000 on many buildings show the unprecedented flood levels in December of that year, when shops were underwater.

Beaux Arts Museum, Quimper.

Allow at least an hour to visit the excellent displays here. Modernity blends in with the antiquity of the building, the former Bishop's Palace. The 16th-century turning stair in the Rohan tower has a carved newel post and parasol finish at the top. The exhibition starts on the ground floor with prehistory, Gallo-Romano deities and Roman coin hoards. Religious art of the Middle Ages includes the tombs of knights and statuary, such as the figure of St-Trémeur holding his severed head. Upstairs there are many examples of Breton costumes in all their intricate details and exquisitely carved wooden furniture, together with a display of Quimper pottery. Look out for 1920s ceramics by Pierre Toulhoat, which manage to amalgamate a plethora of Breton motifs in colourful scenes, and an amusing black and white ensemble of peasants and cow by Mathurin Méheut.

Musée des Beaux Arts

40 place St-Corentin, T02 98 95 45 20, musee-beauxarts.quimper.fr.
Open 1000-1200, 1400-1800, closed Tue (except in Jul and Aug), Nov-Mar closed Sun morning. €4.50. Map: Quimper, p184.

Here you'll find a wealth of Breton domestic and outdoor scenes like the Pardon of Kergoat by Jules Breton with its sharp contrasts of celebration and destitute observers. Another room illustrates Breton legends – 'Les Lavandières de la Nuit' (1861) by Yan Dargent shows an unfortunate traveller ensnared by a herd of flying sheets. The most famous tale is St-Guénolé persuading King Gradlon to throw his daughter Dahut into the waves.

The Salle Max Jacob has a striking portrait by Cocteau, but it's the strange painting showing a sort of martyrdom of Jacob, by Pierre de Belay, that really lingers in the mind. It was painted 10 years before Jacob's death.

Upstairs there are European old masters and the Pont-Aven school (see page 47) Emile Bernard, Sérusier, Seguin and Maxime Maufra are all represented, plus a goose by Gauguin.

Five of the best

Free activities in Quimper

❶ Visit the **cathedral**.
❷ Climb **Mont Frugy**.
❸ Visit the medieval garden in **Locmaria**.
❹ Look at the eclectic display cases in the **Passage de l'Epée** off the **Rue du Parc**.
❺ Admire the displays and enjoy the delicious smells of the **indoor food market**.

Pays Bigouden

Pont l'Abbé

14 km southwest of Quimper.

This very Breton town is set on an estuary with lovely walks down to Loctudy. It's a place of simple appeal, unspoilt by tourism. Each July the Fêtes des Brodeuses (embroiderers) is celebrated with costumed parades and music filling the streets.

This was the crossing point for the monks at Loctudy – hence the name – and Pont l'Abbé retains the formidable keep of the former château of the Barons du Pont, now an excellent museum. It was partly destroyed in the rebellion of the Bonnets Rouge in 1675 (see page 35), and reprisals for that uprising can be seen in the truncated tower of the church of Lambour, with its fine carvings, just across the water. On the riverside near the Eglise des Carmes, which has a resonant 15th-century rose window, is the moving Bigouden memorial of grieving women by François Bazin.

Musée Bigouden (Château des Barons du Pont, T02 98 66 09 03, museebigouden.fr, Apr-May Tue-Sun 1400-1800, Jun-Sep daily 1000-1230, 1400-1830, €3.50). The tall lace coiffe has become an image synonymous with Brittany. The name Bigouden comes from this headdress, and its vital story, linked to Breton identity, is told here, partly in the words and experience of individuals. Visiting this museum of social history also allows a look at

Around the region

Phare Eckmuhl, Penmarc'h.

Penmarc'h

12 km southwest of Pont l'Abbé.

This southwestern tip of Brittany, Penmarc'h ('horse's head' in Breton) was once a major European trading centre, at the turning-point between north and south. The ship motifs decorating the large church here reflect the prosperity brought by the sea in medieval times. Today you can appreciate the extreme difficulties of navigation around this area by climbing the 272 steps of the lighthouse. The magnificent **Phare Eckmuhl** (Apr-Sep 1030-1830) was constructed from Kersanton granite in the 1890s after the daughter of one of Napoleon's generals left a legacy for a lighthouse in a dangerous environment to honour her father's memory.

St-Guénolé

15 km southwest of Pont l'Abbé.

Chaucer's Franklin's Tale begins with reference to the fearful *blakes rokkes* of Penmarc'h, the rocks that Dorigen fears will cost the life of her husband on return from England, so she hires a magician to make them disappear. Follow signs to **Les Rochers**, and climb carefully up to the railing. The iron cross on the rock ahead marks the spot where family members of the Prefect of Finistère were swept away to their deaths when picnicking in 1870.

A safer spot is **Porz Carn**, one of the nicest family beaches imaginable. Opposite the car park is the **Musée de la Préhistoire** (Jun-Sep Mon-Fri 1000-1230, 1400-1730, Oct-May Mon-Fri 1100-1200, 1400-1700) with many indoor and outdoor exhibits from archaeological digs in Finistère. There's a rare Dark Age exhibit, with the remains of some of the first Bretons from the nearby burial ground (c AD 50-1000) of St-Urnel.

the keep of the former château, though it's odd to be looking at a 1960s formica kitchen one minute and climbing a medieval turning stone staircase the next. Interesting exhibits look at the changing world of the area, particularly the role of women and the wearing of the famous headdress, at work and play – watching football, for example. There are some beautiful displays of Breton costumes and lacework, the latter becoming an important source of income for families on the breadline after the failure of the sardine catch in the early 20th century.

Le Guilvinec

11 km southwest of Pont l'Abbé.

The essence of life by the sea is epitomized in Le Guilvinec, third fishing port of France. A visit to **Haliotika: La Cité de la Pêche** (Le Port, T02 98 58 28 38, haliotika.com, Jul and Aug Mon-Fri 0930-1900, Sat and Sun 1500-1830, Mar-Jun and Sep 1000-1230, 1430-1830, Oct Mon-Fri 1500-1800, €5.50/€3.50), gives an insight into the marine world of work with displays on different types of boats, fish of all kinds and a recreation of workers' life at sea. Much is relayed through the life and words of one former fisherman Claude Garo, which gives a personal perspective. There are also colourful exhibits for children and a chance to sit in the captain's hot-seat.

Pointe de la Torche

12 km southwest of Pont l'Abbé.

On the headland itself is a large Neolithic dolmen, in striking contrast with the German fortifications around it. The magnificent beach, exposed to the driving wind and waves of the Atlantic, is a well known surfing mecca, and many come just to watch the performers. If you want to join in, the **Ecole de Surf de Bretagne** (T02 98 58 53 80) has a base here.

You can walk for many miles up the beach, past bunkers and, at Croaz an Dour (3 km), remains of the factory where the Germans ground pebbles into concrete for all their defensive works, at great cost to the natural protective pebble banks of this exposed coast.

Tronoën

11 km southwest of Pont l'Abbé.

The chapel here is often called the Cathedral of the Dunes, as its spire is visible for miles. The calvary is possibly the oldest in Brittany (c 1450). In granite, with statues in darker Kersanton, parts are eroded, but you can clearly make out scenes such as Ste-Veronica and the face of Christ imprinted on her handkerchief, and the three kings bringing gifts. In fact, there are 30 scenes, perhaps the most remarkable being that of Mary with naked breasts and tousled hair on the lower frieze.

Cathedral of the Dunes, Tronoën.

Brest & around

Brest is a lively maritime city, with several ports, many major nautical events and a formidable history. Another draw is Océanopolis, one of the most visited attractions in France. The Rade de Brest is the largest roadstead in Europe, a veritable inland sea protected by a narrow channel from the might of the Atlantic Ocean. The pretty port of Le Conquet thrives on fish and ferries to Molène and Ouessant, which has a lighthouse museum. Inland, near the interesting town of St-Renan, is the king of all menhirs.

Brest.

On first sight Brest is not particularly attractive. A new tramway is being built (to open 2012), after the last one closed some 40 years ago, and the main square, Place de la Liberté, is a wasteland of concrete, surrounded by fast-food outlets. However, there is a lot more to the city and its many attractions than the superficial impression of modern regularity. And it's important to bear in mind the positive symbolism of the city's resurrection from the ashes.

Brest is essentially a post-war place, thrown up in a hurry to re-house the population after devastating bombing in the Second World War when the German submarine base was a prime allied target. Since the 17th century it has been the main French naval base on the Atlantic coast. Allow at least a day for the city itself and another day for visiting Océanopolis.

Rue de Siam

Map: Brest, p192.

This is the main street and principal shopping area, leading up from the Pont de Recouvrance over the river to the Place de la Liberté, where you can find the tourist office. The name comes from the exotic visit of ambassadors from the King of Siam in 1686, on their way to Paris and the court of Louis XIV.

Cours Dajot

Map: Brest, p192.

This long promenade above the commercial port and new docks 'Port du Château' is the best place for a stroll, with fantastic views over the Rade. It was built in 1769 by convicts from the naval prison and later extended to nearly 600 m, starting near the château. The tall monument is to American naval losses in the First World War, rebuilt in identical style after being destroyed by the Germans in 1941. After dark, the Cours is a popular gay meeting place.

Essentials

❶ Getting around It's easy to get around the grid-plan streets in the centre of Brest on foot. Easiest parking (free) is down by the commercial port (five minutes' walk up to the château), or there are underground car parks near the Halles St-Louis and Place de la Liberté.

❷ Bus station The bus station (T08 10 81 00 29) is in Place du 19ème RI. Bus information from Bibus Accueil, 33 avenue G Clemenceau, bibus.fr. You can get a bus (line 15) to Océanopolis, which is 3 km from the centre. Buses also run to Le Conquet (line 31) and St-Renan (line 32). For regional bus travel, see page 274.

❸ Train station The train station (T36 35, sncf.fr) is next to the bus station in Place du 19ème RI. For regional train travel, see page 274.

❹ ATMs Main Post Office,13 avenue Georges Clemenceau, 24 hour at Moulin Blanc.

❺ Hospital Hôpital Morvan, 2 avenue Foch, T02 98 22 33 33.

❻ Pharmacy 36 rue de Siam or 2 place de la Liberté.

❼ Post office 90 rue de Siam or Place Général Leclerc.

❽ Tourist information Office de Tourisme, Place de la Liberté, T02 98 44 24 96, brest-metropolis-tourisme.fr

Eglise St-Louis

Map: Brest, p192.

The first stone of this extraordinary structure was laid in 1955, after an earlier church was destroyed in 1944 by the Germans. It is a huge luminous space, with an incredible capacity of 2500 people, and at 85x27 m, the largest post-war church in France. Most expressive is the vast Wall of Lamentation, a contrast to the light pouring in symbolically from the east through stunning plain-glass windows by Maurice Rocher, with stylized figures – Old Testament greats and four Breton saints – like a design for chess-pieces. Behind a row of towering concrete pillars, the wooden confessionals lining the side-aisle look more like changing rooms or saunas. By the entrance is the decorative blue glass baptistery with its modernist font.

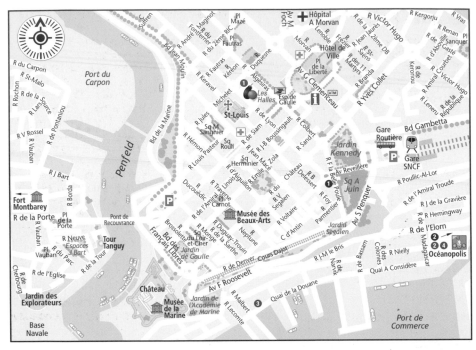

Brest listings

❶ Sleeping
1 Hôtel Agena *10 rue Frégate la Belle Poule*
2 Hôtel La Plaisance *41 rue du Moulin Blanc* (off map)

❶ Eating
1 Amour de la Pomme de Terre *23 rue des Halles St-Louis*
2 Crêperie Blé Noir *Vallon du Stang-Alar* (off map)
3 Le Crabe Marteau *8 quai de la Douane* (off map)
4 Ma Petite Folie *Rue Notre Dame du Bon Port*

Eglise St-Louis.

Jacques Prévert

The poem *Barbara* by Jacques Prévert, published in 1945, is a haunting evocation of Brest before and after the horror of the war, built around a brief glimpse of a young woman in the Rue de Siam running into the arms of a lover, contrasting the soft sea rain over the city that day with the ghastly aftermath: *It rains without stopping in Brest, as it rained before, But no longer the same, for all is destroyed, It rains the terrible desolation of loss.*

Tip…

Visit the Tour Tanguy last, as it will put all that you have seen into context and fill in many of the blanks.

Château de Brest/Museé de la Marine

Rue du Château, T02 98 22 12 39, musee-marine.fr.
Daily Apr-Sep 1000-1830, Oct-Dec and Feb-Mar 1330-1830 (closed Jan). €5.
Map: Brest, p192.

The former château, which remarkably survived the war almost unscathed, is now home of the Atlantic naval command and the National Marine Museum. A Roman *castellum* has left distinctive stonework separated by layers of tiles, visible on the way to the entrance. The castle was held by the English for 50 years in the 14th century during the Wars of Succession, and developed later by Vauban for Atlantic coast defence. The well laid out museum has important nautical exhibits, but the outdoor space is especially interesting with its perspective of the Rade and Penfeld estuary, where the arsenal and construction yards once stood. The Tour Azenor adds a romantic touch, with the legend of a young pregnant wife imprisoned by the jealousy of her stepmother.

Museé des Beaux Arts

24 rue Traverse, T02 98 00 87 96.
Tue-Sat 1000-1200, 1400-1800, Sun 1400-1800, closed Mon. €4.
Map: Brest, p192.

This gallery has an interesting variety of Breton scenes on the ground floor, including many examples of the Pont-Aven school (see page 47). Upstairs are European paintings from the 17th to 19th centuries, and the basement houses temporary exhibitions. The lower rooms are dominated by those essential themes of Breton-inspired art – the sea and women. Bernard and Maufra are well-represented, as are Sérusier, Lacombe and Séguin – look out for the soft and pensive features of the latter's pastel study *La Bretonne*. A study for the ceiling of the theatre in Rennes by Lemordant shows a chain of Breton dancers strutting their stuff up in the clouds. Offerings from Paul Sérusier include a pair of paintings, with women carrying water and laundry bags. A 20th-century perspective is that of the inimitable Mathurin Méheut with his huge brown and grey study of fish (1931).

La Tour Tanguy

Recouvrance.
Jun-Sep daily 1000-1200, 1400-1900, Oct-May Wed and Thu 1400-1700, Sat and Sun 1400-1800. Free.
Map: Brest, p192.

This restored 14th-century round tower on the banks of the Penfeld is now a museum devoted to the history of Brest. The many fascinating exhibits are engagingly visual, such as huge diaporamas including one of the famous battle scene of the Cordelière, a ship built for Anne de Bretagne and blown up by its own commander in a notorious fight with the English at the mouth of the Rade in 1512. A series of photographs of pre-war Brest strike home the incredible transformation of the city, and paintings show the amazing bustle of the port and arsenal in its heyday. It's strange to see pictures of the old tramway – abolished only in 1970 in the interests of modern development and now being reinstated.

Nearby is the **Jardin des Explorateurs**, with a high walkway giving excellent views over the Rade.

Around the region

Moulin Blanc

3 km east of Brest.

This is the pleasure port, the largest on the Atlantic coast. Many major and minor sailing events are held here, and there's a constant buzz of aquatic activity, with lots to watch from the bars and promenade, even for non-sailors. Trips with Azenor start here (see Activities & tours, page 227), and behind the port are the white pavilions of Océanopolis.

Océanopolis

Port de Plaisance, Moulin Blanc, T02 98 34 40 40, oceanopolis.com.
May to mid-Sep daily 0900-1800 (0900-1900 in Jul and Aug), Oct-Apr 1000-1700, closed Mon except in school holidays. €16.50. €11.

This marine life centre is hard to beat for entertainment and education. Apart from the living exhibits, there is an emphasis on the explanatory and informative, with many films and interactive features. Adults and children cannot fail to be entranced not only by perennial favourites, such as penguins and seals, but also the mesmeric tropical shark tanks and luminous jellyfish. Mammals, fish and oceanic plants of every imaginable shape, size and colour are on display. The huge site is divided into Temperate (with an emphasis on Brittany), Tropical and Polar exhibitions.

Conservatoire Botanique National & the Valley of Stang-Alar

3 km east of Brest.

Almost a hidden valley on the edge of the city near Océanopolis, this is a great place to avoid crowds in verdant surroundings. A pretty stream connects a series of lakes over 2 km, with many paths and picnic areas, as well as a good crêperie (see Eating, page 219) and playground. The work of the Conservatoire Botanique National is to preserve endangered species of plants, through conservation and propagation, including threatened native species of the Armorican peninsula. The exhibition room is free, but you pay to visit the greenhouses with their different temperature and soil-type zones (Jul to mid-Sep Sun-Thu 1400-1730), a must for serious plant lovers.

St-Renan

10 km northwest of Brest.

Founded by the Irish monk Ronan (see Locronan, page 203), this town rose to be capital of the area until losing this status to Brest in 1681. It has always been a busy commercial centre, famous for its markets, today held on Saturdays. The Vieux-Marché is surrounded by medieval merchants' houses, the best of all (1641) now housing a crêperie (see Eating, page 219). At the beginning of the 19th century, there were 78 inns for 179 houses here!

The **Maison du Patrimoine** (all year Sat 1030-1200, plus Jul and Aug Tue-Sat 1500-1800) is a little museum of local history in Rue St-Mathieu. There is also a historical trail to follow around the town – a leaflet is available from the tourist office. In the mid-20th century, the excavation of pewter ore became a major, but short-lived, source of prosperity here. The series of lakes around the town are a reminder of this industry, and they now provide good leisure facilities. Lac de Ty Colo has a walking circuit, and fishing and sailing are possible.

Menhir de Kerloas Some 4 km west of St-Renan is the tallest standing stone in France. The Menhir de Kerloas, dating to c 3000 BC, is nearly 11 m high and has the nickname The Hunchback because of two protrusions. Newly-weds would rub against these as part of a fertility ritual, in the hope of having

Tip...

Going to the limit? Not far from St-Renan is the westernmost point of France, the Pointe de Corsen.

sons. The stone on its rise is visible from 30 km away and may have been sited to be seen from the sea, possibly part of a chain with the many other menhirs in this area.

Fort du Dellec

8 km west of Brest.

The Goulet or entry channel to the Rade de Brest is lined by fortifications ranging from Vauban forts to German bunkers. The coastal path passes Fort du Dellec, which is now a public park, open every day. The gun-batteries have become viewing platforms with superb views over the water and across to the Pointe des Espagnols. Despite its history, this is a lovely tranquil spot for picnics or playing games. In term time it is very popular with students from the nearby Technopole.

Le Conquet

22 km west of Brest.

This most picturesque of fishing ports is still a working harbour, and ferries to the islands of Molène and Ouessant leave from here daily. You can watch this spectacle from the Place St-

Conservatoire Botanique National.

A tragic tale

On 16 June 1896 the steamship *Drummond Castle* hit the rocks west of the island of Molène on the last night of its voyage from South Africa to England, and sank within minutes. Fishermen saved two sailors and one passenger, but the other 244 people on board perished. Recovered bodies were buried in the churchyard on Molène. The islanders received practical thanks from Queen Victoria who paid for a cistern, which still stands near the church, to relieve the perennial freshwater problem. A tiny museum on the island tells the story of the disaster.

Christophe, where women used to wait anxiously for the return of the fishermen's ships.

The majority of houses in the village were destroyed in an English attack in 1558, but the fine Maison des Seigneurs (1510) in Rue Troadec (its three stair turrets are visible from across the estuary) survived the onslaught. By contrast, the modern hotel on the hill above the port must be one of the ugliest and most inappropriate buildings in Brittany.

The main church contains the tomb of Michel de Nobletz, the influential 17th-century missionary in Brittany who invented painted 'maps' on sheepskin to tell biblical stories to illiterate peasants. The little chapel of Dom Michel above the port in Le Conquet has some representations of these *taolennou*

Pointe St-Mathieu

There's a dramatic clifftop setting here for the skeletal remains of the ruined Benedictine **Abbaye St-Mathieu**. According to legend, Breton sailors brought the original relic, the skull of the Apostle St Matthew, back from Africa. The impressive fire-tower, which the monks operated as an early form of lighthouse, can still be seen, but is now dwarfed by the 19th-century version. Just below the abbey is a First World War memorial by sculptor René Quilivic. From the coastal path here are some fine views of the islands of Quéménez, Molène and Ouessant, and dolphins are a common sight.

The Crozon Peninsula

Called the Presqu'île de Crozon (almost an island), this long peninsula has many aspects, with the northern coast largely occupied by military installations. The Atlantic seaboard has towering cliffs interspersed by superb beaches, with the GR34 coastal path providing unforgettable views in return for a little exercise. The more energetic will find all manner of water sports readily available in Morgat or Camaret, both delightful ports.

Be aware that in August traffic flows into the resorts as continually as waves lap the shore. Access is either via Le Faou, a scenic route crossing the suspension bridge over the Aulne, or via Châteaulin below the lofty height of Menez Hom.

Crozon Peninsula.

Landévennec

Via D60, 7 km off the main road D791 (on to peninsula from Le Faou).

This tranquil waterside village, empty out of season, enjoys something of a microclimate, with palm trees and exotic flowers. There's a huge 20th-century abbey (the shop sells sweets made by the monks) on the hill, but down by the shore are the impressive remains of an earlier abbey, put into context by an excellent modern museum – **Musée de l'Ancienne Abbaye de Landévennec** (T02 98 27 35 90, musee-abbaye-landevennec.fr, Apr-Jun Sun-Fri 1000-1800, Jul-Aug daily 1000-1900, Sep daily 1000-1800, Oct-Mar Sun 1000-1700, €4.). This vividly presents the life of the Benedictine monks, including a recreated scriptorium with utensils and dyes used to produce the fine illustrated manuscripts. St-Guénolé, one of the most influential Breton saints, first settled here, but the site was later sacked by marauding Vikings in AD 913, as archaeological evidence shows. It's a beautiful spot, with herb gardens and apple orchards.

Crozon

Via D887, both roads into peninsula lead to Crozon.

The hub of the holiday area, Crozon is the place to stock up with provisions – there's plenty of options at the Wednesday market or shops, including a fishmonger, in the pretty centre around the church. The church has an extraordinary altarpiece of the 10,000 martyrs, which has the style of a comic strip, although the story it tells is the tragic one of a whole troop of soldiers put to death for their Christian faith by the Roman emperor Hadrian. The main tourist office for the area is in the former station on the ring road.

Camaret

8 km northwest of Crozon.

The first submarine tests were held in Camaret in 1801 after Napoleon commissioned the American Robert Fulton to develop his idea, but the town's

Swimming

The peninsula is paradise for swimmers, with many golden beaches, but it is essential to respect warning signs, especially on the exposed Atlantic coast. Here the currents and rocks are simply too dangerous. Try the sands around Camaret and Morgat and along the Bay of Douarnenez.

traditional claim to fame has been as a major lobster-fishing centre, and there are plenty of restaurants to sample the catch. The fishing port with its *criée* (fish auction) and the Centre Nautique are on the right immediately as you descend to the town. Ahead lies the natural curving *sillon* which encloses the pleasure-craft harbour. In the little back streets you will discover that Camaret is also a centre for artists of many kinds, with galleries freely open to visitors.

Next door to the tourist office, the **Maison du Patrimoine** (afternoons Jul and Aug) presents many aspects of the marine history of the area. For those not technically minded, the attraction of this workaday display is in the small details, like needles for the making and mending of nets, and fishermen's footwear, conjuring up a former way of life.

Tour Vauban (Apr-end Sep Tue-Sun 1400-1800, Jul and Aug daily, plus 1000-1200, €3). This distinctive terracotta-coloured tower was built under Vauban's auspices not a moment too soon. It saw action in 1694, successfully fending off an English attack that ended disastrously for the invaders (a nearby beach is called La Morte Anglaise). The displays inside the tower illustrate famous examples of Vauban's work in northern Finistère,

Tip...

When parking in Camaret, avoid the scrum at the end of the harbour by turning left at the Hotel Styvel. A usually almost empty car-park is just up ahead.

Beaches

❶ **Kerloc'h** The main road (D8) to Camaret passes this vast sandy beach with spectacular views.

❷ **Trez Rouz** A small sheltered beach, with red earth, pebbles and sand, which is good for sunbathing. It's just north of Camaret (via D335).

❸ **Pen Trez** Miles of sand with a café, not far from Menez Hom (signed off D887).

❹ **L'Aber** At the eastern end of the Bay of Morgat, with a rocky peninsula and fort to explore at low tide.

❺ **Morgat** A good family beach in the town centre.

and a vaulted guardroom has reconstruction paintings of the English offensive. The little marine church of Rocamadour nearby lost the top of its tower to an English cannonball in the same onslaught.

Alignments of Lagatjar/Manoir de Coecilian

Above Camaret on the way to the Pointe de Penhir is the Neolithic alignment of Lagatjar, where 143 stones form three lines, many others having been lost. Birdwatchers, keep your eyes open – there are often choughs to be seen around here. Just visible on the cliff top opposite are the towers of the Manoir de Coecilian. This eerie ruin was a noted centre of culture as the house of poet St-Pol-Roux. In 1940 German soldiers burst in and attacked the old man and his daughter after killing their servant. He died soon after and the house was bombed by Allied aircraft.

Musée de la Bataille de l'Atlantique

On the road between Camaret and the Pointe de Penhir, T02-98 27 92 58.
Jul and Aug 1000-1200, 1400-1800, Easter, Jun, Sep 1400-1800. €3.

Situated in a coastal old bunker, part of the Mur de l'Atlantique or Atlantic Wall, this museum tells the story of the conflict at sea between German and Allied forces, as submarines sought to destroy the supply ships that kept England going. It is a sobering and moving view of terrible loss and destruction. Churchill recognized that this struggle was a crucial factor in the war – 'we must never forget that everything depended on its outcome'.

The **Pointe de Penhir**, nearby, has a huge memorial to the Breton resistance and, beyond, a string of rocks known as the Tas de Pois (pile of peas) stretches out into the ocean.

Morgat & around

2 km south of Crozon.

This idyllic traditional holiday resort with its brightly painted houses was colonized in the 1920s by rich Parisians, whose lavish villas set the style of the surrounding hills. It's perfect for bucket-and-spade activities, with sweets, waffles and nougat stalls taking the place of candyfloss, or water sports. Boats leave from the port here for visits to the extraordinary **marine grottoes**.

Not far away is the **Maison des Minéraux** (Jul and Aug 1000-1900, May-Jun 1000-1200, 1400-1730, closed Sat, Sep-Apr 1400-1730, closed Sat) at St-Hernot, which presents the geology of the Crozon Peninsula. Displays of minerals and fossils hold children's interest too, but the biggest treat is the last room where fluorescent crystals are displayed. Wait for the lights to go out!

It's well worth an excursion to the wild west coast to see the remarkable Iron Age fort at **Lostmarc'h**. Those ready to clamber down – with care – to the beach can marvel at the geological oddity of pillow-lavas, which can be seen embedded in white limestone.

Marine grotto, Morgat.

Sports & activities

Diving

Presqu'ilemersion diving school (T06 18 05 91 76, presquilemersion.com), based in Crozon, is open all year round for exploring the rocky coastline of the peninsula. Novices and experienced divers can enjoy face-to-face encounters with the extraordinary inhabitants of the underwater world in all their weird and wonderful colours and shapes. Equipment can be hired, professional diving instructors accompany and an initiation session costs from €42. Courses for children are also available.

Horse riding

Whether you want to learn to ride in beautiful surroundings or simply enjoy a day on horseback around the lanes, **Les Petites Ecuries** (T06 62 87 13 09, les-petites-ecuries.chez-alice.fr) in Crozon welcomes visitors all year round. They offer an outing of one or two hours by the sea for novices or experienced riders. At the land end of the peninsula, the **Ferme Equestre de Neiscaouen** (T02 98 27 37 11) near Landévennec offers similar options. Phone in advance to make arrangements.

Sailing

Brittany Sail (brittanysail.co.uk), a RYA-recognized sailing school, offers sailing on their yacht, *Cornish Legend*, with as much or as little active participation as you require. For those who want qualifications, there are courses for beginners and serious sailors. The Competent Crew course covers simple manoeuvres, and the Day Skipper course (over five days) concentrates on seamanship, navigation and pilotage. Richard Curtis has been sailing in these waters for 30 years and will introduce you (and non-sailing partners along for the cruise) to the Rade de Brest and the Atlantic islands of Sein, Molène and Ouessant.

Accommodation is available in gîtes – see Sleeping, page 216.

Walking

The coastal path (GR34 – red and white waymarks) gives access to some of the most spectacular walking in Brittany. If you can manage the logistics of linear walking, this is more satisfying than circuits through the not-particularly-attractive interior. An exception to this is at Landévennec, where the forest provides some lovely paths. Much of the northern coast around Lanvéoc and the Ile-Longue submarine station is off-limits for military security. The best walking is from Camaret

to Morgat, a distance of about 40 km, making a fantastic two-day hike, but if you have less time or inclination, the short walk (6 km) from Camaret to the Pointe de Penhir has unbeatable sea views. Continuing to the wonderful sands of Kerloc'h doubles the distance, but you can return along quiet roads directly to Camaret.

The wildest walking is the 10 km from the Pointe de Dinan through Lostmar'ch to the Cap de la Chèvre, an unforgettable route where you will feel alone in the world outside July and August. The *gîte d'étape* for walkers at St-Hernot (see Sleeping, page 216) is easily accessible from the east or west coasts.

Water sports

For a whole variety of water sports, equipment hire and tuition, the **Centre Nautique de Crozon-** **Morgat** (T02 98 16 00 00, cncm.fr) is open throughout the year, with points on the beach and at the port in Morgat. You can enjoy the safe waters of the Bay of Morgat or Bay of Douarnenez for sailing (including motor and catarmaran), surfing and windsurfing, or why not learn to kitesurf? Sea-kayaking (single or double seat) can also be arranged at any time of the year. What a great, hands-on way to discover the fabulous marine grottoes of Morgat!

Douarnenez & Cap Sizun

The energetic town of Douarnenez, with its popular boat museum, is the gateway to Cap Sizun and the Pointe du Raz, one of the westernmost tips of France and an area of steep cliffs and dramatic Atlantic seascapes. It's a great choice for exhilarating coastal walking or cycling on small roads, with the Goyen estuary and Goulien reserve attracting many birdwatchers. For a rural contrast, picturesque Locronan, a location much in demand for filmsets, is just inland.

Construction of a small *crabier.*

Douarnenez

This is an energetic town of three ports: Rosmeur, the working fishing harbour, Treboul, packed with pleasure boats, and in between, the living boat museum of Port de Rhu. **Le Port-Musée** (Jul and Aug daily 1000-1900, Apr-Jun, Sep-Nov 1000-1230, 1400-1800, closed Mon, €6.20) is a fascinating, colourful collection of boats and boating paraphernalia. Outside on the water are further examples, which visitors can explore.

The history of Douarnenez is dominated by the humble sardine. Disappearance of stocks in the bay between 1902 and 1912 caused enormous hardship, forcing the local fishermen to adapt to new ways to fill the gap. 1924 saw a famous strike by sardine workers at the Usine Carnaud over appalling pay and conditions – social action has always been a feature of the town which elected the first communist mayor in France in 1921.

The green oasis of the **Plomarc'h**, which inspired artists such as Renoir and Boudin, has the remains of traditional workers' hamlets, a community farm with animals on show and a Roman factory where garum, a fish sauce, was made and exported. There are also fine views of the Bay of Douarnenez where the island of Ys, the Breton Atlantis, was traditionally situated.

The **tourist office** (T02 98 92 13 35, douarnenez-tourisme.com) is in Rue Dr Mével. The market is held in this square on Mondays, but fresh produce is available daily from Les Halles, the covered market.

Locronan

10 km east of Douarnenez.

Picturesque Locronan (sacred place of Ronan) has been the backdrop for many films, including Roman Polanski's *Tess*. The fine houses are a reflection of wealth brought to the town by the manufacture of sailcloth, first mentioned in 1469.

Locronan has long been associated with the creative arts and there are still many artisans working here today – in sculpture, ceramics, glassware and art.

Carved on the pulpit in the great church you can see the eventful story of St-Ronan, who first set up his oratory in the Bois du Nevet, site of a former Celtic *nemeton* or sacred grove of nature deities. He christianized this into a 12-km circuit representing the months of the Celtic year. Every six years (the next time is in 2013) La Grande Troménie is held – a celebratory walk around the 12 'stations', but each year there's a Petite Troménie

Cap Sizun

Pointe du Millier This point, with its lighthouse, has glorious views, but on the way you should divert into the woods to see the Moulin de Keriolet with an 8-m working wheel. The stream has a mini 'chaos' of granite boulders, and if you step across them and up the bank opposite you will see the stone boat in which Saint Conogan arrived on these shores (allegedly).

Pointe du Van This promontory is less busy than the Pointe du Raz opposite, but just as beautiful. The **Chapelle de St-They** honours a sixth-century monk from Great Britain. According to local legend, the chapel bell rings spontaneously to warn sailors of danger.

Don't miss the breathtakingly beautiful **Baie des Trépassés** (Bay of the Dead) nearby.

Pointe du Raz The visitor centre (required parking €5) is set 500 m back from the point to preserve the natural splendour of one of the most visited sites in France. It's a pity about the hideous statue of the Virgin overlooking the sea. This is not quite the most westerly point of France (see page 194), but the rocky heights are impressive. Offshore, the almost flat Ile de Sein is usually visible.

Cycling tour

This is quite a demanding route of 44 km around Cap Sizun starting from the harbour of Audierne. You'll enjoy pretty chapels, spectacular seascapes and the memorable Baie des Trépassés between the Pointe du Raz and Pointe du Van.

From the centre of Audierne bear right along the harbour towards the Embarcadère. Before that, just past the little chapel of St-Evette, turn right at a mini-roundabout uphill through old houses. At the top, follow right towards the *bourg* and then through the hamlets of Kerhoun, Creac'h, Brignéoc'h and Keromen. After this, turn left at a junction and proceed via Custrein to the **Chapelle de Tugen**.

This exceptional chapel (c 1550) in its walled enclosure has a 28-m tower and elaborately decorated interior. The saint is invoked against rabies and the rabid pain of toothache.

Keep to left of the chapel (signed Pointe du Raz) and continue uphill, bearing left and ahead towards the *bourg* of **Primelin**. At a fork, go right towards the centre. Keep left of the church, then turn left to the hamlet of Kermaléro. Just after it, turn right at the crossroads. At the next junction, go ahead to join the main road (the D784), turning left to cross **Le Loc'h**.

Continue uphill for 100 m (past two turns) then turn very sharp left, signed to Keringar. Go straight through, then turn off left (as the road bends right) through Toramor and on uphill. Where the road splits, either go right to rejoin the main road (500 m ahead) or first divert left uphill for 475 m to the **Chapelle de Notre-Dame du Bon Voyage**, situated on a high viewpoint. This chapel has seats and a picnic table nearby.

At the main road (the D784) turn left and continue to **Plogoff**, which has a bakery and refreshments. Carry on along the same road past the tiny chapel of St-Yves on the left. Continue through Kerguidy and past the **Biscuiterie** (in case you're hungry). Then turn right (the D607), signed Baie des Trépassés.

*Diversion: go straight on (2 km) to see the natural splendour of the **Pointe du Raz**, then return.*

Descend steeply on the D607 to the Etang de Laoual and the magnificent **Baie des Trépassés** (Bay of the Dead).

Diversion: to see the Chapelle St-Tugdual with its fontaine and lavoir in a pretty setting, follow the main road on for 200 m, then branch right and continue for 1 km.

Turn left just before the Relais Hotel and go up a narrow, very steep road all the way to the top – your reward will be spectacular views!

At the top, go left and then follow round right to a T-junction. Then go left to the **Chapelle St-They** and on round to the **Point du Van** (or right for information, toilets and café first).

St-They was a sixth-century monk who came from Great Britain. The T of his name has mutated from D (Dei) – in Cornwall his name is St Day. Return and take the D7 heading east (in the direction of Douarnenez).

Diversion: after 1 km, turn left to Castelmeur (800 m). This peninsula was fortified in the Iron Age, as weapons found here show. The defensive system consisted of four banks and three ditches. Excavation revealed 95 habitations on the slopes behind, indicated by patches of greener vegetation.

Continue on the D7 (past the windmill on the left) for 1.5 km and turn right (on a left bend), signed Poulc'haradeg.

Diversion: for the 40-ha Réserve du Cap Sizun continue ahead on the D7 for 5 km and then turn left where signed. Choughs, shags, fulmars, razorbills and many others make their homes here.

Go right at the split immediately after, on a single-track road, and left 1 km later at a T-junction. Continue to Cléden-Cap-Sizun, visible across a little valley. Then carry on ahead (on the D43) for 1.5 km to Quivillic. The **Chapelle de Langroas** is 300 m beyond on the roadside, by a stream and picnic table. Go straight on through Lezoualc'h (past a superb manor house with a stair turret on the right).

Diversion: 1 km later, go left for 350 m to Goulien, where the church has Celtic stele in its precinct, and nearby is the Maison du Vent, interpretation centre for the wind farm nearby.

Continue for 1.5 km through Kervoen.

Diversion: turn left (on a right-hand bend) for diversion (600 m) to the isolated Chapelle St-Laurent with an unusual triangular calvary, and a menhir nearby.

Continue 800 m to Les Quatre Vents, and turn right (the D43A), signed **Audierne**, and return there via a roundabout at Esquibien.

Morlaix & the Monts d'Arrée

Morlaix, with its attractive pleasure port, is dominated by the viaduct of the Paris–Brest railway, soaring above the medieval heart below. It's the first stop for those off the ferry at Roscoff eager for French coffee and provisions. Nearby is a collection of the best parish closes, a Breton phenomenon mostly found here in the district of Léon. The border between that and Cornouaille is the range of the Monts d'Arrée, the highest hills of Brittany, a special landscape positively oozing with legends and historical gems.

Below: Monts d'Arrée. Opposite: Morlaix's viaduct.

The town has a fabulous food market on Saturday mornings, in the Place Allende, and shoppers will also enjoy the cobbled streets of chic shops in half-timbered buildings. It's an atmospheric place squashed into a deep river valley, with a pleasure port alongside impressive buildings of a former tobacco factory, now being revitalized for cultural use. Above all this is the distinctive pink granite **viaduct**, 60 m high and 292 m long, constructed during the 1860s for the new Paris–Brest railway. It dwarfs the Flamboyant-Gothic **Eglise St-Melaine** (1489) which overlooks the Place des Otages and fine **town hall**. The square commemorates 60 hostages taken by the Germans in reprisal for an attack on an officers' mess. They were deported to Buchenwald, and few returned after the war.

Explore the old town via the *venelles*, stepped passageways criss-crossing three hillsides. The tourist office has a map of routes. Morlaix lost its castle after the Wars of Religion – sadly there's now a bungalow on the spot, but you can climb the steep steps from the Rue de Mur for wonderful views from the little park.

Browse the antique and antiquarian bookshops in the old Quartier de St-Mathieu around **Eglise St-Mathieu** with its original tower of 1584. This attractive church with a restored barrel-vaulted ceiling contains an unusual wooden statue of the Virgin (Notre-Dame du Mur), dating from 1390.

The best of the medieval houses are to be found in **Rue Ange de Guernisac** and **Grand'Rue**, where a superlative example is open to the public (see below). There are also remains of the walls of the *ville close* in Rue de l'Hospice, where there's a picture of the church that once dominated the area with the tallest spire in the region – it fell down in 1806 after stone was removed to sell for building material.

Musée de Morlaix

T02 98 88 68 88, musee.ville.morlaix.fr.
Jul and Aug 1000-1230, 1400-1830, Sep and Apr-May 1000-1200, 1400-1800, Sun 1400-1800, closed Tue, Oct-Mar and Jun 1000-1200, 1400-1700, closed Tue and Sun. €4, family €6.50.

This is currently a split site between Les Jacobins, with changing exhibitions, and No 9 Grand'Rue, a superb 16th-century house. There may be a move to the old tobacco factory on the quay in a few years.

A tragic incident

Allied bombing raids on Morlaix in the Second World War were designed to break the Paris–Brest line of communications via the viaduct. On 29 January 1943, English planes dropped 40 bombs on the town causing 80 deaths and many casualties. The children at the little school of Notre-Dame de Lourdes beside the viaduct were killed, together with their teacher. A chapel – Notre-Dame des Anges – was built on the spot to commemorate the tragedy.

English raid of 1522

The attack on Morlaix took place when the soldiers were away at an army review and the merchants were at a huge fair. English from ships below the port entered the walled city in disguise and paved the way for their armed compatriots who burnt and stole the town. On returning to the port they pillaged all they could from merchants' houses, including much wine. Several hundred stayed to drink in the Bois de Styvel, then fell asleep. They were slaughtered by the returning Morlaisien soldiers; a fountain still visible on the quay is called the Fontaine des Anglais, as the stream feeding it ran red with their blood. The town motto is: '*Si'ils te mordent, mords-les*' (if they bite you, bite them back).

The Château du Taureau was constructed soon after on a rock at the mouth of the estuary to prevent further attacks.

Armoric Regional Natural Park, Monts d'Arrée.

Place des Jacobins

The Jacobins church (not open to the public) is the oldest building in Morlaix. The monastery housed many famous guests such as Anne de Bretagne and Mary Queen of Scots, who arrived as a child in 1548, after a dreadful sea crossing on her way to engagement with the Dauphin. Changing art exhibitions are held here in the adjoining halls.

No 9 Grand'Rue

In a narrow cobbled street, this is an example of a unique architectural type called *maison à pondalez*, from *pont* (bridge) and *aller* (to go). The towering central space with a monumental fireplace rises through four floors with wooden 'bridges' off to each side of an amazingly carved central turning wooden stair. High-quality items of Breton furniture, paintings and panels presenting the history of Morlaix are well displayed. Houses of this kind were urban châteaux for nobles turned merchants in quest of wealth, often in the linen trade which employed thousands in this region. Highly recommended for a visit.

The so-called **House of the Duchess Anne** (May-Sep 1100-1800, 1830 Jul and Aug, closed Sun), in similar style, in the Place Allende, is also open to the public.

Monts d'Arrée

Of these, the highest hills in Brittany, **Roc'h Ruz** (near the transmissions mast) is the topmost point at just over 385 m. Until recent, accurate measurements, **Roc'h Trevezel** was deemed the tallest, unless you count the spire of the little chapel of St-Michel-de-Brasparts, whose silhouette dominates views further west. You can drive up almost to the top of this Mont St-Michel and enjoy panoramic views of Finistère, but particularly of the *landes* (moors) and *tourbières* (peat marsh) which characterize this area. The near view includes the reservoir and first nuclear power station in France (long since decommissioned).

Granite has eroded in this exposed chain of hills and the remaining crags are formed of a mixture of schist and quartzite. The wilderness of the landscape has an eerie appeal and, when the mist lies thickly over the low ground like a silver lake with sharp crags of schist jutting above, it's not hard to understand why it has become a place of legend. The name of a nearby hamlet, Youdig, means 'little porridge', reflecting the dangers of being sucked down into the marsh. The entrance to the Celtic underworld was thought to be here in the Yeun Ellez, and Ankou's spirit looms large. Tales tell of a huge black dog roaming the marshes and, more bizarrely, nocturnal washerwomen calling travellers to help with laundry baskets, thus luring them to their deaths. A line of standing stones known as The Wedding Party wends its way through the heather, said to be drunken revellers petrified by an angry priest who tried to pass them.

Moulins de Kerouat

2 km west of Commana, via D764.
Jul and Aug daily 1100-1900, mid-Mar to May Mon-Fri 1000-1800, Sun 1400-1800, Jun 1000-1800, Sat and Sun 1400-1800. €4.50/2.10.

Set in a peaceful green valley, this eco-museum vividly presents the atmosphere of simple life in rural Brittany in the 17th to 19th centuries. There are waterwheels, mill-machinery and a tannery, with outbuildings containing exhibitions and artefacts that bring home the harsh realities of economic life in the Monts d'Arrée. Don't miss the wonderful examples of huge carved grain chests and box beds.

Maison Cornec

St-Rivoal, via D30/D42.
Jul and Aug 1100-1900, Jun 1400-1800, 1-15 Sep 1400-1800. €1.50/1.

Dating from 1702, this house is in a style called *maison anglaise* (see page 47), with an exterior stone staircase and protruding gable that provided an important extra living space (the family shared the ground floor with their animals). Various paths

The Wolf Museum, Cloître St-Thégonnec.

For children...

Musée du Loup (15 km south of Morlaix at Cloître St-Thégonnec, museeduloup.fr, Jul and Aug daily 1400-1800, Mar to mid-Dec Sun 1400-1800, €3.50/2.50). The wolf museum has an imaginative display honouring wolves, which survived in the Monts d'Arrée until 1906. Some of the material is grisly, but there's lots of fun and humour in sound, pictures, cartoons and interactive stuff.

Menez Meur Nature Reserve (via D342, signed from St-Rivoal and St-Cadou, Menz Meur, Jul and Aug 1000-1900, May, Jun, Sep 1000-1800, Mar and Apr, Oct and Nov Wed and Sun 1300-1730, Dec-Feb 1300-1700 during school holidays, closed 25 Dec, 1 Jan). There are wolves and wild boar (feeding times are posted at the entrance), as well as Breton horses, cows and goats. There's also a play area, picnic tables and several walking trails for all the family.

Huelgoat forest (about 30 km south of Morlaix). Check out the incredible 'chaos' of huge granite boulders in the forest at Huelgoat. It has a timeless fascination for all ages, and kids love to try out the 100-tonne Trembling Rock ... See also page 18.

go around the grounds, preserved in their old form, passing a *lavoir* and little river in the bottom of the valley.

South of Morlaix

St-Thégonnec

12 km southwest of Morlaix.

Built mostly between 1587 and 1682, this most grandiose of parish closes is exuberant in form and feeling. It is dedicated to the sixth-century Welsh monk Conog (Breton form Tegoneg). The legend goes that a wolf killed the stag that was pulling Conog's cart full of building stones so the monk forced the wolf to take the stag's place. This appears in iconography here on the porch and calvary and again inside.

Through the stolid triumphal gate, the verticality of the overall design is striking – everything points symbolically upwards. The church oddly has two towers, one the remnant of a former structure, and the main one, built in competition with that of Pleyben, another fine *enclos*. The ossuary is encircled by an inscription, the key words being '*hodie mihi, cras tibi*' (I die today, you will tomorrow). Inside in the crypt a *mise en tombeau* scene has amazingly expressive mourning faces.

The calvary (1610), shows 40 figures in nine scenes of the Passion, from Jesus' arrest to his Resurrection. There is a marked contrast between brutish faces (like the idiot with the lolling tongue), showing the ugliness of sin, and the serenity of the women, secure in their faith. Contemporary fashion detail can be gleaned from the costumes, such as the rounded hats. The cross shows angels taking the sacred blood of Christ, origin of the Holy Grail legend.

Inside the church the glorious density of ornamentation captures the attention. A fire in 1998 badly damaged the interior – a display of charred remains near the organ shows the extent

Parish closes

The *enclos paroissal* is a phenomenon particularly linked to northern Finistère. It arose out of an increase in wealth in the 16th and 17th centuries, thanks largely in the region of Léon to the linen trade with England. Farmers, weavers and merchants put their money into grandiose expressions of faith and pride rather than individual ostentation. Thus small villages came to have huge and elaborate churches, with rivalry between different communities leading to outrageously competitive building and decoration.

The ingredients of this mini city of god are the church, calvary, ossuary for the bones of the dead and an encircling precinct, originally containing the cemetery, with symbolic triumphal entrance. The same basic elements make up each parish close, but there is huge degree of variation and presentation from church to church. Three of the best known are in close proximity and generally open to visitors every day, except when services are taking place.

of the restoration project – so cleaning and repainting have vivified the altarpieces and statuary. In the north transept is a Retable du Rosaire with a statue of Saint Louis IX, king of France, because the altar was ordered on the saint's day. Adam and Eve, driven from Eden, are shown, with Purgatory and the fires of hell graphically displayed. The main figures are the Virgin Mary, with Ste-Catherine to one side and St-Dominic on the other. The little dog with a torch in his mouth is a word-play symbol – the Latin *Dominicani* separates into *domini cani* (dogs of the Lord) guarding the faith.

Guimiliau

16 km southwest of Morlaix.

A beautiful ensemble here, but it's the calvary (1581) that draws visitors from all over the world. More than 200 figures are depicted in a medieval

What the author says

On a drizzly October afternoon the little chapel on top of Mont St-Michel-de-Brasparts is lost in mist, the lake below dark and gloomy. I'm on my way to St-Rivoal, a Monts d'Arrée village, where the Fête de Pomme is taking place. It's an annual ritual for me and a few hundred others. The setting is the Maison Cornec, one of my favourite places for its simplicity and integrity. Musicians are playing as I enter the throng – accordions, a violin, and the *bombarde*.

Everyone is here. The older generation lean on sticks as they talk in Breton, happy children eye the cake stalls, dogs roam gregariously. Calm, good humour reigns. Suddenly the sun peeps out, new musicians begin to play with an insistent beat and a wave of laughter comes from the little makeshift bar where cider is served.

Stalls of many local craftspeople offer wood sculpture and pottery, cider and jam.

A baker sells country bread, glossy buns and succulent apple cakes.

The entertainment is simple – guessing the number of apples in a basket and watching the basket-weavers or the wheel of the old apple press turned by hand for instant juice. The smell of a great mass of apples mingles with that of sausages ready for crêpes, local cheeses and the wet grass all around.

A group goes off quietly for a tour of the land, with its original low stone walls, small fields and orchards, ancient *fontaine* and pretty river down in the valley. In the crowd, local associations explain their activities, with commitment and enthusiasm – so many people are involved in benefiting the community.

Returning, the mist has lifted. Rocky outcrops stand sharp and hard against the mirror of water below. Maybe a harsh landscape, but brimming with life. This is my Brittany.

---

fashion parade. In addition to the usual scenes of the Passion and Resurrection, there is a graphic scene of the naked figure of Katel Gollet (Mad Kate) being gobbled up by the monsters of hell. Details on the frieze include the tender image of Mary touching her baby's foot on the flight into Egypt, and Veronica holding up her handkerchief with an image of Christ. There are many little touches of realism, like Jesus' rolled-up sleeve as he washes the disciples' feet, or the Last Supper showing hungry disciples and Judas with a bulging purse.

The façade of the south porch (1606-1617) has numerous carvings illustrating Old Testament scenes, such as Adam and Eve's fall and a delightful little vignette of Noah's Ark. Inside the porch is a fine collection of the Twelve Apostles, each with their special attribute. The small frieze below contains some oddities – the birth of Eve with God pulling her from Adam's rib, and the 'Cock King', in reference to a medieval cock-fighting ritual.

The interior boasts an exceptional organ (c1690) by Englishman Thomas Dallam, whose family fled to Brittany from Cromwell's Puritanism. Nearby are two remarkably preserved 17th-century processional banners (carried in the pardon) in glass cases, one with St-Miliau, patron of this church.

His story is told in an altarpiece to the right of the main altar area. This sixth-century saint, once ruler of Cornouaille, was beheaded on orders of his jealous brother Rivoad. There's a poignant image of the saint holding his own head, supported by his wife.

The Altarpiece of St Joseph commemorates a royal decree of 1661, setting a public holiday for St Joseph. Above the main image of Joseph holding his son Jesus by the hand, is St-Laurent shown carrying his own portable barbecue. He was martyred by being roasted alive, allegedly calling out to his torturers to turn him over because one side was done. Below is the lawyer St-Yves, patron saint of Brittany, conventionally

shown between a rich and a poor man, symbolizing his fairness of judgement.

Lampaul-Guimiliau

19 km southwest of Morlaix.

This *enclos* has a relatively simple exterior with a narrow triumphal entrance, plain calvary, and ossuary with a superb doorway interestingly uniting a Tree of Life with the inscription *momento mori*. The truncated bell tower (1573) was one of the highest in Brittany until lightning struck in 1809. An ornate Gothic entry porch, with a good set of Apostle statues, is a taste of things to come, for the interior of this church, dedicated to St-Miliau and St-Pol (Paul Aurelien), is most impressive.

At the rear is a *mise en tombeau* scene of exceptional quality in *touffeau*, with each figure lost in their own emotions. Mary looks on in suppressed anguish as John offers wordless comfort; a greater complexity of feelings is shown on the face of Mary Magdalene. Next to this are two remarkable processional banners surviving from the 17th century and, opposite, is a bright baroque baptistery (1650) in octagonal form, which has a riot of details from twisting vines to mini-statues of the Apostles and Christ's own baptism.

The nave is dominated by its glowingly decorative *poutre de gloire* (beam of glory) with scenes from the Passion on one side and the Annunciation on the other, a poignant contrast. Ahead, the main altarpieces are of John the Baptist and the Passion. Here, a highly elaborate display shows Miliau decapitated by his brother, holding his own head. On the left, there's a rare depiction – Anne resting in bed having given birth to the Virgin Mary, while midwives wash the baby. The patron saint of Brittany has her own altarpiece on the north wall. Another female saint, Margaret, is also honoured on the south. Punished for her faith, she was swallowed by a dragon, but she used her cross to scratch his stomach and he coughed her up. She became the patron of childbirth, as mothers prayed for such an easy delivery.

Listings
Sleeping

Quimper

Hôtel Gradlon €€€-€€
30 rue de Brest, Quimper, T02 98 95 04 39, hotel-gradlon.com.
Map: Quimper, p184.
Best choice for central Quimper, with quiet off-street rooms available around a pretty interior courtyard garden complete with fountain. Rooms are tastefully decorated and well equipped, while the public areas are rather old fashioned. There's no restaurant, but there is a comfy bar and an excellent buffet breakfast can be eaten in or overlooking the garden. Impeccable service. Parking available (paid).

Hôtel Oceania €€€-€€
17 rue du Poher, Quimper, T02 98 90 46 26, oceaniahotels.com.
Map: Quimper, p184.
This modern hotel has spacious rooms with sleek modern decor, air conditioning and comfortable beds. Facilities include an outdoor heated swimming pool (summer months only), free parking and Wi-Fi (unusually with a charge after 15 minutes). Catering is not that special – the restaurant kitchen can be very slow even when it's not especially busy, and you can get much better value for money breakfasts at the nearby commercial centre.

Escale Oceania €€
6 rue Théodore Le Hars, Quimper, T02 98 53 37 37, oceaniahotels. com.
Map: Quimper, p184.
A cheaper Oceania hotel, and not a place of great beauty, but it's in an excellent position for the cathedral and centre, just across one of the river passerelles. Rooms are decent, and there's a good restaurant, although you're well placed for access to many others. A useful multi-storey car park is right next door.

Self-catering/camping
Orangerie de Lanniron
Allée de Lanniron, T02 98 90 62 02, lanniron.com.
The most beautiful setting in the grounds of a (private) château for this 'one-stop shop' for accommodation, with camping, chalets to rent and even overnight hotel facilities. On the banks of the Odet, there's also a large outdoor swimming pool, and bikes for hire. The little boathouse for two is ideal for a romantic holiday. Camping is €19-32 per night, chalet rental €315-966 a week.

Pays Bigouden

Hôtel/Restaurant Le Poisson d'Avril €€€-€€
19-21 rue Men Meur, Le Guilvinec, T02 98 58 23 83, lepoissondavril.fr.
Well-positioned hotel near the port and Haliotika discovery centre. The bedrooms are in rustic/marine chic style with colourful fabrics and good bathrooms. A suite of two rooms is available for a family. Try to get a room with a private terrace and fantastic sea views. If you can't get one of these, the outdoor dining area offers the same thing.

Brest

Hôtel La Plaisance €€
37/41 rue du Moulin Blanc, T02 98 42 33 33, hotel-plaisance.fr.
Map: Brest, p192.
Overlooking the pleasure port at Moulin Blanc, this is a perfect base for Océanopolis (200 m) or for taking a boat trip around the Rade. The hotel is modern and plain, but the comfortable rooms are a decent size, many with sea views, some with little balconies. Friendly staff work around the clock, if you want a drink or cup of tea in the middle of the night.

Hôtel Agena €€-€
10 rue Frégate la Belle Poule, T02 98 33 96 00, agena-hotel.com.
Map: Brest, p192.
If you want a reasonably priced, basic stopping place near the lively commercial port area, this is a good choice. No frills, but acceptable rooms with nautical motifs and a bar area. It's fairly easy to park in the vicinity, and handy for the Cours Dajot. It's only a short walk to the ferries to catch the early boat to Molène or Ouessant.

Ferme Insulaire de Quéménès €€€

T06 63 02 15 08, iledequemenes.fr.
This small island in the Mer d'Iroise is the object of a durable development project. The sole inhabitants, David and Soizic, run a farm, and offer *chambres d'hôtes* with full board. There are only three rooms, with one bathroom between them. Visitors are collected by boat (weather permitting) from the island of Molène. Minimum stay is two nights, which will cost €350-400 all in for two. You will need to book a long time in advance.

Hostellerie de la Pointe St-Mathieu €€€-€€

Pointe St-Mathieu, T02 98 89 00 19, pointe-saint-mathieu.com.
It is a real treat to stay in this hotel near the fabulous Pointe St-Mathieu. Rooms have sea views, some overlooking the lighthouse and ruined abbey on the clifftop. Decor is mostly marine themed, both smart and comfortable, with a jolly bar in ocean-liner style. The antiquity of the building is apparent in the restaurant with its exposed stone walls and fireplace.

Self-catering
Le Village Vacances de Beauséjour
Le Conquet, T02 98 89 09 21, lesvillagesmer.com.
Open all year.
Well placed for a stroll into town or to the coastal path, this park has good-quality units to rent and is popular with walkers and cyclists. Chalets for 10 (five bedrooms) or for four to five (two bedrooms), both types with kitchen/sitting areas and small outdoor space. Excellent value at €280-530 a week for the smaller model. Short breaks also possible.

Crozon Peninsula

Trouz ar Mor €€
Kerloc'h, T02 98 27 83 57, trouzarmor.com.
Perfect for a spot of self-indulgence, this retreat is perched above the fabulous beach of Kerloc'h. The breakfast room and front bedrooms enjoy the lovely view. The bright house has a calm and happy atmosphere. There's a yoga room, large sauna and fitness equipment. Hosts Galya, Frédéric and Karen keep the emphasis on relaxation, with a range of massage treatments available.

Hôtel de la Plage €
42 bd de la Plage, Morgat, T02 98 16 02 16, presquile-crozon.com/ hotel-de-la-plage.

Good value at this friendly hotel on the seafront, newly refurbished for 2010. The first-floor restaurant has panoramic views, and a bar terrace across the road allows you to sip your drinks beachside. Book in advance to be sure of getting a room with a sea view.

Hôtel Styvel €
2 quai de Styvel, Camaret, T02 98 27 92 74, camaret-sur-mer.com/ les-hotels-et-residences.php.
Open all year.
Excellent position for this hotel/ restaurant overlooking the sea and Tour Vauban. Try to get a room in the front, not only for the views but to avoid the noise of the kitchen at the back. No 2 is the nicest, with a good-sized bathroom. You won't be disappointed with the food at dinner (see Eating, page 220), and the hotel is good value for money, apart from the breakfast.

Chambres-d'hôtes/ self-catering
Gîtes-St-Hernot €
St Hernot, T02 98 27 15 00, presquile-crozon.com/ gites-saint-hernot.
Invaluable stop, much used by walkers as it is not far off the coastal path. Jacqueline Le Guillou, a characterful host, offers *chambres d'hôtes* and a *gîte d'étape* (very basic, about €15 a night) behind the bar-restaurant

in this little village. The three letting bedrooms are in an apartment which can be rented as one unit. Kitchen facilities are available, but the restaurant is excellent value, and one of the packed lunches will keep you going all day along the cliffs.

L'Ancrage
Kergalet, Lanvéoc, T02 98 17 01 31, brittanysail.co.uk.
Open Apr-Sep.
Richard and Sue Curtis have two gîtes (sleeping six and two to three) at their sailing school base near Crozon, and a family house (for eight) to let at Camaret. The gîtes are in outbuildings converted to a very high standard. The larger one has bedrooms downstairs and a living room above to take advantage of the country views. Guests are welcome to share the peaceful gardens. Prices range from €295-425 for two, and €425-575 for six.

Camping
Camping Plage de Trez Rouz
Camaret, T02 98 27 93 96, trezrouz.com.
Open mid-Mar to mid-Oct.
Superb position for this pleasant site, by the 'Red Beach', so called for its striking cliff colour (or for English blood from 1694, according to gorier versions). There are good facilities and children's activities. Mobile homes have terraces with sea

Eating & drinking

views and a rental of about €450 for four people in late June or early September.

Douarnenez & Cap Sizun

Hôtel de la Baie des Trépassés €€
Plogoff, T02 98 70 61 34, hotelfinistere.com.
A superb location right on the beach of this bay at the end of the world. Sleep in a comfortable room facing the ocean, with the sound of the waves breaking gently outside – it's great for a romantic break or for walking the coastal path. The hotel also has a decent restaurant with that priceless view.

Morlaix

Le Manoir de Coat Amour €€€
Route de Paris, T02 98 88 57 02, www.gites-morlaix.com.
The name Coat Amour (Wood of Love) lends an appropriately romantic air here. Bed and breakfast in palatial rooms is available at this impressive *manoir*. It's a short walk to the restaurants in town, but an evening meal is available if booked in advance. There are luxurious gîtes in the gorgeous gardens. The units (one for six or seven, the other for two) have everything for a relaxing holiday in this oasis of calm. Outdoor

swimming pool in summer. Small gîte €395-699, large gîte €599-999.

Hôtel du Port €€
3 quai de Léon, T02 98 88 07 54, lhotelduport.com.
Great value for this super-friendly hotel, very popular with British visitors. It's situated by the river in the centre of Morlaix, perfectly placed for restaurants and sights. Rooms are simply decorated with good facilities like plasma TV and internet access (Wi-Fi). Jean-Christophe Rollet and his team are rightly proud of their welcoming establishment.

Monts d'Arrée

Chambres d'hôtes de Brézéhant €
Lac du Drennec, T02 98 78 02 32, chambres-hotes-brezehant.fr.
This gem of a place is in the heart of the Monts d'Arrée and very near Lac du Drennec with its swimming beaches. The 17th-century weaver's house is full of original art and choice furniture, as you'd expect in the home of a professional artist and potter. The guests' sitting room has a huge ancient fireplace, and bedrooms are strikingly individual. Andréas and Catherine Merényi will be happy to advise on things to see and do in the area.

Quimper

L'Epée €€
14 rue du Parc, T02 98 95 28 97, quimper-lepee.com.
Daily 1030-2300 (food served 1200-1430, 1900-2200).
Map: Quimper, p184.
A suave brasserie by the river with flavoursome food and cheerful service. Modern decor and music set the scene for varied menus, with a three-course lunch just over €20. A puff pastry artichoke tart might be followed by crisp-skinned cod and imaginatively cooked vegetables. The chocolate pannacotta is a richly satisfying dessert. Good ambience, popular with all ages.

Le Saint Co €€
20 rue du Frout, T02 98 95 11 47.
Lunch and dinner all year Mon-Sat, closed Feb.
Map Quimper, p184.
This restaurant behind the cathedral has set menus at €20.50 and €26.50 offering oysters, scallops and salmon as well as steak with a choice of sauces. Tender pork fillet in mustard sauce comes with chunky potato wedges and a selection of vegetables. Don't be deterred by the poky interior, as there is also an upstairs room.

Crêperie du Sallé €
6 rue du Sallé, T02 98 95 95 80.
1200-1400, 1900-2230, closed
Sun and Mon.
Map: Quimper, p184.
In the heart of the old town,
with tables on the street or
a dining room with ancient
beams and Breton-themed
decorative plates. The menu is
fairly basic, but crêpes are tasty
with quality fillings. Particular
recommendations include pear
and hot chocolate, and apples
with salted caramel. At busy
times of year queues form at
lunchtime, so get there early,
although service is pretty brisk.

Cafés & bars
Bistrot à lire €
*18 rue des Boucheries, T09 63 00
19 53.*
Mon 1400-1900, Tue-Sat
0900-1900.
Map: Quimper, p184.
A bookshop with café. Simple
lunches and cakes available.

Café des Arts €
*4 rue Ste-Catherine, T02 98 90
32 06.*
Mon-Fri 1100-0100, Sat and
Sun 1500-0100.
Map: Quimper, p184.
On the quieter bank of the river,
with a cathedral view from the
outdoor tables, this café/bar is
popular with arty types and
young people. Linger over
hot drinks, beer and cocktails
(including non-alcoholic).
You can even try Guinness
with a squirt of caramel syrup.

Auberge du Port €€-€
74 rue de la Marine, Le Guilvinec, T02 98 58 14 60.
Mid-Mar to mid-Sep, lunch and dinner every day.
Slightly old-fashioned feel for this family-run restaurant, with dark blue paint and tablecloths, but the food is excellent, particularly a huge plate of *fruits de mer* (shellfish) fresh from the port. A simple meal of flavoursome fish soup, white fish fillet of the day in tangy seaweed sauce and home-made crème caramel costs all of €16!

Crêperie Les 4 Saisons €
2 rue Burdeau, Pont l'Abbé, T02 98 87 06 05.
Daily 1130-1830, except mid-Sep to Apr closed Sun.
An unpretentious place just off the main street with memorable offerings, from the savoury *blé noir* with goat's cheese, streaky bacon and a sort of creamy prune sauce to the Bigouden speciality dessert crêpe *'au riz au lait'*, a sweet rice pudding filling flavoured with caramel or chocolate or apple.

Brest

Le Crabe Marteau €€
8 quai de la Douane, T02 98 33 38 57, crabe-marteau.com.
Tue-Sat, lunch and dinner.
Map: Brest, p192.

In the commercial port where there are many restaurants, this is really one for the seafood lover – the crab and hammer sounds like a gimmick, but the quality and quantity of fresh crab, served with bread, local organic potatoes and sauces on a wooden board is quite an experience. The hammer is more of a wooden mallet! Other fish and shellfish dishes available if you can't face the hard work.

Ma Petite Folie €€
Rue Notre Dame du Bon Port, T02 98 42 44 42.
1200-1400, 1930-2200, closed Sun.
Map: Brest, p192.
A fun place to eat, on board an old boat. The main dining room is the lower deck, with timbers and portholes. If you prefer the upper deck with views over the port, book specifically in advance. The menu is predominantly fishy, with a daily special, but the pork with stir-fried vegetables and the gingered lamb are supremely tender. Set menus have very limited choice for the main course, but there's plenty on offer à la carte.

Amour de Pomme de Terre €€-€
23 rue des Halles St-Louis, T02 98 43 48 51.
1200-1430, 1900-2200.
Map: Brest, p192.

A good central place to eat, with huge platters of food figuring the eponymous potato in some form or other. The atmosphere is cheery, with an open kitchen, and chunky rustic tables packed into the small room. There's also a rather basic outdoor terrace opposite. Daily specials may be meat or fish, and the salads are also substantial. Try and find room for the banana tarte tatin if it's on the dessert board. This is not a place for dieters!

Crêperie Blé Noir €
Vallon du Stang-Alar, T02 98 41 84 66.
Daily from 1200.
Map: Brest, p192.
The restaurant is near the parking area for the Stang Alar valley, with a lake and playground nearby. Crêpes, salads and a few gratin dishes, such as scallops à la Bretonne available. Tasty choice of pancakes like La Bretonne, which has artichokes with ham and cheese. It's a very pleasant place to eat or have a drink outside, not far from Océanopolis.

Around Brest

Crêperie La Maison d'Autrefois €
7 rue de l'Eglise, St-Renan, T02 98 32 67 91.
1145-1400, 1900-2130, Sep-Jun closed Wed.

You can enjoy this remarkable 15th-century house and really good crêpes at the same time. Sit out in the square and admire the unusual 'helmet' roofline, or in the beamed dining room with turning stair. The speciality Dolmen has sausage from Molène, fried apples, *salicorne* and a glass of Chouchen spirit. Friendly service, recommended.

L'Armen €
9 rue Lieutenant Jourden, Le Conquet, T02 98 89 07 03.
Open 1200-1500, 1830-2200, Sep-Jun closed Tue.
A pizzeria that also serves a range of traditional dishes in set menus, such as fish terrine followed by turkey escalope in cream sauce. Friendly and good-humoured service creates a pleasant ambience here, as pizza deliveries stream in and out. Might be worth trying a takeaway to eat by the estuary.

Les Korrigans €
7 rue Lieutenant Jourden, Le Conquet, T02 98 89 00 45.
Open 1200-1400, 1900-2130.
This crêperie is in a lovely old building, so it's a shame that the atmosphere can sometimes be spoilt by one surly waitress. Food is good enough though, with excellent crêpes, especially those stuffed with seafood, as you'd expect in a fishing port.

Crozon Peninsula

Le Langoustier €€
1 esplanade Jim Sevellec, Camaret, T02 98 27 99 00.
Daily Apr-Sep, lunch and dinner.
Many dishes here are distinctively herb flavoured, so wafts of rosemary, thyme and garlic follow servers out to the terrace overlooking the *sillon*. Try the meltingly delicious tuna steak or pork fillet with vanilla sauce. The lunchtime *menu du pêcheur*, with a starter/dessert and fish of the day is a bargain. The restaurant is extremely popular, so get there early.

Restaurant – Hôtel Styvel €€
2 quai de Styvel, Camaret, T02 98 27 92 74.
Daily lunch and dinner.
You can eat in the dining room with its nautical-themed paintings, or out on the terrace here. The emphasis is naturally on fish and shellfish, although there are a few meaty options, such as duck. One perfectly balanced main course is salmon and pollack in a light cream herb sauce, served with potato stack and delicate carrot flan.

Saveurs et Marée €€
52 bd de la Plage, Morgat, T02 98 26 23 18.
Open 1200-1400, 1900-2200, Oct-Mar closed Mon and Tue.
In the heart of the town with great sea views, this restaurant offers fishy delights, in soup, salad or starring role. Lobster and *choucroutrie de mer* are specialities, but there are other options such as veal and duck.

Goustadig €
Landévennec, T06 15 71 10 20.
Mid-Jun to mid-Sep, otherwise Sun and school holidays.
A cheap and cheerful *salon du thé* and crêperie by the old abbey, with rustic decor, simple well-cooked food and a good atmosphere. The menu is basically a 'create your own' format from lists of sweet and savoury fillings, but with suggestions like goat's cheese with home-made green tomato chutney and Roquefort with blackberry jam. Preserves are the house speciality.

Le Korrigan Crêperie €
Route de Postolonnec, Morgat, T02 98 27 14 37.
Jul and Aug daily, Sep-Jun closed Mon.
A fabulous setting for this crêperie overlooking the bay, and a large outdoor terrace to make the most of it and watch the seagulls wheeling over the water as you eat. The eponymous crêpe has goat's cheese, Roquefort and nuts with a green salad; La Peskette is packed with smoked salmon and chives in a cream sauce. Service and food are excellent.

Café du Port
Morgat.
This little café/bar is around the curve of the beach towards the port, so not quite so frenetically busy in summer as many others. Its small terrace is a pleasant place to sit and watch activity in the bay.

Douarnenez

Chez Fanch €€-€
49 rue Anatole France, T02 98 92 31 77, chez-fanch.com.
Jul and Aug daily 1200-1400, 1900-2200, Sep-Jun closed Thu.
Breton flags, multilingual menus and whimsical drawings greet you on arrival. Just a few paces up from the port, the restaurant has a very attractive interior, with roaring fire in winter. Set menus from €11-41 are excellent value, with good choice. The *soupe de poissons* is a flavoursome starter.

La Trinquette €€-€
29 quai du Grand Port, T02 98 92 11 10.
Open 1200-1400, 1900-2130, closed in winter.
As you'd expect in the town's fishing port area, a fish menu with everything fresh. Maybe start with *rillettes* of sardines dressed with balsamic vinegar, followed by a thick tuna steak in chilli tomato sauce with saffron rice. Prawns, scallops and oysters also feature on a changing menu of specials, according to supply.

Le Mercure bar in the Tréboul port area is popular with young people in the evening; likewise **Les Docks** (bd Jean Richepin, T02 98 92 21 95) and **Le Banana Boat** (47 quai du Port Rhu, T02 98 92 10 43).

Morlaix

L'Estaminet €€
23 rue du Mur, T02 98 88 00 17.
Daily 1200-1400 and 1900-2200.
Once you get used to sitting in a leather armchair to eat, you'll appreciate the comfort and stylish decor of this café/brasserie. Service is attentive, the food of chef Patrice Cabioch original and full of fresh tastes. There are diverse specials such as *entrecôte* steak or fish-stuffed chilli peppers with orange pepper sauce. Salads are fabulous. Highly recommended.

La Terrasse €€-€
31 Place des Otages, T02 98 88 20 25.
Mon-Sat 1200-1400, 1930-2130, closed Sun.
La Terrasse is very popular with British visitors just off the ferry at Roscoff, but it's hard to get a consensus on the quality of the food and service, as both are variable. Steak and chips is reliably good. The belle epoque decor inside is definitely worth seeing, however, with a wrought-iron staircase, huge mirrors and murals. People-watching from the terrace is the best fun here.

Cheese & Co €
13 Place des Otages, T02 98 63 18 49.
Tue-Sat 0930-1930, Sun 1000-1300 (evening Fri and Sat, reservation only).
Just by the tourist office, this superb delicatessen specializing in cheese also offers a light but elegant menu, such as *tartines* or a plate of cold meat with cheese of choice. Jérôme Grill is passionate about his products and you'll appreciate his skill when stocking up with ingredients for your picnic. Nice stop for a coffee too!

Crêperie Hermine €
35 rue Ange de Guernisac, T02 98 88 10 91, restaurantmorlaix.com.
Mon-Sat 1200-1400, 1900-2130 (Fri and Sat 2200), Sun 1200-1330, 1900-2130.
Perhaps the most popular crêperie in town, with a wide menu and efficient service in one of Morlaix's ancient houses. The seafood speciality fillings are fresh from Roscoff, and you can become better acquainted with

some of Brittany's 600+ varieties of seaweed, which make a surprisingly tasty contribution to many kinds of fish and shellfish.

Enchanted Crêpe €
26 rue Ange de Guernisac, T02 98 88 69 59.
Jul-Aug daily, Sep-Jun Tue-Sat 1200-1400, 1900-2200.
This place suffers unfairly from being too near the long-established Hermine, but our preference is for the unpretentious style and really delicious food found here, whether it's well-filled crêpes, well-cooked steak or *plats du terroir*. Local sources of ingredients are noted in the menu, which is always a good sign. Friendly service and pleasant atmosphere.

South of Morlaix

Krampouez Breizh Crêperie €
21 place Aristide Briand, Huelgoat, T02 98 99 80 10, creperie-krampouez-breizh.com.
Thu-Tue lunch and dinner (Sep-Mar closed Fri lunch).
The best crêperie in town, according to numerous regulars, combining an atmospheric setting in a beautiful old house with Gaelle's friendly service and delicious crêpes. The cheesy fillings are very good here – perhaps Roquefort, Emmenthal and *chèvre* with walnuts.

L'Autre Rive Café/Librairie €
Restidiou Braz, T02 98 99 72 58, autrerive.hautefort.com (blog).
Wed-Sun 1100-2100, school and public holidays daily 1100-2200 (but hours vary).
A lovely café/bookshop with sofas and internet access, in an idyllic forest setting just outside Huelgoat. Marc is a genial host and the whole atmosphere is relaxed and civilized. A light menu of savoury cake (various flavours made with chestnut flour) and salad, or soup or a cheese/fish/meat plate is available at any time. Yummy ice cream too!

Cafés & bars
Saveurs de Guimiliau
Guimiliau.
Daily 0630-1800, mid-Sep to Easter closed Mon.
This bakery just by the famous parish close has delicious bread and cakes. It also offers tea, coffee and hot chocolate at outside tables or in a pretty upstairs room. Excellent fare, served by very nice people.

Quimper

Festivals & events
Festival de Cornouaille
festival-cornouaille.com.
Jul.
This iconic annual festival (programme and tickets from March) fills the historic centre with music, song and dance. A chance to learn Breton dancing, listen to traditional instruments and watch children parade in colourful costumes. Many events are free.

Music
Le Ceili
4 rue Aristide Briand, T02 98 95 17 61.
Mon-Sat 1030-0100, Sun 1700-0100.
Map: Quimper, p184.
The best place for traditional music in a lively ambience. Also worth a visit for the choice of more than 20 beers, including the pick of local brews.

Théâtre de Cornouaille
1 esplanade François Mitterand, T02 98 55 98 55, theatre-cornouaille.fr.
Season runs Sep-Jun, closed Sun and Mon.
Map: Quimper, p184.
Concerts, theatre and spectacles all year round. Many modern and innovative productions, with world music well represented. You can book online.

Shopping

Pays Bigouden

Festivals & events

Fêtes des Brodeuses
Jul.
This festival of embroiderers is celebrated in Pont l'Abbé with costumed parades and lively music filling the streets.

Brest

Bars & clubs

If you're looking for lively bars, music and impromptu performances, take an evening stroll around the streets by the Port de Commerce.

Brest also has a lively gay scene. **The Pink Sauna** (35 rue Duperré, T02 98 80 68 57, daily from 1200 – from 1300 Sat and Sun – until late) is a popular meeting place with its bar, jacuzzi and sauna rooms and generous opening hours. Of the bars, the pick is **L'Happy Café** (193 rue Jean Jaurés, T02 98 33 62 93, Tue-Sat 1700-0100), a gay bar with dancing and theme nights, and **Le Melting** (89 rue de Glasgow, T02 98 43 90 59, Thu-Tue 1700-0100).

Festivals & events

Fête Maritime Internationale
Jul. Every 4 years (next 2012).
Attracts thousands of boats and hundreds of thousands of visitors to Brest.

Music

Espace Vauban
17 av Clémenceau, T02 98 88 20 25, espacevauban.com.
A basement cabaret venue with a mainly young crowd. Saturday night is for dancing with a DJ mixing old favourites and current smashes. There's a good jazz programme too.

La Carenne
30 rue Jean-Marie Le Bris, T02 98 46 66 00, lacarenne.fr.
Home of contemporary music in Brest, with performance space and recording studios. Good place to hear new bands and innovative sounds.

Le Quartz Theatre
Place de la Liberté, T02 98 33 70 70, lequartz.com.
Tue-Sat 1300-1900, later on performance nights, closed Jul and Aug.
The traditional arts centre near the tourist office, with a programme of plays, concerts and dance.

Les Jeudis du Port
In July and August, every Thursday evening is music night in the commercial port area with several stages and lots of street entertainment. International artists feature and recent star-turns include the Yardbirds.

Quimper

Arts & crafts

Henri Faience
Locmaria, Quimper, T02 98 52 22 52, hb-henriot.com.
Open 1000-1900, closed 1300-1400 out of season.
This is an outlet for the famous Quimper pottery. Factory tours are also possible.

Food

Les Halles
Rue St-François.
The indoor market has all manner of good things – sushi, Moroccan specialities, local meats and cheeses, organic bread, fruit and vegetables. Also many takeaway options for salads, sandwiches and savouries. Crêpes are freshly made in front of you, but go before or after the 1200 rush.

Les Macarons de Philomène
13 rue Kéréon, T02 98 95 21 40, macaron-quimper.com.
Open 0900-1900, closed Sun and Mon.
This shop is something of an institution and queues in the street are not unknown. Macaroons taken to an art form, in every colour imaginable.

Océane Alimentaire
Le Port, St-Guénolé, T02 98 58 43 04.
Daily in summer, varied hours in winter.
Lots of fish products, such as *rillettes* of mackerel and tuna, seaweed items to eat or to indulge the body in the form of creams and gels. Free exhibition.

Brest

The tourist office has a leaflet – Brest Shopping – which lists by category the main shops (especially clothing) in the city centre and a few restaurants. The covered market, Halles St-Louis, with many food stalls, is open daily except Sunday afternoon.

Books
Dialogues
Forum Roull/rue de Siam, T02 98 44 88 68.
Mon-Sat 0930-1930, closed Sun.
The best and largest bookshop in northern Finistère.

Souvenirs
Roi de Bretagne
12 quai de la Douane, T02 98 46 87 67, roidebretagne.com.
Mon-Sat 0930-1230,1330-1900.
Regional products from food to crafts and beauty products.

Crozon Peninsula

Clothes
Armor Lux
Route de Camaret, T02 98 26 27 90.
Summer hours Mon-Sat 1000-1930, otherwise Mon-Fri 1400-1900, Sat 1000-1230, 1400-1900.
Just outside Crozon, this outlet of the best-known Breton clothing retailer has a large shop, also selling regional products.

Sports equipment
Absolute Surf
4 rue Kreisker, Morgat, T02 98 17 01 96.
Mon-Sat 1000-1300, 1500-1900, Sun pm only, irregular hours out of season.
Buy or hire water sports gear and equipment.

Douarnenez

Penn Sardin
7 rue Le Breton, T02 98 92 70 83, pennsardin.com.
Open 0930-1200, 1430-1900, closed Tue out of season.
A truly Breton experience, the sardine shop! Superb products and decorative tins.

Morlaix & Monts d'Arrée

Arts & crafts
Ferme des Artisans
Nr Mont-St-Michel-de-Brasparts, on D785, T02 98 81 46 69.
Jul to mid-Sep daily 1000-1930, mid-Sep to Mar Sat and Sun 1030-1900, Apr-Jun Mon-Fri 1400-1830, Sat-Sun 1030-1900.
A huge shop on two floors with mostly locally produced, good-quality arts and crafts, plus books, jewellery, food and drink, hats, pottery and furniture.

Activities & tours

Brest

National Marine Naval Base
Porte de la Grande Rivière, La Corniche, T02 98 22 06 12.
Free visits without reservation to the marine base from mid-June to mid-September (arrive between 1400 and 1500), but you must have a passport or identity card for a country in the European Union. Guided in groups, the visit lasts two hours, often with the chance to go on board a warship.

Boat trips
Azenor
Port de Plaisance (also Port de Commerce), T02 98 41 46 23, azenor.com.
This company has daily cruises on the Rade in high season, lasting 1½ hours at a cost of €15.50 (€11.50). There is also a longer option going around the Bay of Camaret, and lunch/dinner events.

Penn ar Bed
Port de Commerce, Brest, or Ste-Evette, Audierne, T02 98 80 80 80, pennarbed.fr.
Boats go to Molène and Ouessant from Brest (or Le Conquet) all year round. About €30 return June to September, or €18.40 October to May. Leaving from Brest gives a wonderful trip around Pointe St-Mathieu. For the little island of Sein, boats go from Audierne.

Crozon Peninsula

Peninsula le Labyrinthe
Route de Dinan, Crozon, T02 98 26 25 34, peninsulalabyrinthe.com.
Jul and Aug daily 1000-1900, Apr, Jun and Sep daily 1400-1800, Oct-Mar Wed, Sat, Sun and national holidays 1400-1800.
Humorous and well-planned entertainment designed for children, but fun for adults too: a wooden panel maze with story-board clues. Exhibition about mazes and games for youngsters too.

Monts d'Arrée

Horse riding
The **Village Equestre de Bécherel** (contact Aurore and Julien Goachet, T02 98 99 77 24, or drop in) near Huelgoat offers a day out on horseback (full day €70/half day €45) and/or can teach you how to ride. Special packages with accommodation (gîte) and riding available, from €180 for a weekend.
The **Centre Equestre de Cranou** (T02 98 26 90 27, centre-equestre-du-cranou.com) on the western edge has similar options, plus a *gîte d'étape* and camping.

Walking
The association **ADDES** (T02 98 99 66 58, arree-randos.com) has various guided walks with an emphasis on nature and legends, including one by night (carrying lanterns) on the moors, when you may even meet a korrigan.
Brittany Walks (brittanywalks.com) offers guided walks in English for individuals or families, or advice about walking in the area.

Contents

Morbihan

Old houses in the main street of Rochefort-en-Terre.

Introduction

Morbihan means 'little sea', appropriate for the almost landlocked gulf, dotted with islands, where cruising and boat-watching are fruitful pastimes. At the head is the beautiful town of Vannes, which wows its host of international visitors with ancient architecture, contemporary culture and a busy pleasure port.

Megalithic marvels are strewn around the coastal area, from the World Heritage Site of Carnac to a single burial chamber on the island of Gavrinis. But there are also impressive Neolithic sites that are much less well known around Erdeven and the Presqu'île de Rhuys.

This sheltered southern district of Brittany has a rich sylvan landscape and many small towns of exceptional character, like gorgeous Rochefort-en-Terre, centre of arts and crafts. The Nantes–Brest canal, engineering feat transformed into modern leisure resource, crosses Morbihan, passing the mighty towers of Josselin's château and Pontivy, a thriving commercial centre. In the countryside are quirky gems, such as the only troglodyte chapel in Brittany and the zany workings of an ironmonger poet. It's also home to that most Breton of foods, the andouille sausage of Guémené-sur-Scorff.

With all this going on, Lorient doesn't get much of a look-in here, except as the home of one of Brittany's top festivals – the Festival Interceltique each July.

Alignements de Kerzerho, Erdeven.

What to see in…

…one day
Visit the cathedral and medieval quarter in **Vannes**, with a seafood lunch by the port. Take a boat to the **Ile d'Arz** from the Gare Maritime or the famous Neolithic chamber on **Gavrinis**. Wander among the megaliths at **Carnac**, then go to a surfing beach on the Quiberon Peninsula. Take a long browse in **Pontivy**'s Monday market followed by a walk along the Nantes–Brest canal. Check out the arts and crafts at beautiful **Rochefort-en-Terre**.

…a weekend or more
Stay a night on the **Ile-aux-Moines** and walk the coastal path. Take a tour of all the megalithic sites to compare the stones. Visit the château at **Josselin**, **Lizio**'s unusual museums and the exceptional church windows in **Malestroit**. Cycle, swim and taste local products on the Quiberon Peninsula.

Vannes & the Gulf of Morbihan

Vannes is very much more than a base for leisure activities around the gulf. It's a soft, sweet city, with interest around every corner, scenic rampart gardens and two excellent museums in ancient buildings. The port area gives a flavour of the maritime past and present, with the Gare Maritime just downstream in the Parc du Golfe, the watery gateway to cruises and island visits in the Gulf of Morbihan. Here you can forget the car and enjoy island life on the Ile d'Arz or Ile-aux-Moines, strolling, cycling or simply watching the graceful yachts pass by.

Gulf of Morbihan.

The best place to start exploring Vannes is by the harbour in the **Place Gambetta**, where the Porte St-Vincent leads straight into the old quarter – relics of the walled medieval town that grew up around the cathedral mound. The well-preserved ramparts and imposing **Tour du Connétable** are an impressive sight, together with the colourful French-style gardens laid out below along the Marle stream, where art is displayed in summer. Vannes was a favoured place of ducal residence, with Jean IV building the **Château de l'Hermine** as an integral part of the town's defences. It was here that the Treaty of Union between Brittany and France was signed in 1532. The existing building is an attractive 18th-century replacement. Near the Porte Poterne are the restored *lavoirs*, with the Jardin de la Garenne opposite, a good photo spot.

When Parliament was exiled from Rennes to Vannes in the 17th century (see page 35), **La Cohue** (indoor market) was modified for political meetings, amid a veritable building boom when grand stone houses were constructed for all the important incomers. The finest example is the newly restored **Hôtel Limur** in the Rue Thiers.

A most alluring cluster of medieval streets lies between the Porte de St-Vincent and the cathedral. At the corner of the Rue Noé in the Place Valencia is the carving of a happy couple traditionally known as *Vannes et sa femme*. The square was named for the birthplace of St Vincent Ferrier – there's a little statue of him by the name plate. Stroll in the atmospheric Rue St-Salomon, Rue des Halles and the Rue du Bienheureux Pierre-René Rogue, or for even older examples of houses, look around the area of St-Patern outside the 15th-century Porte de Prison. Here the church is dedicated to one of the founding saints of Brittany, and has a Tro Breiz chapel (see page 40).

Essentials

❶ Getting around The compact centre is easily manageable on foot but there is a pick-up and drop-off bike scheme (velocea.fr) if required with advance registration and deposit. The easiest, and free, parking is by the river. Park then walk up to the town.

❷ Bus station Place de la République, with an Infobus point (T02 97 01 22 23). There are bus links to other parts of the gulf and megalithic sites. For regional bus travel, see page 274.

❸ Train station Place de la Gare, T36 35, sncf.fr. Journey time one hour 20 minutes to Nantes, three hours to Paris, 2½ hours to St-Malo (via Rennes). For regional train travel, see page 274.

❹ ATMs Crédit Agricole, 3 rue St-Vincent, 22 rue Thiers; BNP Paribas, 16 rue F Decker.

❺ Hospital 20 bd Gl Maurice Guillaudot, T02 97 01 41 41.

❻ Pharmacy 19 rue Thiers, 14 rue St-Vincent.

❼ Post office Place de la République, rue St-Nicolas.

❽ Tourist information Quai Tabarly, T08 25 13 56 00, tourisme-vannes.com. July and August 0900-1900, otherwise Monday-Saturday 0930-1230, 1330-1800. Morbihan region: morbihan.com.

Cathédrale St-Pierre

Open 0900-1800.
Map: Vannes, p234.

Tightly embraced by a network of old streets, the cathedral looms benevolently over the town. The Spanish missionary saint Vincent Ferrier, who died in Vannes in 1419, seems to have elbowed out St-Pierre in terms of coverage. His elaborate chapel (under restoration) in an uncommon Renaissance-style tower dominates the north aisle and the north transept window is dedicated to him.

From the large ambulatory you can see the luxuriant Chapel of St-Sacrament at the east end. The oldest part of the cathedral is the Romanesque tower to the left of the west door.

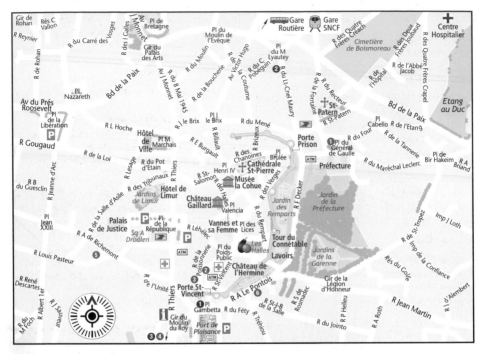

Vannes listings

❶ Sleeping
1 **Hôtel Le Marina** *4 Place Gambetta*
2 **Hôtel Manche Océan** *31 rue du Lt-Cnel Maury*
3 **Hôtel Mercure** *19 rue Daniel Gilard* (off map)

❶ Eating
1 **Dan Ewen Crêperie** *3 place du Général de Gaulle*
2 **Café de la Poissonnerie** *21 place de la Poissonnerie*
3 **La Table de Jeanne** *13 place de la Poissonnerie*
4 **La Saladière** *36 rue du Port* (off map)
5 **L'Eden** *rue Louis Pasteur*
6 **Les Remparts** *6 R A le Pontois*

Vannes.

Musée la Cohue (Musée des Beaux Arts)

Place St-Pierre, T02 97 01 63 00.
Oct to mid-Jun 1330-1800, mid-Jun to end Sep
1000-1800. €4.20 (€6 for 2 museums).
Map: Vannes, p234.

This amazing 13th-century structure was a market,
with law courts on the upper floor. The exiled
Parliament of Brittany used to meet in a room with
a superb oak ceiling. You can see the interior while
viewing works of art mainly from the 19th and 20th
centuries, including artists Monet and Boudin, with
abstracts downstairs and more classical works
above. Temporary exhibitions of contemporary
local artists are also shown here.

Château Gaillard

Rue Noé, T02 97 01 63 00.
Mid-Jun to end Sep 1000-1800, mid-May to
mid-Jun 1330-1800. €4.20 (€6 for 2 museums).
Map: Vannes, p234.

The superb quality and rarity of the archaeological
exhibits here underlines the importance of the Gulf
of Morbihan area in Neolithic times. It's also well
worth seeing the interior of the 15th-century
Château Gaillard, built by Duke Jean V's chancellor
Jean de Malestroit. The ground floor has changing
displays, such as medieval religious objects, with
an impressive fireplace in the first room. Up the
narrowest of stone stairs the huge carved beams of
an unpainted ceiling are revealed and the amazing
archaeological section begins.

It seems incredible that such perfect, polished
jadeite axes were made more than 5000 years ago
– that is, until you see the variscite funerary
jewellery from the Tumulus de Tumiac, and the
delicate shell necklaces from the Mesolithic period
(10,000-6000 BC). On the third floor, there's a real
library and a strange one made of papier maché,
plus a little room of wooden cabinets with painted
panels, illustrating religious figures like the Desert
Fathers. Up in the attics, with upturned-boat style
roof timbers, are many curiosities brought back
from all corners of the world by 19th-century
travellers, evidence of the collectors' insatiable
thirst for knowledge and wonders.

Aquarium de Vannes

Parc du Golfe, T02 97 40 67 40, aquarium-du-golfe.com.
Jul and Aug 0900-1930, Apr-Jun and Sep
1000-1200, 1400-1800, Jan-Mar and Oct-Dec
1400-1800. €10.30, children €7.20 (€15.10,
children €10.60 for a joint ticket to the Butterfly
Garden nearby).

A warm, wet world of exotic fish. Even to reach the
ticket desk you have to cross a pool of sharks and
giant turtles. There is a fantastic display of fish from
around the world and closer to home with the
Breton blue lobster. A recreation of a coral reef is
one of the biggest attractions. Visit in the morning
or when the sun is shining to avoid the crowds.

Gulf of Morbihan

This inland sea is littered with well over 100 islands
and islets. The two largest, where you can
disembark, are the **Ile-aux-Moines** (310 ha) and the
Ile d'Arz (324 ha). The latter is less populated and
generally quieter, with a tide mill and former salt
marshes. Its busier neighbour has an attractive
bourg and various dolmen. Both have places to stay
and eat, and good walking on the coastal paths
(and cycling inland).

The most famous island is probably tiny
Gavrinis (gavrinis.info), which has a Neolithic cairn
with extraordinary carvings. A trip here will also
pass Er Lannic with its rare stone circle, half in and
half out of the water. Boats (Jul and Aug 0930-1230,
1330-1900, Apr, Jun and Sep 0930-1230, 1330-1830,
May 1330-1830 plus Sat and Sun mornings, Mar, Oct
and Nov 1330-1700 and closed Wed, €12, family
€28) go from Lamor Baden for the short crossing,
included in the price of a site visit.

See Activities & tours on page 269 for trips on
the gulf. It's best to book in advance and arrive in
plenty of time on any day in summer.

Around the region

Presqu'île de Rhuys

This is the least known part of the Gulf of Morbihan, forming an embracing southern arm. It offers many things to see and do whether you seek activity, history or relaxation. Once on the D780, the watery nature of the region soon becomes apparent with the tide mill at Noyalo. Accessible at low tide, the Ile Tascon at **St-Armel** is a well known spot for watching winter bird migrants. In July and August a little passenger ferry runs across to Sené (near Vannes) where there is a nature reserve. Nature lovers will also appreciate the former salt-working marshes (Réserve du Duer). **Sarzeau** is the main settlement on the peninsula with shops and services.

Continue on the D780 all the way out to the end at **Port Navalo**, from where you can take a cruise on the gulf or enjoy a walk out to the lighthouse from the little beach. The former *criée* (fish auction) here is now a year-round exhibition centre with both artistic and heritage displays.

For an ideal picnic and boat-watching spot, head to the **Pointe Bilgroix** nearby where you are on the dividing line between open sea and the gulf. **Port Crouesty**, by contrast, is a busy pleasure marina, with an excellent tourist information office (T02 97 53 69 69).

Maison du Cidre

Route de Lann-Vrihan, Le Hézo, T02 97 26 47 40, museeducidre.com.
Jul and Aug open all day and Sun 1500-1800, Apr-Oct 1000-1200, 1430-1830, closed Sun. €5 (children free).

One of the best cider museums around, with a genuine desire to share knowledge and traditions, not just get you in the shop. Every stage of the cider-making process is explained through exhibitions and traditional utensils in the many outbuildings. You can also stroll in the orchards to discover numerous varieties of apple and what each is best used for. Production here includes delicious cider and apple juice, which can be tasted as part of the visit. Other local products such as salt, cider vinegar and honey are also on sale.

Petit Mont

South of Arzon.
Jul and Aug 1100-1830, Apr-Sep 1430-1830, closed Wed. €6, children €3.

This is an exceptional Neolithic cairn. A guided visit puts the site in its context, with access to tomb carvings characteristic of the period, such as

Petit Mont.

serpentine forms and axe-heads, and rarer idol shapes. The cairn was used as a German bunker in the Second World War. This promontory is also a good place for a walk, with many footpaths and excellent views over the gulf.

Tumulus de Tumiac

Southeast of Arzon, just by the main D780 road.

This low, rounded hill is more commonly known as the Butte de César. Tradition has it that from here Julius Caesar watched the sea battle against the Vénètes in 56 BC when the Romans finally overcame tribal resistance in this area. It's unlikely he'd have seen much if he did. In fact, the mound covers a Neolithic burial chamber (c 4500 BC). You can climb to the top for good 360-degree views.

Château de Suscinio

Sarzeau, T02 97 41 91 91, suscinio.info.
Apr-Sep 1000-1900, Oct, Feb and Mar 1000-1200, 1400-1600, Nov-Jan 1000-1200, 1400-1700.
Family ticket €15, adults €7, children €2.

One of the unusual things about this magnificent château is its coastal situation on low, wet marshland. The elaborate *logis* building from the 15th century reflects its prime purpose as a place of pleasant sojourn for the duke and his family, with widespread hunting grounds. Much of the fabric of the château was sold off to builders after the Revolution, but restoration has enhanced the site admirably and you can visit rooms with displays of the castle's history and ducal lifestyle. Most notable are the colourful decorative medieval tiled floors rescued from the vanished chapel. There are good views over the marsh from the *chemins de ronde*.

Abbaye de St-Gildas-de-Rhuys

Open daily.

This abbey church is one of the best Romanesque examples in Brittany. The story is that St-Gildas' body was washed across from the island of Houat

to the shore here and buried where the church now stands. A more famous connection is that of Abélard, the scholar who was abbot here in 1125. He wrote to Héloïs of the uncultured nature of their lifestyle, regarding the Presqu'île as a rude desert. Not surprisingly he made himself very unpopular, and finally ran away in fear of his life.

Two huge stoops that are former capitals from the original church stand near the narrow night stair for the monks, a reminder of the former abbey. The simplicity of the 11th-century high, rounded arches contrasts with an 18th-century nave; the overwrought baroque altar in Loire stone in the south transept looks particularly out of place. There are many tombstones from the 14th and 15th centuries including that rare thing, one for a woman, Jeanne de Bretagne, daughter of Jean IV. The tomb of St-Gildas himself is in the ambulatory. The abbey (abbaye-de-rhuys.fr) next door is a cultural and spiritual retreat centre.

Auray & megalith country

The big draw of this area is Carnac, the world-famous site of Neolithic alignments and burial places. It's hard to travel any distance without finding a monument of one sort or another, and Locmariaquer has equally fine remains in evocative settings. The Quiberon Peninsula too has megaliths, but the coast has a starring role here with wild surfing spots, gentle family beaches and dramatic routes for walkers and cyclists.

Auray is an interesting town in its own right and an excellent base for Vannes, megalith country or the interior of Morbihan. The pretty harbour of St-Goustan is the perfect place for a relaxing evening meal and waterside stroll.

St-Goustan, Auray.

This fine old town has many handsome buildings in and around the Place de la République, including a former prison (1788). It also has the most picturesque little port imaginable at **St-Goustan**. The two are connected by the Rue du Château, a steeply sloping street of attractive houses, which leads to the old bridge and an enclave of half-timbered dwellings by the harbour. The former castle fortifications rise above the water on the town side, where you can walk up to the **Belvédère** for views over the estuary.

The harbour flourished in the 15th to 18th centuries with cargoes of grain, fish, iron and, later, pit-props for south Wales, but its prosperity dwindled as Lorient's rose. Settlers left from Auray for America in 1632, and Benjamin Franklin stopped here in 1776 on his way to seek help for the American War of Independence, as a quayside plaque on a restaurant records. It's worth exploring the narrow streets up to the church and a very 'grotty' chapel of Notre-Dame de Lourdes.

In a park on the edge of Auray is the lavish **Mausoleum of Georges Cadoudal**, the Chouan leader who was executed in 1804 (see page 36). Opposite is the house he was born in, and the adjoining hamlet Kerléano has some delightful old houses.

Musée de la Chouannerie

15 km southwest of Auray, Route de Quiberon, Plouharnel, T02-97 52 31 31.
15 Jun-15 Sep daily 1000-1200, 1400-1800, Apr-15 Jun Tue-Sat 1300-1800. €5.

This museum is based in a large Second World War German bunker. In the claustrophobic interior, connecting rooms present a wealth of material concerning the Chouan uprising against the aims of the French Revolution (see page 36), and their fanatical royalist, religious determination is evident in what is shown here. There is also a detailed presentation of the fateful events of 1795 when English troops landed on the Quiberon Peninsula

Auray street.

to bring support to the counter-revolutionaries. Unfortunately Marshal Hoche was more than ready for them and they were trapped, forced to surrender and many were shot.

The approach to the Presqu'île along a narrow strip promises a stunning coastline, but it's after the pinch-point at Penthièvre and its imposing fort (still a military installation), that you enter a world of two contrasting aspects. To the west is the Côte Sauvage, wild and rocky, pounded by strong waves and howling winds, while the east is much gentler (and more built up) with safe sandy beaches, tucked into the Bay of Plouharnel. If you like walking, a hike on the wild side down the GR34 is highly recommended, but don't swim or be

Sauzon harbour, Belle-Ile.

tempted into the surf without being aware of the serious risks. For family bathing and sand-castle building, head for the beaches of the south or east.

Côte Sauvage

The little village of Portivy is the gateway to the Côte Sauvage. On the way to its port – the only point of shelter down this side of the peninsula – have a look at the delightful little chapel Notre-Dame de Lotivy. This suffered in the 18th century at the hands of the English, and then French soldiers who used its beams for firewood. From Portivy, squiggle on down the coast road with its increasingly breathtaking views. There are car parks at Port Blanc (Gwen), Port Rhu and Port Bara, with access to footpaths and many warning signs about the dangerous waters. As you approach Quiberon, the Vivier (see Eating, page 263) is prominent on your right and soon after, a series of menhirs on the left.

Quiberon & St-Pierre-Quiberon

Quiberon itself is not a place of great beauty, as the sight of the prominent Château Turpault, a 19th-century fantasy, indicates. Beyond Port Maria and the Gare Maritime (boats to Belle-Ile and the small islands Houat and Hoëdic) is Grande Plage, a perfect family beach. To get away from the sunning hordes, continue around the coast past the huge thalassotherapy centre to the Pointe du Conguel, an unspoilt fingertip jutting out to sea with fine island views. The next step is to Port Haliguen – above the beach just before it is the memorial to the royalists who surrendered here in 1795. There's a tourist office (quiberon.com) at 14 rue de Verdun.

St-Pierre-Quiberon is a little port with a lovely enclosed beach, and much more of a village atmosphere than its big brother. If you want to get in the megalith mood, follow signs to the Cromlech of St-Pierre, part of an enclosure around modern gardens. But don't miss the unsigned, more spectacular alignments just behind (follow roads around a triangle to find them). The Rue du Dolmen has a large burial chamber with massive top stones, sitting nonchalantly among the houses.

Belle-Ile

A 45-minute boat trip from Quiberon leads to the largest Breton island and its main town Le Palais, where the defences of the Citadelle Vauban dominate the harbour entrance. One of the most famous residents was actress Sarah Bernhardt, who first came here in 1894 and fell in love with the "wild, grandiose beauty". It is indeed a good place for walking, with a full circuit of about 90 km.

You need a few days to appreciate all aspects of the landscape, culture and life here. There's the pretty port of Sauzon, the classical music festival Lyrique-en-Mer (in July and August), and the great Tour Cycliste de Belle-Ile at the end of September.

Compagnie Océane (compagnie-oceane.fr) has year-round sailings from Quiberon. For an evocative glimpse, see belle-ile.com.

Megalith country

There is such a bewildering number and variety of megaliths in Morbihan that it helps to stop first at the excellent **Musée de Préhistoire** in Carnac or the **Masion des Megaliths** (see page 242 for details of both) near the alignments. This will help to establish what you'll be looking at in a general context, and what you need to look out for to get beyond the superficial impression of an awful lot of bits of stone. The Musée de Préhistoire gives a strong sense of everyday life in the Neolithic period (see also page 29), which helps greatly in imagining the sort of ceremonies and spectacles they might have organized; it also gets rid of the completely false notion of hairy Druids in long white robes. On display are many of the objects found inside the burial chambers on excavation. The three main sites to visit here are Carnac, Erdeven and Locmariaquer, but there are also many individual monuments. The places that give a real sense of experience are singled out below.

Tip...

Take a torch with you if you're a serious megalith explorer.

Carnac

There are three main groups of alignments – Alignements du Ménec, de Kermario and de Kerlescan, dating back to a pre-Stonehenge 4000 BC. Le Petit-Ménec may be an extension at a changed angle – don't miss this enchanting site a little off the beaten track.

Interspersed are numerous burial places and other enclosures or single menhirs, whose relationship to the main lines is uncertain. The Tumulus de Kercado and Tumulus de St-Michel contain burial chambers covered by mounds of earth, and in the area are hundreds of dolmen whose stone chambers are now exposed. It may be that a general cult of the ancestors made this a major ceremonial meeting place, which is the likely purpose of the alignments.

The sheer scale is what impresses at Carnac, and even if the whole of the site is not accessible now, for reasons of conservation, you can still get the sense of awe that such an elaborate construction must have inspired – even more so 6000 years ago, when there were no other permanent constructions on the face of the earth.

There's a viewing tower at Kermario for an aerial perception. You might also try the simple exercise of entering the Kerlescan alignments at the eastern end and walking up one of the rows, gradually going uphill and seeing the stones of the enclosure coming nearer, so close together that your view of what might be happening beyond is obscured. Did the crowd stay outside and watch an event? Was it a religious ceremony, a ritual dance or even a sporting/hunting contest? The design suggests huge gatherings and ritual movements, with many tribes coming together for seasonal festivities or competitions. Perhaps different groups built

St-Cornely & the ox

One explanation for the menhirs is that they are lines of Roman soldiers turned to stone by the saint when he could go no further to escape their pursuit. At one point he hid in an ox's ear to avoid detection, and in gratitude is said to have established a cult of the beast in this area. The church in Carnac has an unusual exterior tableau with a colourful statue of the saint flanked by two pictures of oxen standing self-consciously among the standing stones. Could this legend connect to dim ancestral memories of ancient religious practice? The roof-slab engraving at Gavrinis certainly seems to show a graceful picture of curving horns, which may represent the masculine aspect of the forces of nature and fertility.

Five of the best

Megalithic experiences

❶ **Les Géants de Kerzerho**, Erdeven.

❷ **Les Pierres Plates**, Locmariaquer.

❸ **Le Tumulus de Kercado**, Carnac.

❹ **Musée de Préhistoire**, Carnac.

❺ **Le Petit-Ménec**, Carnac.

different parts and this is a microcosm of the use of menhirs as boundary markers across Brittany.

It's worth taking a walk through the wood to the Géant de Manio menhir and nearby quadrilateral enclosure of Crucuno, with its contrasting coloured stones. You can go inside the Tumulus de Kercado (c 3800 BC) and see the carvings with the help of an electric light, and there's a riot of decorative detail to be seen in the underground tomb of the group at Mané Kerioned to the north.

Maison des Megaliths (Jul and Aug 0900-2000, May-Jun 0900-1900, Sep-Apr 1000-1700, free). This information centre at the Alignements du Ménec provides an invaluable little leaflet with diagrams of the whole complex, which ranges over several kilometres, as well as a model showing the interrelationship of the various alignments.

Musée de Préhistoire J-Miln, Z-Le-Rouzic (10 place de la Chapelle, Carnac, T02 97 52 22 04, museedecarnac.com, Jul and Aug daily 1000-1800, Apr-Jun and Sep 1000-1230, 1400-1800, closed Tue, Oct-Mar 1000-1230, 1400-1700, closed Tue, €5). The museum is named after its founder, James Miln, a Scottish archaeologist who carried out significant work here in the 1880s, and his assistant/successor.

Paleolithic and Mesolithic finds from the area provide an interesting comparison with later Neolithic objects, where the big leap forward in production, technique and artistry is very apparent. The stages and development of burial practices are outlined, with some fantastic artefacts from local sites like the Tumulus of Kercado. The corridor is more of a Neolithic art gallery, with full-size reproductions of engraved stones.

The second room contains a superb display of items, both beautiful and functional, from everyday life in the New Stone Age. These are helpful images to bear in mind when viewing the megalithic sites, giving a strong sense of their not-so-simple lives. One of the star exhibits consists of four jadeite axes found on the beach in St-Pierre Quiberon in 2007, made of stone from the Italian Alps, and therefore prestigious for their rarity. Upstairs the galleries cover the Bronze and Iron ages, and Gallo-Roman period.

Locmariaquer

12.5 km east of Carnac, Route de Kerlogonan, T02 97 57 37 59.
Jul-early Sep 1000-1900, May-Jun 1000-1800, otherwise 1000-1230, 1400-1715. €5.

Locmariaquer has an important site with three megaliths grouped together. The largest known menhir, Le Grand Menhir Brisé, now lying broken into three pieces, was once nearly 20 m high and weighed 280 tons, a remarkable feat of engineering to extract, shape and erect. The tumulus of Er Grah shows remains of an enormous cairn structure and the Dolmen de la Table des Marchands (c 3000 BC) is a large tomb with fine decorative carvings. The latter has a ceiling stone in the chamber with half an animal engraving, the other half is in the tomb at Gavrinis 4 km away, and that in turn has a design where the other half was found in the Tumulus d'Er Grah. In other words, an engraved menhir about 14 m high was broken up and used in bits at different sites – a bit of Neolithic recycling.

There are many other megaliths around this area, but the dolmen of Mané-Lud is well worth seeing. Also, don't miss the large coastal tomb of Pierres Plates, where a long access corridor adds to the experience. Take a torch and mind the puddles.

Erdeven

9 km northwest of Carnac.

Erdeven has a large alignment of enormous stones, cut through by the main D781. There is unrestricted access to this evocative site. Look for the little sign to the Géants de Kerzerho away to the left behind the parking area – they are suitably gigantic. An 8-km circular walk takes in most of the megaliths here, including one called Caesar's Chair and a group of dolmen at Mané Braz.

It's also worth looking at the large Dolmen de Crucuno beside a house near Erdeven, which has an enclosure of menhirs 400 m beyond in a field. The three tombs at Mané Kerioned (you need a torch to see the exuberant engravings down the steps in the underground chamber) are only a little further on.

Carnac.

Pontivy & around

This area is a rural delight, from the Blavet valley to the wooded countryside around the famous Chapelle Ste-Barbe in the west. The focus is bustling Pontivy, once a military centre at the time of post-revolutionary unrest, with its Napoleonic grandeur balanced by a fine medieval château and narrow period houses. Le Faouët has long been an artistic community, its bucolic atmosphere and remarkable chapels attracting important painters such as Maurice Denis. A more down-to-earth fame has come to Guémené-sur-Scorff as the home of the best Breton tripe sausage.

Place du Martray, Pontivy.

The town is a busy place, full of pigeons and bustling with young people. It is the commercial centre for the surrounding district, with a well-known Monday market. A visit to Pontivy today presents two distinct facets of Breton history: its medieval château and old streets contrast sharply with the grid-plan Napoleonic development of the post-Revolution period. It became a military centre at that time to deal with extensive Chouan activity (see page 36) in the area. Several times during the 19th century, the name was changed to Napoléonville, depending on shifting politics. The **tourist office** (T02 97 25 04 10, pontivy-communaute.fr) just past the château is in a building that was once a leper house.

The name Pontivy supposedly comes from the bridge made over the Blavet river by the British monk Ivy in the seventh century, when he founded a monastery here.

Le Château des Rohans

Rue Général de Gaulle.
Mid-Jun to Sep daily 1030-1830, Oct and Nov Wed-Sun 1400-1800, Feb-Easter Wed-Sun 1400-1800, Easter to mid-Jun daily 1000-1200, 1400-1800, closed Dec and Jan. €3.70.

This Rohan family château dates from the late 14th century, with only two of a possible four original towers remaining. It was built by Jean II de Rohan, with later modifications in the 17th and 18th centuries, such as the many windows of the façade, which were added to improve living conditions. The huge internal courtyard has a smart double sweeping staircase, added in 1738 in the style of the day, but oddly placed in a corner. The little chapel has vacillated between Protestant and Catholic faith according to the vagaries of the Rohan family.

Inside there are summer exhibitions on the ground floor and in the upper galleries. The Salle d'Honneur has an imposing 16th-century painted

Chateau de Rohans.

stone fireplace, with its heraldic devices showing no connection to the Rohans – not surprisingly, as it is not original, but a piece rescued from elsewhere. The superb roof timbers in the upper tower room are the real thing, uncovered in the 1960s and restored. A good view of the town can be obtained from the *chemin de ronde*.

Medieval quarter

Many half-timbered houses remain in the showpiece **Rue du Fil**, a blaze of painted façades and flags. The Place du Martray has the Maison de Roscoët with a fine Renaissance doorway from 1578, its blazons effaced – a common fate of coats of arms at the time of the Revolution. The Maison des Trois Pilliers is now a newsagents and,

Around the region

opposite, a very fine half-timbered house with wooden pillars is not enhanced by modern glass shop panels.

The **Rue du Pont** leading down to the water has a more subdued but equally interesting chain of ancient edifices. No 14, once the home of the seneschal of the Viscount de Rohan, has a beautiful 1577 doorway. In nearby Place Anne de Bretagne, No 14 has a superb swathe of wood carvings with faces and decorative patterns dating from the 16th century.

Napoleonic quarter

Here, the broad streets and neoclassical façades proclaim the order and conformity so prized by Napoleon's imperial regime. The **Rue Nationale** is 1 km long, topping Place Aristide Briand, an enormous square which once acted as a parade ground for 10,000 soldiers. Civic buildings, such as the town hall, the law courts with their Ionic columns, and the former commander's residence, line the square. Just across the river is the old

Blavet river valley, near St-Nicolas-des-Eaux.

barracks, manned in 1811 when Chouan unrest still simmered.

Further along the Rue Nationale is the neo-Gothic Eglise St-Joseph, paid for by Napoleon III in 1858. Have a good look at the gargoyle on the left by the entrance porch – it's the Empress Eugénie. There are some fine imperial stained-glass windows inside. Behind the church is the former hay store for the cavalry horses, said to have a roofline modelled on the pyramids.

The Blavet

The river was part of the grand canalization plans of the early 19th century, when Napoleon wanted a safe internal waterway to link the arsenals at Nantes, Brest and Lorient. It comes down to the town from the north and Lac de Guerlédan, providing a pleasant walk past the cascade, although much of the canal is neglected further on. To the south 28 locks provide a navigable route to Hennebont.

Northwest Morbihan

St-Nicolas-des-Eaux & Site de Castennec

15 km southwest of Pontivy.

This village is one of the most attractive stopping places on the Blavet. Pause for a stroll, a meal or a spell on the water in a kayak. Just up the road is the Belvédère at Castennec, marking the spot where the earliest Rohan fortification stood, and giving great views over the valley below. A delightful but steep walk (allow at least 30 minutes there and back) leads down to the only troglodyte chapel in Brittany, La Chapelle St-Gildas, by the water. You can get nearer in a car, following signs from the Bieuzy-les-Eaux road.

Village de l'an Mil

About 2 km from Melrand, follow signs, Lann Gouh Verrand (old Melrand), T02 97 39 57 89, melrand-village-an-mil.info.
Jul and Aug 1000-1900, end Feb-end Jun, Sep and Oct 1100-1700 (1800 weekend). €5.

This is the former site of a village from the year 1000, a time when the feudal system was developing. From the remaining foundations, certain parts have been recreated using ancient techniques and materials to give a realistic idea of how people lived and worked then. The hill-top situation posed problems for sourcing water – this may have been why the village was abandoned in the medieval period in favour of the current location of Melrand.

There are also reconstructions of charcoal and pottery-making and a tannery with leathers and dyes on show. If you are interested in how things were done in the distant past, this place has many answers and may pose a few questions you hadn't thought of. Children will enjoy the exhibits and animals. There's also a large garden area, showing former uses of plants, and alongside graze *pie noir* Breton cows and hardy Ouessant sheep. It's a low-key kind of place, but pleasant to stroll around, with good explanatory panels and often something practical going on, like children having an outdoor archaeology lesson. Go for a guided visit (in summer months) if you prefer a more animated perspective; there may even be medieval ploughing to watch.

Guémené-sur-Scorff

20 km west of Pontivy.

A modest but rather charming little town which rambles downhill towards the valley of the Scorff, where there are pleasant walks. Guémené is famous in Breton gastronomy for the *andouille*, a sausage made of cows' intestines, and a visit to the

Artists at Le Faouët

In the mid-19th century François-Hippolyte Lalaisse produced a series of lithographs showing local costumes, and he was soon followed by artists seeking the traditional and the quaint in this quiet corner of Brittany. In 1886 Emile Bernard wrote that Le Faouët was "a town of painters, where life is cheap and the setting picturesque". A group of painters established themselves here in the early 20th century, including friends Germain David-Nillet and Charles Rivière, and the deputy mayor organized the first collection of their work in 1913. Local hotels, such as the Lion d'Or, set up studios and darkrooms to encourage the trend, and well-known painters like Maurice Denis, one of the Nabis, and later Mathurin Méheut (see page 47) produced work here. Typical subjects can be seen in the museum's permanent collections – the *jubé* (rood screen) of St-Fiacre, peasants by the market hall, women at the *fontaine* of Ste-Barbe or a hideously romanticized apple harvest.

Les Halles, Le Faouët.

Maison d'Andouille (see Shopping, page 267) is recommended. There are many remnants of a prosperous past – from the sections of ramparts and the unusual Les Bains de la Reine (the hypocaust room of a former château bathhouse) by the Hôtel de Ville, to the Rohan gate, which is a mixture of military and religious style. The central streets contain many old houses, notably the decorative Hôtel des Princes, a *maison à pan de bois*, and the Relais de Diligence, which is enhanced by amusing modern sculptures further up the street. Higher still in the Rue Mazé is L'Echoppe, with its cap roof for the half-timbered upper floor.

Le Faouët

This little rural town is certainly blessed with a fine heritage – two of the best chapels in Brittany, and a huge market hall in the centre. The **Musée du Faouët** (Apr-Oct Tue-Sat 1000-1200, 1400-1800, Sun 1400-1800, closed Mon except in Jul and Aug, €4) in a former Ursuline convent at the corner of

the main square has a small permanent exhibition of the group of painters based here in the late 19th/early 20th century, when Brittany was a fashionable artistic area.

See page 250 for information on the tourist office and walks around the sights.

Les Halles One of only three surviving 16th-century market halls in Brittany, this one is particularly distinguished by its great size – 940 sq m (53x19 m). Dating from 1542, it represents the strong commercial traditions of this town. Stalls of shoes, linen, vegetables and flowers would have been under the shelter of the *halles*, while animals had their own allotted area outside – pigs in the Place de la Corderie and sheep in the corner where the Rue du Château starts. The granite columns around the outside holding up the supporting beams of the elaborate oak and pine roof structures have unusual aesthetic detail for such a utilitarian building.

Chapelle Ste-Barbe (Jul and Aug daily 0930-1230, 1400-1900, Apr-Jun, Sep-Oct 1000-1200, 1400-1800, Nov-Mar Sat-Mon 1400-1615). The extraordinary location of this chapel is attributed in legend to the successful appeal of Jehan de Toulbodou to the protective powers of Ste-Barbe during an electric storm while on a hunting expedition. In return he built the chapel on a narrow ledge of rock. The building took 25 years, a short time for those days, and was constructed without the benefit of the access road, which was built in the 17th century. Apparently, each night a pair of magnificent red oxen magically brought the necessary materials for the following day.

The chapel was built in Flamboyant-Gothic style in 1489. The most striking feature of the ensemble is the later stone staircases (1700) that link the separate elements of church, oratory and bell. Traditionally the bell was rung to ward off lightning – you can have a go at pulling the cord yourself. The oratory is also a later addition, and the metal rings in the walls were once threaded with rope to allow pilgrims to make a dangerous 'tour' of the exterior.

In its strange position between the rocks above the River Ellé, the chapel has no room for a nave and consists only of choir and transept, with a double door entrance and stone vaulting unusual for that early date. Above the main altar a window from 1889 shows scenes from the life of the saint, while to the left there's an ancient window (c 1525), with the same theme. Among the votive offerings are two ostrich eggs, symbolic of lightning bolts, and paintings. One dark canvas shows a carriage overturned – when the pregnant wife of the lord of Faouët survived, the family gave financial aid to the chapel.

Some 500 m downhill is the *fontaine* (1708) with a statue of the saint in her tower. Traditionally girls came to see if they'd be married within the year by throwing a hairpin or coin into the water, hoping it would fall into the little round opening.

Chapelle St-Fiacre (Apr-Nov daily 1000-1200, 1400-1800, Nov-Mar Sat-Mon 1400-1700). By

Sainte-Barbe

The ghastly story of Sainte-Barbe originates from Turkey. A young girl converted to Christianity against the wishes of her pagan father, who then imprisoned her in a tower – often seen in the saint's iconography. When he tried to force her into marriage, she refused all suitors and was eventually subjected to various tortures by her father. She continued to declare her faith and her wounds healed miraculously. Finally, he cut off her head, and was then killed himself by a lightning strike – hence Sainte-Barbe is invoked against storms and sudden death, and she became the patron of those who confront the danger of fire.

contrast with the simple devotional concept of Ste-Barbe, this chapel, with its odd asymmetrical façade, has a clear political significance. It was built between 1450 and 1480 by the noble family of Bouteville, and may well have attracted the financial support of the dukes of Brittany too. The Montforts (see page 32) sponsored many religious initiatives to match the pious image of Charles de Blois, their beaten opponent. Above the entrance is the word 'Dux' (duke) and at the back of the chapel, the banner and ermines of the ducal family. The fabulous *jubé* (rood screen) was made by Olivier de Loergan, an artisan who had been elevated to the nobility by the Montforts. This shows deadly sins on the choir side and biblical scenes towards the nave, interspersed by numerous creatures, both realistic and fantastic. The church also has some excellent statuary from the 15th to 17th centuries and windows from the 16th century, including the life of St-Fiacre, an Irish monk, and an even older Tree of Jesse.

Dance of death

The lovely church at Kernascléden between Le Faouët and Guémené is especially famous for its wall paintings, including the *Danse Macabre* or Dance of Death in the transept. The architecture is equally worth seeing for a supreme example of the Flamboyant-Gothic style.

Walking around Le Faouët

This little country town is a perfect starting point for agreeable rural walks. Well-marked circuits pass the two famous chapels in the vicinity, as well as sacred springs, old pilgrim paths, a Roman road and the traces of a medieval château. The Ellé valley, with its granite 'chaos' of tumbling boulders, is a particularly attractive sight. Generally the terrain is hilly and wooded, most beautiful in spring and autumn, but peaceful and quiet in all seasons. Remember that paths may be slippery after wet weather. For a flatter and less demanding route, try the Circuit de St-Fiacre, a 7-km tour starting at the remarkable Chapel le St-Fiacre.

Starting and finishing your walk in Le Faouët provides many refreshment options, or the chance to stock up for a picnic along the route. The **tourist office** (3 rue des Cendres, T02 97 23 23 23, open all year), has individual circuit maps, which you can browse before choosing, or you can buy a collection of 32 walks covering the whole district for about €15. So lace up those walking boots, fill the water bottle in your rucksack, and set out boldly on the pilgrim trail…

Circuit des Chapelles

Allow up to four hours for this 12-km walk, which has steep sections. It starts along the Rue des Halles and continues via an underpass below the D769 before climbing a rough paved pilgrim path to the extraordinary setting of the Chapelle Ste-Barbe. After visiting the *fontaine* in the wood below, the route descends to cross the D132, then follows a rural trail parallel to the main road, before looping round the Moulin Berzen and swinging west cross-country to St-Fiacre. A short diversion takes in the famous chapel, before returning north to Le Faouët, with a section of the former railway line, part of the GR38. The last stretch is along a minor road to regain the town centre.

Circuit de St-Sébastien

This rural walk of 12 km passes over the countryside north of the town, above the valley of the Ellé to Villeneuve Barrégan, after which the route passes the remains of the castle on its mound and the *fontaine/lavoir* just beyond. The Chapel of St-Sébastien is a little over 1 km ahead, a good spot for a pause, with a picnic table. The next hamlet, Coat Queven, has some good examples of local architecture. After a further country ramble, the way lies close to the main road before a last uphill flurry. At the top there's the choice of either turning right, back down to the town, or of taking a 600-m detour ahead to see the Chapelle Ste-Barbe before returning.

For something more strenuous

Leave the Circuit St-Sébastien for a demanding but very scenic alternative, of 8.5 km. After the *lavoir* at Barrégan, turn left, and left again at the road. Where it bends left soon after, go straight ahead on a footpath. Continue into a wood and, after

Roches du Diable, south of Le Faouët.

100 m, turn right and then right again to descend to the edge of the trees near the river. At the road turn right (with the water station on your left), then left into a pine wood. Ignore the river bridge and continue ahead with care. An up-and-down section of about 1.5 km passes the 'chaos' of rocks in the river. Where the path flattens out, turn right up the hillside, rising steeply to the Fontaine Ste-Barbe. From there go ahead at a junction of tracks up the old stony pilgrims' path to the chapel. A very pleasant *auberge* may offer the chance of refreshments here.

Cross the grass ahead (*auberge* and car park on your right) and pick up another pilgrims' path down through the trees. Pass the bee museum and take the underpass beneath the D769, then continue back to the centre of Le Faouët.

Eastern Morbihan

Five little towns in eastern Morbihan certainly share visual appeal, but they also each have a distinct personality and environment to offer the visitor. Arts and crafts thrive in Rochefort-en-Terre, Josselin's château contains the surprise of a doll museum, Ploërmel retains some of its former ducal splendour and Malestroit is on a beautiful stretch of the Nantes–Brest canal. And for the biggest themes, life and death, the area also has the unmissable Resistance museum and the unforgettable mechanical fantasies of an iron-working poet.

Astronomical clock of Brother Bernardin, Ploërmel.

Ploërmel

The busy town of Ploërmel is an interesting mixture of ancient and modern, often in the same building. Glimpses of the walls of the original *ville close* survive, as well as the **Tour Thabors**, one of the original 12th-century towers. In the Rue Beaumanoir you can see the **Hôtel des Ducs de Bretagne**, once part of the ramparts and home of famous figures like Duke Jean I and the Duc de Mercoeur (see page 33). Opposite, and with wonderful carved figures, is the **Maison des Marmousets** (1586), and nearby the **Maison des Quatre Soldats**, now a café. By the tourist office, the former Convent of the Carmelites, destroyed at the Revolution and then rebuilt, has been modernized. The glass-box *médiathèque* is bizzarely placed inside the **17th-century cloister**, which you can still walk round. The 'Blue Chapel' with its shiny windows, is now an exhibition centre.

Eglise St-Armel (open daily). The Flamboyant-Gothic church of St-Armel has a superbly decorated north door and an impressive square tower from the 1730s. Inside, the marble tomb of Dukes Jean II and Jean III (to the left of the altar), marks the political importance of the town in medieval times. In the transept is the tomb of Philippe de Montauban, chancellor of Anne de Bretagne, and his wife, with some individualistic carvings of monks around the base. The wooden vaulted ceiling is particularly fine, with carved beams and decorative figures.

Astronomical clock The former establishment of the Brothers of Christian Instruction in the Place Mennais is in fact a college, but you can enter the courtyard (signed Horloge) to see the curious astronomical clock in its glass house. This wonder was created in 1850 by Brother Bernadin, and is a working model of the solar system, also showing every aspect of current time. Phases of the moon, year of the century, sign of the zodiac, stars over Ploërmel – the detail and correlation of the parts is mind-bogglingly complex, yet apparently straightforward enough to be shown in 10 dials.

Lac du Duc This large lake, 1.5 km north of Ploërmel, offers year-round leisure facilities with a well-organized **Club Nautique** (T02 97 74 14 51, club-nautique-ploermel.com) that has sailing, kayak and waterskiing. For keen walkers, there's a 16-km circuit right around it, and strollers following the 3-km Circuit des Hortensias can be sure of something in bloom at almost any time of year. Cyclists will appreciate the Green Way running up the eastern side of the water, and there's a golf course at the Hôtel Roi Arthur beside the lake.

Mi-Voie – Column of the Thirty

Midway between Ploërmel and Josselin on the D724 there is a huge column commemorating the infamous set-piece battle of 1351, the most celebrated incident of the Wars of Succession (see page 32). Some 30 knights, led by Jean de Beaumanoir, captain of the Josselin garrison, faced 30 knights led by Englishman Thomas Bemborough, based at Ploërmel. The column lists the names of those on the Breton side. In fact, there were also Bretons on the other side although most were English and German mercenaries. A humbler memorial cross is behind the column.

Josselin

12 km west of Ploërmel.

Château de Josselin (Jul and Aug 1000-1800, Apr-Jun and Sep 1400-1800, Oct Sat and Sun 1400-1800, €7.40). The fabulously austere façade of the château with its three round towers looms over the River Oust. Jean de Beaumanoir led out his knights to the Battle of the Thirty in 1351 from here. Later, Olivier de Clisson IV, Constable of France and one of the most powerful men of the day, was responsible for the original fortifications. At the time of his death in 1407, the château came into the hands of the Rohan family, who still live there today. The resplendent inner face (1490-1510) shows the potential beauty of stonework in Flamboyant-Gothic style.

The Protestant Rohans incurred the wrath of Cardinal Richelieu after the Wars of Religion – he had a whole section of the outer fortifications blown up, not so easy in those days, and it took two weeks. The tower now called the *tour isolée* was later used as a prison – many Englishmen in the 18th century stared at the walls here. Only guided visits to the château (45 mins) are available (sometimes in English). It's worth the hefty entrance fee to see the courtyard façade, but slightly disappointing in that there's limited access to the interior and the tour is rather swift. Rooms are in '19th-century-meets-medieval' style with quality period furniture and paintings, indicating Rohan family pride. In the former stables is a doll museum with a remarkable collection displaying hundreds of dolls in porcelain, wood and leather, dating from the 17th century onwards. A double ticket is available.

Basilique de Notre-Dame du Roncier (open daily). The strange name 'Our Lady of the Brambles' derives from an ancient legend that says a workman founded a statue of the Virgin while clearing the site. He took it home, but it returned to the original spot – stained-glass windows in the church tell the story. The statue certainly had a powerful legacy – the workman's blind daughter was cured after touching it, and centuries later it was the only thing to soothe the turbulent spirits of the 'barking women' (*Les Aboyeuses*) of Josselin. A beggar was reviled by washerwomen here, and they set their dogs on her. It turned out to be Our Lady in disguise and she condemned them to bark like dogs. Even in the 19th century there were many documented examples of women, especially in religious frenzy during processions, howling and whining.

The earliest part of the church retains its Romanesque pillars and delightful relief carvings, including a dog chasing a rabbit. The tomb of

What the locals say

On summer Sundays the Morbihanais flock to tiny chapels, tucked away in isolated hamlets and cared for by locals, for the pardons. A pardon will start at the well for a sprinkling of saintly water and finishes with a feast, served to hundreds of people by volunteers. It's then followed with singing and dancing. There might be a special theme (harvest or black pudding) or activity (pig racing, tractor blessing) and in the evening there'll be a *Fest Noz*, with more music, food and drink.

Then there are the *Noces Bretonnes*, re-enactments of the weddings of yesteryear – they involve costumed processions, ceremonies at the Mairie and chapel, dancing and *kir Breton* before the wedding feast, which is cooked in great vats over fire-filled trenches. See you there? You're sure of a warm Breton welcome.

Martin Green, Morbihan resident.

Olivier de Clisson and his wife is in the south chancel. At certain times the tower is open for good views over the town.

The Pardon of Notre-Dame du Roncier (7-8 September) lasts for two days with a superb torchlight evening procession followed by a day-time parade of sacred banners and the statue of Our Lady.

Lizio

12 km south of Josselin.

A delightful village with a marvellous assortment of 17th- to 18th-century granite houses, a picturesque church and an insect museum (insectarium-de-lizio.com). Lizio also has a well-attended festival of arts and crafts on the second Sunday in August. The Val Jouin, with its lakes, offers lovely walks, especially the tranquil and verdant Sentier Botanique (3 km or 7.5 km). Nearby are two fascinating museums.

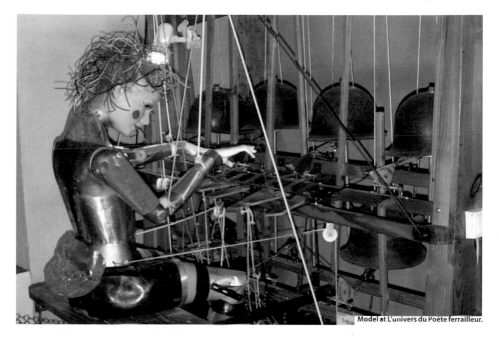

Model at L'univers du Poète ferrailleur.

L'univers du Poète ferrailleur (La Ville Stephant, 2 km from Lizio, T02 97 74 97 94, poeteferrailleur. com, Jul and Aug daily 1030-1900, 1-15 Sep daily 1400-1800, Apr-Jun and 15 Sep-Nov, Sun, public holidays 1400-1800, €6, €5 children). This 'iron-working poet's' fantasy land is an amazing place to visit. The models themselves are extraordinary enough, but each has a button for you to press and set in motion – the combination of colour, sound and movement is entrancing. Once you've finished marvelling at the imaginative concept, you start looking at what bits and pieces Robert Coudray has used to create them – individual parts begin to emerge from the whole – a tap, a fork, a bed-spring … even German helmets rung like bells. Outdoors there are many more pieces, making use of wind and water power, with a more serious, educational look at energy and ecological building.

There's everything here – skill, imagination, humour and a vibrant sense of simply being alive. Don't miss it!

Ecomusée des Vieux Métiers (Ste-Catherine, 3 km from Lizio, T02 97 74 93 01, ecomuseelizio.com, Jul and Aug 1000-1200 and 1400-1900, Feb-Jun, Sep-Oct and 20-31 Dec 1400-1800, closed 25 Dec, €5.80, children €4). This is one of those remarkable collections that reflect the passionate commitment of an individual. For more than 20 years Alain Guillard has worked at assembling a vast array of items from Breton life over the last two centuries. The exhibition covers far more than the usual traditional rural crafts, with domestic interiors, clothes, fully equipped shops and workshops for every imaginable trade, a school-room and even a 1950s garage complete with petrol pump. The sheer number of exhibits is almost overwhelming, so allow plenty of time to savour it all. Nostalgia fans and those with a curiosity about Breton life will love this, and there's something to surprise and amuse everyone, especially if you take the guided tour. Now why does that wooden sabot have its heel at the front of the foot?

Malestroit

14 km south of Ploërmel.

The combination of the **Nantes–Brest canal** and a charming historic centre of half-timbered houses makes Malestroit an appealing destination. Now a relaxing sort of place, it was a centre of commerce for many centuries thanks to the Oust, which widens impressively here around a vast weir. Across the river is the ruined **Chapelle de la Madeleine**, where a famous treaty was signed in January 1343 between Edward III of England and Philip VI of France to bring a lull to the fighting of the Wars of Succession in Brittany.

The town retains signs of former wealth in the quality of the church and houses, as well as mill buildings by the bridge. In the corner of the central Place du Bouffay, the **Maison La Truie qui File** (The Spinning Pig) has funny carvings including the eponymous pig and a hare playing the bagpipes. In summer there are free outdoor concerts on Friday evenings.

Eglise St-Gilles (open daily). Built on the site of a sacred source (see the old fountain outside), the church was mostly reconstructed in the 16th century after a fire, with a double nave. It contains a most beautifully expressive Pietà, carved from a single piece of wood. This was saved from burning at the Revolution by a local who, with a pleasing irony, paid for it in firewood.

The church is well known for its stained-glass windows – a dramatically rich Tree of Jesse (16th century) over the south door contrasts with a modern (1960s) mystical rosary theme by Hubert de Sainte-Marine behind the altar. Most impressive of all is the subtly pale 15th-century window telling the life of St-Gilles, including an anachronistic scene where he receives Charlemagne's confession. This is not the only oddity here – the pulpit has prominent semi-erotic mermaid figures.

Musée de Résistance Bretonnne (St-Marcel, 3 km from Malestroit, T02 97 75 16 90, resistance-bretonne.com, 15 Jun-15 Sep daily 1000-1900,

Rochefort-en-Terre.

16 Sep-15 Jun 1000-1200, 1400-1800, closed Tue, €6.90). This is one of the most important museums in Brittany, on the site of a resistance stronghold in the Second World War, with vast indoor and outdoor exhibitions. Essentially it commemorates a particular wartime struggle here, but the issues raised and territory covered are much wider. The emotive power and density of the displays leaves one with a sense of real experience. Documents, artefacts and audio-visual material (English subtitles) bring home not just the facts of the savage battle fought here between the Free

French forces and German troops in July 1944, but also the whole psychology of occupation and resistance. Weapons, uniforms, period vehicles and communication equipment figure largely, but it's the small things that linger – the little wooden coffin sent as a warning to collaborators, the recreated restaurant scene showing the reality of rations and a photograph of fighters of necessity wearing clogs. It's hard not to start thinking about the true nature of liberty and the many different sorts of deprivation.

Rochefort-en-Terre

30 km east of Vannes, 16 km south of Malestroit.

The most beautiful village in Brittany perches on a rocky height above the Att valley. It's home to numerous artists and artisans and is famous for its flowery cobbled streets, which are lined by stunning houses from every period. It's also a gourmet's delight with many good places to eat. But the best thing about Rochefort-en-Terre is that the deluge of visitors hasn't swept away its soul – if ever a little town repaid time and observation, it's this one. The **Rue de Porche** and the **Place du Puits** with the striking **Tour du Lion** are most notable but the back-streets offer treasures too.

Rochefort became a cultural centre before the First World War thanks to a group of artists based at the Auberge Lecadre (now the Hôtel Pelican, see page 261). American painter Alfred Klots has left his mark in many ways, and the village is now a centre of arts and crafts, with the shops and workshops of artisans lining almost every street, so you'll have no trouble finding some original souvenirs to remind you of your visit.

Château de Rochefort-en-Terre (T02 97 43 31 56, Jul and Aug daily 1100-1900, Jun and Sep 1400-1830, May and public holidays Fri-Sun 1400-1800). Alfred Klots purchased the ruins of the château here in 1907, and went on to create a completely new one, using parts from other old buildings in the locality, such as the Renaissance *lucarne* windows. A visit includes views of its exquisite façade from the courtyard, which has a remarkable tree-topped well. An octagonal artist's studio can be seen from outside, and the alluringly decrepit chapel is sadly visible only from afar at present. The widow of Klots' son Trafford sold the château to the Department of Morbihan, which now welcomes American artists to continue the tradition.

The original château suffered a chequered history of dismantlement and rebuilding in medieval times. It was finally destroyed by the Republicans in 1793, after being held by the Chouans. A large painting by Alexander Bloch (1886) showing this hangs above a magnificent fireplace in the only remaining finished room of the old building, now part of the museum. Other exhibits are paintings relevant to Rochefort-en-Terre, and a collection of *coiffes* (Breton headdresses) and furniture.

Eglise de Notre-Dame de Tronchaye (open daily) The church is lower than the village, on the side of a hill. Its name – 'trunk' – refers to a wooden statue of Our Lady, found in a tree in the 12th century after being hidden during the Viking invasions. The (replacement) figure of Our Lady has turned black over time and with restorative treatments.

The building of 1533 is in Flamboyant-Gothic style, although the Romanesque square tower is the oldest part. The calvary outside also dates from the 16th century, and the three tombs to the left of the door are from a time when the graveyard surrounded the church. The graphic skull carvings behind the pulpit once formed the base of a cross symbolizing Golgotha (place of the skulls) which may have marked the former ossuary. A subtle and moving altarpiece (in the left transept) by Alfred Klots in the form of a triptych is a memorial to the tragedy of the First World War, with representations of loss and grief.

Vannes

Hôtel Mercure €€€
Le Parc du Golfe, 19 rue Daniel Gilard, T02 97 40 44 52, mercure-vannes.com.
Map: Vannes, p234.
This plush hotel, one of a large chain, lacks individuality, but it is comfortable and spacious, with all the amenities you'd expect. For a view over the gulf you need to ask (and pay more) for a *chambre privilège* on the upper floors. The main advantage of staying here is that the Gare Maritime is on the doorstep.

Hôtel Manche Ocean €€
31 rue du Lt-Cnel Maury, T02 97 47 26 46, manche-ocean.net.
Map: Vannes, p234.
The bright, comfortable bedrooms here are tastefully decorated – you can pay a little extra for greater space, a minibar, separate toilet and good-sized bathroom. Special praise for the excellent breakfast buffet, and smilingly helpful service. The only disadvantage is the busy road outside. It's just a five-minute walk to the ramparts and old quarter.

Hôtel Le Marina €€
4 place Gambetta, T02 97 47 22 81, hotellemarina.fr.
Map: Vannes, p234.
An atmospheric place to stay with the Place Gambetta's bars and restaurants always busy. It's the nearest hotel to the port and also right by the Porte St-Vincent, which gives access to the old city. The hotel is good value, with decent decor and most rooms overlooking the marina, but it can be noisy at night. Sipping a drink on the terrace, you'll certainly feel at the heart of life in Vannes.

Gulf of Morbihan

Self-catering

Pierre & Vacances
Presqu'île de Rhuys, Port de Crouesty, 56640 Arzon, T02 97 53 85 35, pierreetvacances.com.
A large complex of well-equipped apartments on the Presqu'île, with good facilities and many arranged activities. **Bretagne Douche** has direct access to the beach and sailing school, but the newer and more spacious **Cap Océan** development with pretty apartments overlooks the pleasure port and has a very nice swimming pool. Prices (from about €500) are fully inclusive.

Auray

Hôtel Le Marin €€
1 place du Rolland, T02 97 24 14 58, hotel-lemarin.com.
Just a few paces from the lively port area of St-Goustan with all its bars and restaurants, this friendly small hotel is in a quiet location. It's very clean and well kept. Decor is generally on a blue marine theme, with each room named after a different Breton island, which is depicted in superb photos on the walls. The town centre is a short uphill walk across the river.

Quiberon Peninsula

Hôtel Restaurant Europa €€€-€€
Port Haligue, Quiberon, T02 97 50 25 00, europa-quiberon.com.
Apr-Nov (restaurant until end of Sep).
In a calm position, with beaches and the coastal path just across the road. Rooms at the front have balconies and sea views. It's spacious, with charming staff, and a restaurant offering guests a panoramic perspective of the Bay of Quiberon. Recommended for relaxation, with an indoor pool, sauna and jacuzzi.

Hôtel Albatros €€
19 rue de Port Maria, Quiberon, T02 97 50 15 05, hotel-albatros-quiberon.com.
Closed mid-Nov to mid-Dec.
Of the many two-star hotels along the front, the Albatros is best placed for the Gare Maritime, just a few paces away, for boat trips. It's a friendly place, with bar and restaurant on the ground floor and decent rooms above. All at the front have balconies with sea views, and a scenic breakfast buffet is served on the first floor.

Camping

Camping du Conguel
Boulevard de la Teignouse, T02 97 50 19 11, campingduconguel.com.
Apr-Oct.
A great beachside location for this quality campsite. It's not the cheapest in the area, but the sea is on the doorstep and there's a terrific swimming pool. Activities for children and evening entertainment in high season, plus a restaurant, shop and internet point. Tent/camping spot from about €15-45 depending on the month and a mobile home for rent (up to six people) at €458-741.

Megalith country

Hôtel des Alignements €€
45 rue St Cornély, Carnac, T02 97 52 06 30, carnac-hotel.com.
About 100 m from the Neolithic alignments, this is a Logis de France with spacious rooms and a good restaurant. The road in front is not that busy, but bedrooms at the back overlooking a small garden have balconies with table and chairs – and evening sunshine. Decor is generally plain, enlivened by some beautiful framed photo-prints of Breton seascapes.

Plume au Vent €€
4 venelle Notre Dame, Carnac, T06 16 98 34 79, plume-au-vent.com.
A truly individual place, thanks to the personality of Elisabeth Rabot, an enthusiastic and knowledgeable hostess, who really cares about the quality of your stay. The old house is full of interesting artwork from nautical themes to comic-strip, and exudes relaxation. Breakfast is delicious. The location is handy for the megaliths or for the Gulf of Morbihan.

Pontivy

Hôtel de Rohan €€
90 rue Nationale, T02 97 25 02 01, hotelpontivy.com.
Warm attentive service sets the tone for a stay in this delightful hotel. Just a short walk from the centre of town, it has charming rooms in distinctive individual styles with lots of attention to detail in the decor. Good bathrooms and beds contribute to a sense of comfort. There a little bar and garden for drinks outside, and a generous breakfast buffet.

Mme Prouff €
9 rue de Lourmel, T02 97 25 07 52.
Open all year.
Mme Prouff offers two large bedrooms in her beautiful 18th-century house, with turning staircase and the fine proportions of the period. The decor is classic chic with subtle contrasts of colour and texture. The very attractive en suite rooms are separated by a library area for guests' use. There's a secluded loggia in the walled garden for breakfast on summer mornings. A very convenient location by the château.

Self-catering
Tranquility
18/20 rue du Pont, T02 97 07 05 01, tranquility-gites.com.
Open all year.

Two small gîtes right in the old centre of the town in a 16th-century house. An independent entrance leads up to the first floor where each apartment has an open-plan living-room/corner kitchen. Stairs lead up to a bedroom and bathroom in the attic. Good value and perfect for couples, although one has a sofa bed and could sleep four. Under €300 in high season.

Eastern Morbihan

Hôtel Le Roi Arthur €€€-€€
Le Lac du Duc, Ploërmel, T02 97 73 64 64, hotelroiarthur.com.
If you feel like a touch of luxury, try this smart hotel beside the Lac du Duc, with balconies overlooking the lake or golf course. You can pay more but the standard 'classic' room has everything (except a minibar) to provide a comfortable stay. There's also a spa with pool, sauna and treatments such as massage and reflexology on offer. A cheaper stay is available at the Lancelot (it has the same management) next door with rooms and modern 'cottages'.

La Tour du Lion €€€-€€
10 rue du Porche, Rochefort-en-Terre, T02 97 43 36 94, latourdulion.com.
Staying in one of the most imposing historic buildings, with its 16th-century tower, right in the centre of the village is an experience in itself. The five historically themed rooms, one on the ground floor, are all spacious, with quality furnishings. On the ground floor, there's a very pleasant tea room, with irresistible cakes.

Château de St-Malo €€
Ploërmel, T02 97 73 58 20, chateau-saint-malo.com.
This imposing 19th-century château with stair tower is completely hidden from the road, in wooded grounds by the Lac du Duc. Inside, all has been lovingly restored to a very high standard of decor and furnishings, with superb original wooden floors. Rooms are vast, and each beautiful bedroom is strikingly different, one including a four-poster bed. Guests are welcome to walk in the grounds and the owners will be happy to tell you about the history of the house.

Hôtel Le Cobh €€
10 rue des Forges, Ploërmel, T02 97 74 00 49, hotel-lecobh.com.
The name comes from Ploërmel's twinning with the Irish town of Cobh. Audrey and Michael Suire have created a very welcoming atmosphere for guests, and an outstanding restaurant (see Eating, page 264).

Rooms are colour-themed in red, blue or green and the sumptuous decor reflects history and legend, such as the Arthurian connection with Brocéliande. Rooms (family suite available too) are all well-equipped. Excellent value for this quality of service and comfort, and you won't meet nicer hosts.

Hôtel-Restaurant Le Pélican €€
Places des Halles, Rochefort-en-Terre, T02 97 43 38 48, hotel-pelican-rochefort.com.
In a former existence this hotel was the centre of the artistic movement that first brought Rochefort to prominence. Now a Logis de France, it's still a very nice place to stay. The side-entrance is a dull start, but once inside the charm of the building and the staff makes a big impression. There are seven bright and well-furnished double bedrooms, a little bar area for guests, and an excellent restaurant (see Eating, page 265).

Manoir de Mongrenier €€
Coet Bugat, Guégon, Nr Josselin, T02 97 73 02 54, manoir-de-mongrenier.com.
This beautiful manorhouse near Josselin dates back to the 13th century and has been lovingly restored by Carol and Chris Sealey to create the most idyllic

setting for a holiday. The accommodation is in the adjoining farmhouse – there are two B&B rooms and a gîte (complete with Godin stove) sleeping six, with a separate romantic little cottage for two nearby. Exposed stonework, fine antique furniture, large grounds and an outdoor swimming pool all add to an ambience of luxurious relaxation.

Hôtel du Château €€-€
1 rue Général de Gaulle, Josselin, T02 97 22 20 11, hotel-chateau. com.
The location is the biggest plus point for this Logis de France. It's nothing special in terms of the rather dull decor and sometimes chilly service, but if you can get a room overlooking the water and château, opening the curtains in the morning will make up for it. The food in the restaurant here is good and worth trying, although it can feel a bit lonely at times in the huge dining room.

La Maison Blanche €
2 rue Madame Malestroit, T02 97 72 29 09, alamaisonblanche.eu.
You'll get a warm welcome from Jean and Adrian, who have created a comfortable haven beside the Nantes–Brest canal. Two large double rooms at the front have a view of the river, and there's a smaller twin room at the back. Jean is a linguist, and pleased to have an international

clientele. Here you can sit outside on the flowery terrace watching boats and towpath activity. A pleasant place to stay.

Le Rêve B&B €
Ste Catherine, Lizio, T02 97 74 99 25, brittanybedandbreakfast. co.uk.
This pretty cottage is in a very peaceful location, a good base for exploring the area. Sue and Alan offer a welcoming home-from-home for their guests with one large family room (bathroom downstairs) and a romantic double en suite. Drinks' trays are provided in the rooms and a buffet at breakfast. There's a separate children's bedroom with toys and books. Very good value for money.

Camping
Domaine du Roc
Rue Beaurivage, Le-Roc-St-André, T02 97 74 91 07, domaine-du-roc. com.
Apr to mid-Sep.
This campsite not far from Lizio is situated alongside the Nantes–Brest canal, making a good base for walking/cycling on the towpath. Fishing, riding and canoeing can also be arranged, and there's a heated swimming pool on site. As well as tent sites and the rental of mobile homes (€250-570), for something more unusual you can also stay in a cabin in the tree-tops.

Eating & drinking

L'Eden €€
3 rue Louis Pasteur, T02 97 46 42 62.
Open 1200-1400, 1930-2130,
closed Sat lunch and Sun.
Map: Vannes, p234.
Not far from the tourist office,
the rather odd exterior leads to a
stylish brown and cream dining
room. Food is both refined and
full of flavours, the service
fastidious. For under €20 you can
enjoy a three-course lunch that
might include fish of the day or
pork fillet. More expensive menus
and a good wine list are also on
offer. It's one of the best places to
eat in Vannes these days.

Les Remparts €€
6 rue A Le Pontois, T02 97 47 52 44.
Tue-Sun 1200-1400, 1930-2200
(wine bar from 1800) closed
Sat lunch.
Map: Vannes, p234.
A convenient location just
opposite the ramparts for this
restaurant/wine bar. At lunch
there's a €15 set meal, but you
may not be able to resist
sampling the sophisticated
seasonal menus. Many local
products include fresh oysters
and scallops. Wine lovers can
simply enjoy a glass with a
plate of cheese.

La Table de Jeanne €€-€
13 place de la Poissonnerie,
T02 97 47 34 91.
Open 1200-1400, 1900-2130,
closed Sun and Mon.
Map: Vannes, p234.
Excellent quality and variety here
on a constantly changing menu.
The set lunch is a two-course
affair (starter/dessert plus main
dish) which might include
roasted fillet of sea bream with
lentils or chunky lamb with
couscous. If available, try the
delicious pannacotta dessert. The
service can be on the inattentive
side, but the food makes up for it.

Café de la Poissonnerie €
21 place de la Poissonnerie,
T02 97 47 15 58.
Lunch until 1500, closed Sun
and Mon, except in Jul and Aug.
Map: Vannes, p234.
This café by the fish market is
rightly famous for the biggest,
finest *croque monsieur* available.
You'll never look at a toasted
sandwich in the same way again.
Croque madame and other
versions too are great. In the
highly unlikely event of a

carbohydrate vacuum afterwards, try the *riz au lait*.

Dan Ewen Crêperie €
3 place du Général de Gaulle, T02 97 42 44 34.
1130-1530, 1900-2200, closed Sun (and Mon out of season). Map: Vannes, p234.
In an ancient house, this crêperie has a good atmosphere, with Celtic-style music in the background, pleasing decor and an interesting range of crêpes. Seven of the specials are named after the founding saints, the others after Celtic countries. The Ecosse has smoked salmon and potatoes with salad dressed in raspberry vinegar.

La Saladière €
36 rue du Port, T02 97 42 52 10, lasaladiere-vannes.com.
Daily 1200-1400, 1900-2130. Map: Vannes, p234.
In the port area, this is a great place for a group that includes vegetarians, with the emphasis on plentiful gourmet salads. Some come with smoked fish or meat, and there's a shortlist of grills available too for fresh-vegetable haters. The ambience is bright and cheerful.

Auray

The old port St-Goustan in Auray has a whole string of bars and restaurants in a beautiful waterside setting, with something to please everyone.

L'Eglatine €€
Tue-Sat, lunch and dinner.
This refined place has a pretty pink interior and gourmet cooking – their version of *boullaibasse* is recommended.

Bistrot du Port €
Open daily.
A no-nonsense catch-all with crêpes, pizzas, steaks and *moules*, all good value for money.

Quiberon Peninsula

Le Vivier €€
Route de la Côte Sauvage, Quiberon, T02 97 50 12 60.
Closed Dec and Jan, Mon out of season.
More a bar with food than a restaurant, but the small dining room overlooks a fantastic rocky seascape. The menu is mostly shellfish, but what fresh and oceanic offerings! The rich, gutsy fish soup with its accompaniments of croutons, cheese and *rouille* (like a spiced mayonnaise) is almost a meal in itself.

La Criée Maison Lucas €€-€
11 quai de l'Océan, Quiberon, T02 97 30 53 09, maisonlucas.com.
1215-1400, 1915-2200, closed Mon (and Tue out of season).
Right by the port, this is the restaurant of the Maison Lucas, a company famed for its smoked fish. In a nautical-style dining room you can enjoy a mighty *assiette de fruits de mer* or a range of super-fresh fish dishes, such as salmon and camembert, or curried prawns in layered pastry. Booking advisable.

Megalith country

La Côte €€€-€€
Lieu-dit Kermario, Carnac, T02 97 52 02 80, restaurant-la-cote.com.
Jul and Aug 1215-1415, 1915-2115, closed Mon, Tue lunch, Sep-Jun also closed Sat lunch and Sun evening.
Easily the best place to eat around Carnac, opposite the alignments of Kermario. Pierre Michaud has made quite a name for himself as a culinary star, and this is a place where the food is both serious and fun. Just reading the menus makes your mouth water. Opt for the light selection at €24 or a more expensive feast (various menus up to €80) – it's all creative and exciting.

Hôtel Les Alignements €€-€
45 rue St Cornély, Carnac, T02 97 52 06 30.
Carnac is not exactly stuffed with good eateries and you could do a lot worse than dine here. A cheap three-course menu is under €15 and for less than €20

you can enjoy a substantial meal such as chicken and mushroom pastry followed by cod with wild rice and crème brûlée, all well cooked and nicely presented. The pleasant service is also a plus.

Cafés & bars

Chevillard Boulangerie Pâtisserie

2 rue du Tumulus, Carnac. **Daily.**

If you just want a snack, the *salon du thé* attached to this excellent bakery has good sandwiches or pizza/quiche with salad, followed by a quality cake for less than €7. Recommended option for picnic food too.

Pontivy

La Pommeraie €€-€

17 quai du Couvent, T02 97 25 60 09. **Open 1200-1330, 1900-2230, closed Sun and Mon.**

An unobtrusive façade for this restaurant on the quay, but what a shame to miss such gourmet cooking, where presentation is not rated higher than flavour – everything looks and tastes superb. Succulent fillet of cod and robust *bavette* of beef are cooked with the same fine judgement; roast figs with a Breton biscuit and ice cream form the most mouth-watering dessert. The wine list is serious, with a changing

recommendation at a special price. Highly recommended.

Le Martray €€-€

32 rue du Pont, T02 97 25 68 48. **Open 1200-1345, 1915-2130, closed Tue (and Wed out of season) and first 2 weeks of Jul.**

A traditional restaurant in the centre of town, this is very popular with locals and visitors. Warm, cosy atmosphere and a range of menus encompassing *produits du terroir*. There are fishy choices – *gratinée de fruits de mer* is a great starter – but it's also a place to eat quality steak, veal, lamb, sausage and rustic pâté. Good-value set menus start at €15.50.

La Petite Bretonne €

20 rue du Fil, T02 97 25 73 49. **Open 1200-1400, 1900-2130, closed Tue and Mon evening out of season.**

Situated in the picturesque Rue du Fil, this is one of the best crêperies in town, a warm, welcoming sort of place. Lots of meaty fillings on offer, including the *andouille* of Guémené in various combinations, but an alternative would be the odd-sounding combination of goat's cheese with salted caramel – surprisingly pleasant! The restaurant is very popular, so go early for lunch or dinner.

Northwest Morbihan

Thon Kiri €€

23 rue du Soleil, Le Faouët, T02 97 23 21 67. **Open 1200-1400, 1900-2200, closed Mon.**

A stylish establishment, with dining facilities on three floors in an attractive old building. The food is described as *cuisine du monde* and there is certainly a fusion of styles in the menu – *pissaladière, millefeuille* of goat's cheese, tempura of prawns and asparagus or lamb with prunes. Good food, service and ambience.

Le Chalet €

3 bis promenade des Estivants, St-Nicolas des Eaux, T02 97 51 88 87. **Open all year, closed Mon out of high season.**

You expect to emerge from this wooden cabin on to snowy slopes rather than the delightful Blavet riverside. Apart from the attractive setting, there are excellent crêpes, with a wide choice of combinations. It's a family-friendly establishment, with a useful children's play corner, and even a clown crêpe with bananas and smarties.

Eastern Morbihan

Hôtel Le Cobh, Restaurant €€€-€€

10 rue des Forges, Ploërmel, T02-97 74 00 49.

It's hard to believe that the chef here is only in his mid-20s –

Cédric Rivière is certainly a name to watch for in future in the world of gastronomy. The whole dining experience here is memorable, with the pretty red and yellowy-cream decor creating an intimate, relaxed atmosphere, and impeccable service. The great-value *menu du midi* might include fillet of sea bass, lentils and chorizo. Desserts are fantastic. Recommended.

Hôtel-Restaurant Le Pélican €€€-€€
Places des Halles, Rochefort-en-Terre, T02 97 43 38 48, hotel-pelican-rochefort.com.
A fabulous dining room – heavy beams, chandeliers, huge fireplace, gleaming copperware – is the setting for some seriously good food, all beautifully presented. Very varied menus offer everything from tripe and *andouille* to sea bass and red mullet, lamb and duck. The dessert *Délice Breton* certainly lives up to its name. Recommended.

La Table d'O €€-€
9 rue Glatinier, Josselin, T02 97 70 61 39.
Open 1200-1400, 1930-2100, closed Wed and Sun evening.
Not only a superb view of the canal and château, but creative, quality food, plus a good wine list. Popular for local family celebrations, the yellow-walled dining room is bright and

inviting. Salmon and soy bean stuffed *nems* with a creamy mushroom sauce and slice of surprisingly delicate-flavoured *andouille* is an exceptional starter; followed by medallions of monkfish with *cocos de Paimpol* and tarragon, it's a feast. You may have to book at busy times.

L'Olivier €€-€
5 rue Gal de Gaulle, Guegon, nr Josselin, T02 97 75 64 99.
Daily.
Five minutes from Josselin, this wonderful family restaurant is a real find. The set lunch menu is ridiculously cheap at under €12, with a buffet of imaginative home-made starters and a 'chariot de desserts' where you can help yourself to chocolate or fruit confections and unusual treats like pears in mint-flavoured juice. The *plat du jour* might be meat or fish, or choose *à la carte*. Everything is fresh, well cooked and well served. Highly recommended.

Crêperie Grill Bar du Puits €
4 place du Puits, Rochefort-en-Terre, T02 97 43 30 43.
Open 1200-1400, 1900-2130, closed Tue evening, Wed in winter.
The warm decor of this ancient house includes a monumental fireplace, old implements hanging on the walls and a range of original artwork (for sale).
 The menu is crêpes and grills, with especially good-quality

meat; try the entrecôte steak (various sauces) or grilled Breton sausage with lentils and bacon.

Crêperie le Mael Trech €
13 place du Bouffay, Malestroit, T02 97 75 17 72.
Open all year, 1200-1400, 1900-2130, closed Tue and Wed out of season.
Sit outside in the main square and enjoy people-watching as you eat. This is more than just another crêperie, as the menu also features plenty of main course salads and a few sturdy meat dishes such as *boudin noir* (a sort of black pudding sausage) with apples cooked in salted butter. Friday is *moules frites* night. Good cider from the Val du Rance. In high season this place is packed, so go early.

Entertainment

Le Café Breton €
8 rue du Porche, Rochefort-en-Terre, T02 97 43 32 60.
15 Jun-15 Sep daily, Apr, May and end Sep, closed Wed morning and Thu, winter Mon-Wed lunch only, Fri-Sun all day, closed Mar.
The interior of this fine old house is the main attraction. Feast your eyes on the local frescoes by Alfred Klots before tucking into excellent crêpes. The dessert ones are especially good here – try La Brocéliande with *chouchen*, apples and cider-flavoured ice cream.

Les Ateliers Gourmands €
7 rue Beaumanoir, Ploërmel, T02 97 72 10 76.
Tue-Sun lunch and dinner (from 1830).
In one of the oldest houses in the town, La Maison des Marmousets, you can eat in the upstairs dining room or walled courtyard at the back, with an eclectic selection of background music. The menu revolves around savoury tarts, gratins (salmon, potato, creamed leeks and cheese is very tasty), salads and crêpes. Nice people, good value for money.

Vannes

Bars & clubs
The liveliest evening spot in Vannes is the port area around the Place Gambetta. It's always busy with a mix of young people and international visitors from the pleasure port. Otherwise, you'll find locals enjoying an evening drink or two in the many bars in a more downmarket atmosphere in the old quarter around the Church of St-Patern, near the Porte Prison.

Music
Festival Jazz A Vannes
mairie-vannes.fr.
Jul.
At the end of July, this music festival hosts concerts, performances and jamming sessions for all lovers of jazz.

Gulf of Morbihan

Festivals & events
La Semaine du Golf
semainedugolfe.asso.fr.
May-Jun.
A two-year cycle (next 30 May-5 June 2011) for this vintage boat festival in the Gulf of Morbihan with vessels of all kinds from bi-planes to pleasure craft, plus concerts and exhibitions.

Shopping

Food

Côte Sauvage
ZA de Kergroix, St-Pierre
Quiberon, T02 97 30 73 38,
saumonsauvage.com.
Tue-Sat 0930-1230, 1430-1800.
Smoked wild salmon to taste and
buy, plus factory visits on offer.

La Quiberonnaise
5 quai de Houat, Quiberon,
T02 97 50 12 54
Daily Apr-Oct 1000-1215,
1530-1900.
All manner of conserved fish
products, such as soup, sardines
and much more. Good for
souvenirs and presents.

Megalith country

Food

Chantier Ostréicole Tibidy
171 route du Pô, Carnac, T02 97
52 08 15, tibidy-huitres.com.
Open all year.
Excellent oysters and all kinds of
shellfish on sale here straight
from the producer.

Northwest Morbihan

Food

Maison de l'Andouille
5 rue de Bellevue, Guémené-sur-
Scorff, T02 97 51 21 10, andouille-
guemene.com.

Quiberon Peninsula

Bars & clubs
Nightclub Suroit
29 rue de Port Maria, Quiberon,
T02 97 30 56 69.
If you fancy a good bop, there's
chart and funky-disco beats on
Fridays and Saturdays from 2330,
while Sunday night is 1950s-
1980s rock and salsa, from 2200.

Northwest Morbihan

Festivals & events
Fête de l'Andouille
Guémené-sur-Scorff.
Aug.
Every August the home town of
the best *andouille* in Brittany
celebrates its famous product
with all manner of gastronomic
feasts, music and dancing.

Open 0900-1230, 1415-1900, closed Sun and Mon.
The famous tripe sausage is smoked in the chimney here, according to a family tradition dating back to 1931. They'll even gift-wrap a present for you.

Eastern Morbihan

Rochfort-en-Terre is full of artists, artisans and attractive shops, many open all year.

Espace Kaleo at 6 place des Halles (open daily Jul and Aug, closed Mon out of season and Jan and Feb), has a good selection of quality craft products, including jewellery.

The bag and basket shop (*vannerie*) in the Rue du Château is also worth a look, and **Le Terroir Gourmand** (1 place du Puits) and **Entre Ciel et Art** (5 chemin du Tertre) will satisfy food lovers.

Books
English Bookshop
36 rue des Trente, Josselin, T02 97 75 62 55.
Jun-Sep, Tue-Sat 1000-1800, Oct-May 1100-1600, closed Mon-Wed.
You will find a huge range of English books, new and second-hand in this well-run, friendly shop right in the centre.

Very useful for guidebooks and the history of Brittany, or a novel for your holiday reading.

Food & drink
Brasserie de Lancelot
La Mine d'Or, Le Roc-St-André, T02 97 74 74 74, brasserie-lancelot.com.
Tue-Sat 0930-1230, 1330-1800 (Fri 1700).
A well-known brand of beer is made here, with seven different types in constant production and five specials from time to time, including one just for Halloween. This company also created Breizh Cola. The shop is open every afternoon and guided visits are also on offer.

Activities & tours

Gulf of Morbihan

Boat trips

Golfe Croisières (T02 97 57 15 27, golfecroisieres.com) offers tours from Lamor-Baden with or without a stop on the Ile-aux-Moines. Prices start from €12.

Navix (T08 25 13 21 00, navix. fr) has a wide range of tours from various ports, plus dining options (from about €50). Mini-tours start at €15.

Vedettes Angelus (T02 97 57 30 29, vedettes-angelus.com) is based at Port Navalo and Locmariaquer. A five-hour circuit of 35 km with a lunch stop on the Ile-aux-Moines costs about

€26, or there's a mini-cruise past Gavrinis and Er Lannic for €13.

The Gare Maritime in Vannes is at the **Parc du Golfe** (T08 20 05 60 00, smn-navigation56.com). The **Compagnie des Iles** (T08-25 13 41 00, compagniedesiles.com) has a range of gulf options from here, plus trips to Belle-Ile and the Ile de Groix further afield.

Walking

The tourist office in Vannes has a free folder – Tour du Golfe – covering 16, mostly linear, walks around the Gulf of Morbihan.

Quiberon Peninsula

Water sports

Plunge into those compelling breakers with the **Spirit Surf Club** (T06 35 43 50 55/spirit-surf-club.com). They offer many options, with English-speaking instructors. The **Surfing Paradise School** (T02 97 50 39 67, quiberonsurfingparadise.com) also offers individual tuition (two hours, €30) or a weekend break. Or go deeper with the **Quiberon Diving Club** (T02 97 50 00 98/quiberon-plongee. com) at Port Haliguen.

Northwest Morbihan

Cultural

L'Art dans les Chapelles
artchapelles.com.
From first weekend in Jul to mid-Sep, open every afternoon except Mon.

Each summer modern artists exhibit in ancient chapels in north Morbihan – a simple idea that brings some glorious juxtapositions and incongruities. For details of events, see the organization's website or ask at any tourist office.

Tip...

La Route des Ducs de Bretagne is a tourist route around the eastern Morbihan that links some highlights of ducal Brittany including châteaux, museums and memorials. You also get additions, such as the animal park at the Château de Branféré and the doll museum at Josselin, which are both great for children. An illustrated leaflet is available from tourist offices.

Inland waterways

The Nantes–Brest canal is navigable from Redon to Pontivy (184 km and 106 locks). Boats can be hired at Redon or La Gacilly (see page 131).

The Blavet Canal runs for 58 km between Pontivy and Hennebont, passing 28 locks.

See canaux-bretons.net for more information, and ninarion.fr for boat hire at Inzinzac-Lochrist. Canoes and kayaks can be rented at the Base Nautique (T02 97 51 50 33) in Rohan.

Contents

Practicalities

Ploumanac'h, Côtes d'Armor.

Getting there

Air

From UK & Ireland
Two budget airlines connect the UK to Brittany. You can fly to **Dinard** airport (near **St-Malo**) from the East Midlands or Stansted with **Ryanair** (ryanair. com). Prices are from €20 one way. Dinard airport is at Pleurtuit, and does not have a shuttle service, so taxis will be necessary to get to the nearest big centre at St-Malo (9 km/allow €20).

    Flybe (flybe.com) has budget flights into **Rennes** airport from Southampton, Manchester, Leeds, Edinburgh, Glasgow and Belfast, from €40 one way. The airport is 20 minutes by bus (No 57) from the centre.

    Both **Ryanair** and **Flybe** have flights to **Brest** (Guipavas). From here a bus shuttle service (€4.60) goes to the city centre and station. (These flights are not year round, so check websites for details.)

    AerLingus (aerlingus.com) flies from Dublin to **Rennes** and **Aer Arann** (aerarann.com) from Ireland to **Lorient** and **Brest**.

Air France (airfrance.fr) provides a regular service to Paris and also flies from Paris (Charles de Gaulle airport) to the regional airports of **Rennes**, **Brest**, **Lorient**, **Lannion** and **Quimper**.

From North America
There are flights to Paris with **Air France**, **British Airways**, **Delta**; then go via Air France to regional airports, or take the train to the major towns around Brittany.

Airport information
Dinard airport (T08 25 08 35 09, best information is from the unofficial site dinardairport.net); **Brest airport** (T02 98 32 86 37 for parking info, airport. cci-brest.fr); **Rennes airport** (T02 99 29 60 00, rennes.aeroport.fr); **Lorient airport** (lorient-aeroport.fr).

    Car-hire facilities are available at all the airports. The companies with offices in major towns are **Hertz** (hertz.com.fr), **Avis** (avis.fr), **Europcar** (europcar.fr) and **Sixt** (sixt.fr).

Rail

You can travel by **Eurostar** from St Pancras to Paris, Gare du Nord in 2½ hours, and then continue by high-speed TGV from Gare Montparnasse to all the major towns in Brittany (Rennes two hours, Brest and Quimper four hours). Changing from the Eurostar at Lille and proceeding direct to Rennes is easier, avoiding the station change in Paris.

European Rail (europeanrail.com) and **Rail Europe** (raileurope.co.uk) have details of timetables, fares and ticket booking. Discount passes are available for young people and senior citizens.

For timetabling information within France, see the rail network **SNCF** site, voyages-sncf.fr.

Road

Bus

Eurolines (eurolines.co.uk) provides coach services to Rennes, St-Brieuc and Brest.

Car

Driving from the Channel ports will take up to seven hours from Calais and about three hours from Caen and Cherbourg. Allow three hours from Paris to Rennes (348 km), or five hours to go on to Brest (593 km). There are no motorway tolls once you get into Brittany.

Michelin (viamichelin.com) are the standard road maps and they have a route-planning service.

You must have a valid driving licence, car registration documents, insurance and a nationality plate.

Sea

Direct ferries to Brittany are run only by **Brittany Ferries** (brittanyferries.com), with sailings to St-Malo from Portsmouth (9-10 hours, usually overnight from England), or from Plymouth to Roscoff (six to eight hours). There is also a service from Cork in Ireland to Roscoff. The website has a timetable and prices, but these do vary according to how far in advance you buy a ticket. Off-season schedules are published only briefly in advance.

This monopoly makes fares expensive, so an alternative route is to cross the eastern end of the Channel or to Cherbourg and then drive. This takes about seven hours from Calais, 4½ hours from Dieppe and three hours from Caen or Cherbourg, but there will be the added cost of motorways tolls and petrol, so weighing up the benefits is an exercise in precision. The relatively easy access of Plymouth by motorway in the UK, avoiding the southeast, could also be a factor in opting for the Roscoff route.

Other cross-channel ferry companies are **P&O** (poferries.com), **Condor** (condorferries.com), **Speed Ferries** (speedferries.com) and **LD Lines** (transmancheferries.co.uk). **Ferrysavers.co.uk** is worth a look for getting the best deal, as there are many permutations according to season and choice of crossing ports. **Irish Ferries** (irishferries.com) sail from Rosslare to Roscoff and Cherbourg.

Getting around

Rail

The state rail network **SNCF** has a good TGV (high-speed) service within Brittany connecting the main towns. The northern route goes through Dinan, St-Brieuc, Guingamp and Morlaix to Brest. Rennes has a link with Quimper, or there's a southern route via Nantes to Vannes and Quimper. You can check routes, timetables and price options or book tickets on voyages-sncf.fr.

Within the region, the **TER** network (ter-sncf.com/Bretagne) connects coastal spots including St-Malo, Roscoff and Quiberon and important towns such as Pontivy and Carhaix-Plouguer, but in general rural central Brittany is not well served by public transport. The website has details of the Korrigo card, which can be used on regional trains, and other public transport networks.

When travelling around, you must validate (*composter*) your train ticket at the orange machine on the platform before getting on board.

Various discount schemes are available from SNCF, including the 'Carte 15-25 ans' for young people, and the over 60s 'Tarif Découverte'. Some restrictions of travel may apply. There is also a less well known 'Découverte à deux' which gives 25% off for two people travelling together.

To view facilities for disabled passengers, see the Mobilité Réduite information on voyages-sncf.fr.

Bicycles can only go on certain trains – check for the symbol on timetables before booking.

Ille-et-Vilaine There's a good train network in Ille-et-Vilaine. You can arrive by ferry at St-Malo and get a train to Rennes (1 hr, €13) or Redon. Paris to Rennes is just over two hours. Visit voyages-sncf.fr.

Côtes d'Armor The Paris–Brest TGV line has main stations at Lamballe, St-Brieuc and Guingamp. For times and fares, see voyages-sncf.com.

There are local lines from Guingamp to Paimpol (45 mins) and Lannion (35 mins), and from Lamballe to Dinan (35 mins). For details, see ter.fr.

Finistère Trains link Brest with Morlaix, Quimper and Paris. The TGV from Paris to Brest via Morlaix takes 4½ hours. Details on voyages-sncf.fr.

Morbihan There is a major TGV train route through Vannes, with Paris just under three hours away. From Vannes to Auray is 10 minutes and to Pontivy about one hour. Details on voyages-sncf.fr.

Road

Bicycle

The main towns have cycle lanes. Rennes and Vannes have bike (*vélo*) schemes whereby you can pick up a bicycle from one of the special ranks and drop it off at another elsewhere in the town. The bikes have baskets and some have child seats. Rental times vary from an hour to a day or a week, but advanced registration and a large deposit are needed. The relevant tourist offices have details, or see levelostar.fr (Rennes) and velocea.fr (Vannes). Brest is probably the least cycle-friendly of the large centres.

Most towns of any size, and places in the coastal holiday areas, have bike hire from cycle shops or camping sites. Tourist offices will have details. There's a useful list of providers near Green Ways at randobreizh.com. The largely car-free islands have bike hire near the arrival port.

Bus/coach

Each district has its own transport network, with urban and rural routes. The system is reliable and efficient, although the countryside is not especially well served. More buses cover coastal routes in summer when demand is high. The local bus station (*Gare routière*) will have information, and there are special offices to provide help in big towns. For general information T08 36 35 35 35.

Ille-et-Vilaine (illenoo-services.fr. Rennes: T02 99 30 87 80, star.fr). Buses are frequent and efficient. There are more than six buses a day from Rennes to Paimpont – consult star.fr. The website illenoo.fr will help you plan any journeys around the department of Ille-et-Vilaine.

Côtes d'Armor (tibus.fr). St-Brieuc is at the hub of the Tibus network – for a plan and timetables consult the website. A single journey ticket is €2, or €40 for a monthly card.

More buses serve the coastal resorts in summer. There are three daily services from Lannion to Paimpol (about one hour), via Tréguier, and Line 15 will take you all around the Pink Granite Coast.

Finistère (Brest: T02 98 44 46 73, bibus.fr, Quimper: T02 98 90 88 89, qub.fr). For journeys further afield, check viaoo29.fr.

Morbihan (morbihan.fr. Vannes: T02 97 01 22 10, Lorient: T02 97 21 28 29). For details of the bus network TIM (€2 or 10 trips for €15), the website morbihan.fr has interactive maps and links. Line 4 covers Josselin, Ploërmel and Malestroit from Vannes. There are buses from Vannes, Auray and Quiberon to Carnac for visiting the megaliths.

Car

Driving in Brittany is a pleasure, with generally good roads, no expressway tolls and comparatively little traffic. You must give way to traffic from the right at junctions, unless otherwise indicated. It is not often the case in the countryside, but be extra vigilant in towns.

From Roscoff or St-Malo, the rest of Brittany is easily accessible via express routes – N12 in the north (Brest, Morlaix, St-Brieuc), N164 in the centre (Carhaix-Plouguer to Rennes, still with some single-lane sections) and N165 in the south (Quimper, Lorient, Vannes). Rennes is at the hub of the major routes.

Parking Parking is usually pay and display in central town areas, and you must get a ticket from the machine (*horodateur*). Be especially careful not to park overnight in squares where markets are held early the following morning. Blue-lined parking bays mean you must buy a limited time disc from a *tabac*. These are useful if you're spending several days in one place.

If you are planning on staying a while in Rennes or Brest it makes sense to use the huge central underground paying car parks. Even several days' parking will come to little more than €20, and the machine will usually take credit cards.

Regulations Police can impose on-the-spot fines for offences, such as not stopping properly at a stop sign or running a red light. Pay strict attention to drinking and driving regulations (0.5g/L) and speed limits – patrols and testing are common.

You must carry a red warning triangle and at least one reflective safety jacket – this is obligatory. Don't forget that you must have your headlight beam adjusted to the right, or buy special stickers to achieve the same effect.

Maps The best maps are **Michelin** (michelin.com). **IGN** (ign.fr) have orange departmental driving maps, but these do not mark places of interest. Their blue topographical Cartes de Randonnée with walking routes marked are useful for driving on smaller roads and worth buying if you are based in one particular area.

Practicalities
Directory

Customs & immigration

UK and EU citizens do not need a visa, only a valid passport or identity card. US and Canadian citizens must have a valid national passport. US citizens can check the customs situation through their Customs Service (customs.ustreas.gov).

Disabled travellers

Brittany is gradually providing better access and facilities for disabled visitors. The regional tourist board (tourismebretagne.com) has a download of accommodation adapted for reduced mobility. For wide-ranging information on equipment, activities, including sporting options, transport possibilities and accommodation, have a look at bretagne-accessible.com. This also provides localized details.

Emergencies

Ambulance (SAMU) T15, **Fire service** (Pompiers) T18, **Police** T17. The pan-European emergency number from any phone is T112.

Etiquette

Brittany is still a traditional place with strong social bonds. Good manners are the norm here – it's common to say a general *bonjour* on entering a small shop or the post office, or to people in the street in rural areas. Bretons respond well to a smile and a greeting. Showing respect for religious buildings by speaking quietly and keeping children under control in a cathedral or chapel will also go down well. And do ask before taking a photograph of someone performing their job, whether it's a fisherman or crêpe-maker.

Families

Brittany is just as family friendly as the rest of France. Children are welcomed in restaurants and hotels, and special provision is happily made if necessary. Discounts are usually offered at attractions for children up to 16 years old, and those under four are often given free entrance. Tickets for a *famille nombreuse* give a price for three or more children who are accompanied by two parents.

Health

Comprehensive travel and medical insurance is recommended. EU citizens should apply for a free European Health Insurance Card or EHIC (ehic.org), which entitles you to emergency medical treatment on the same terms as French nationals. Note that you will have to pay all charges and prescriptions up front and be reimbursed once you return home. If you develop a minor ailment while on holiday, a visit to any pharmacy will allow you to discuss your concerns with highly qualified staff, who can give medical advice and recommend treatment. Outside normal opening hours, the address of the nearest duty pharmacy (*pharmacie de garde*) is displayed in the pharmacy window. The out-of-hours number for a local doctor (*médecin généraliste*) may also be listed.

In a serious emergency, go to the accident and emergency department (*urgences*) at the nearest Centre Hospitalier (numbers listed in the Essentials section at the beginning of each chapter) or call an ambulance (SAMU) by dialling T15.

Insurance

Comprehensive travel and medical insurance is strongly recommended, as the European Health Insurance Card (EHIC) does not cover medical repatriation, ongoing medical treatment or treatment considered to be non-urgent. Check for exclusions if you mean to engage in risky sports. Keep all insurance documents to hand; a good way to keep track of your policies is to email the details to yourself. Make sure you have adequate insurance when hiring a car and always ask how much excess you are liable for if the vehicle is returned with any damage. It is generally worth paying a little more for a collision damage waiver. If driving your own vehicle to France, contact your insurers before you travel to ensure you are adequately covered, and keep the documents in your vehicle in case you need to prove it.

Practicalities

Money

The French currency is the euro. There are plenty of ATMs all over Brittany, in banks, commercial centres, main post offices and often in ferry terminals. Credit and debit cards are not accepted everywhere (look for the signs at restaurants beforehand) so it's a good idea to have cash as well. Small sites and private attractions and even some shops may refuse plastic. Traveller's cheques can be cashed at post offices and banks, in theory, but problems are sometimes experienced and using a cash card will certainly be easier.

Police

The Municipal Police are based in towns and deal with parking, transport issues and civic events. The Gendarmerie deal with traffic and criminal offences and general law and order, while the Police Nationale deal with crime in large towns.

Post

Generally the postal system is reliable and efficient. A letter or postcard to the UK requires a €0.70 stamp, and an €0.85 one for the US and Canada.

Bars usually sell stamps, but these will not be for foreign destinations.

Safety

Brittany is a low-crime area, although common-sense precautions should be taken in cities and at night. Avoid small alleyways and parks after dark. Be sure to lock cars (and bicycles) and don't leave valuables in sight or in the boot. If you are worried about valuables in hotels, ask at reception for safe facilities. Personal safety is unlikely to be an issue.

Telephone

To call France from abroad, dial T00 33 then the number minus the initial 0. The Brittany area code is 02 followed by eight digits. You need to dial the whole number within France. Departmental codes are 96 (Côtes d'Armor), 97 (Morbihan), 98 (Finistère) and 99 (Ille-et-Vilaine). Information calls may begin 08.

Public phone booths take prepaid cards, obtainable from a bar/tabac, newsagents and post offices.

The mobile phone network, split mainly between Orange, SFR and Bouyges Telecom, is reasonable but coverage can be patchy.

Time difference

France uses Central European Time, GMT + 1.

Tipping

Service is almost always included in restaurants and there is no need to leave a tip, although simple rounding up is appreciated rather than waiting for a few cents of change. This is especially true when taking coffee outside a bar. Tipping in hotels is not expected. For other services such as taxis, tip up to 15%.

Voltage

France functions on a 220v mains supply. Plugs are the standard round two-pin European variety.

Language

Basics

hello *bonjour*
good evening *bonsoir*
goodbye *au revoir/salut* (polite/informal)
please *s'il vous plaît*
thank you *merci*
I'm sorry, excuse me *pardon, excusez-moi*
yes *oui*
no *non*
how are you?
  comment allez-vous?/ça va? (polite/informal)
fine, thank you *bien, merci*
one moment *un instant*
how? *comment?*
how much? *c'est combien?*
when? *quand?*
where is …? *où est …?*
why? *pourquoi?*
what? *quoi?*
what's that? *qu'est-ce que c'est?*
I don't understand *je ne comprends pas*
I don't know *je ne sais pas*
I don't speak French *je ne parle pas français*
how do you say … (in French)?
  comment on dit … (en français)?
do you speak English? *est-ce que vous parlez anglais?/Parlez-vous anglais?*
help! *au secours!*
wait! *attendez!*
stop! *arrêtez!*

Numbers

1	*un*	7	*sept*
2	*deux*	8	*huit*
3	*trois*	9	*neuf*
4	*quatre*	10	*dix*
5	*cinq*	11	*onze*
6	*six*	12	*douze*

Breton glossary

aber estuary
beg summit, headland
bihan/vihan small
braz/vras large
enez island
ker village/hamlet
koat/coat/coët wood
kozh/koz/coz old
krampouezh/krampouz crêpes
kreizh centre
marc'h horse
ménez mountain
meur/veur large
nevez new
pen/penn head/headland
poul pond/pool
plou parish
Saoz English
ti/ty house
Yec'hed Mat Cheers!

See page 49 for more information on Breton.

13	*treize*	30	*trente*
14	*quatorze*	40	*quarante*
15	*quinze*	50	*cinquante*
16	*seize*	60	*soixante*
17	*dix-sept*	70	*soixante-dix*
18	*dix-huit*	80	*quatre-vingt*
19	*dix-neuf*	90	*quatre-vingt-dix*
20	*vingt*	100	*cent*
21	*vingt-et-un*	200	*deux cents*
22	*vingt-deux*	1000	*mille*

Shopping

this one/that one *celui-ci/celui-là*
less *moins*
more *plus*

expensive *cher*
cheap *pas cher/bon marché*
how much is it?
  c'est combien?/combien est-ce que ça coûte?
can I have …? (literally 'I would like') *je voudrais…*

Travelling

one ticket for… *un billet pour…*
single *un aller-simple*
return *un aller-retour*
airport *l'aéroport*
bus stop *l'arrêt de bus*
train *le train*
car *la voiture*
taxi *le taxi*
is it far? *c'est loin?*

Hotels

a single/double room
  une chambre à une personne/deux personnes
a double bed *un lit double/un grand lit*
bathroom *la salle de bain*
shower *la douche*
is there a (good) view?
  est-ce qu'il y a une (belle) vue?
can I see the room?
  est-ce que je peux voir la chambre?
when is breakfast?
  le petit dejeuner est à quelle heure?
can I have the key?
  est-ce que je peux avoir la clef?/La clef, s'il vous plaît

Time

morning *le matin*
afternoon *l'après-midi*
evening *le soir*

night *la nuit*
a day *un jour*
a week *une semaine*
a month *un mois*
soon *bientôt*
later *plus tard*
what time is it? *quelle heure est-il?*
today/tomorrow/yesterday
  aujourd'hui/demain/hier

Days

Monday *lundi*
Tuesday *mardi*
Wednesday *mercredi*
Thursday *jeudi*

Friday *vendredi*
Saturday *samedi*
Sunday *dimanche*

Months

January *janvier*
February *février*
March *mars*
April *avril*
May *mai*
June *juin*

July *juillet*
August *août*
September *septembre*
October *octobre*
November *novembre*
December *décembre*

Index

Index

Index

credits

Footprint credits

Project editor: Felicity Laughton
Text editor: Jen Haddington
Picture editor: Kassia Gawronski
Layout and production: Jen Haddington
Maps: Gail Townsley
Proofreader: Sally Somers
Series design: Mytton Williams

Managing Director: Andy Riddle
Commercial Director: Patrick Dawson
Publisher: Alan Murphy
Publishing Managers:
Felicity Laughton and Jo Williams
Design and images:
Rob Lunn and Kassia Gawronski
Digital Editor: Alice Jell
Marketing: Liz Harper,
Hannah Bonnell
Sales: Jeremy Parr
Advertising: Renu Sibal
Finance and administration:
Elizabeth Taylor

Print

Manufactured in India by Nutech
Pulp from sustainable forests

Every effort has been made to ensure
that the facts in this guidebook are
accurate. However, travellers should still
obtain advice from consulates, airlines etc
about travel and visa requirements before
travelling. The authors and publishers
cannot accept responsibility for any loss,
injury or inconvenience however caused.

Publishing information

FootprintFrance
Brittany
1st edition
© Footprint Handbooks Ltd
May 2010

ISBN 978-1-906098-90-2
CIP DATA: A catalogue record for this
book is available from the British Library

® Footprint Handbooks and the Footprint
mark are a registered trademark of
Footprint Handbooks Ltd

Published by Footprint
6 Riverside Court
Lower Bristol Road
Bath BA2 3DZ, UK
T +44 (0)1225 469141
F +44 (0)1225 469461
footprinttravelguides.com

Distributed in North America by
Globe Pequot Press